Who's Your
Hoosier Ancestor?

Indiana. From George Pence and Nellie C. Armstrong, Indiana Boundaries *(Indianapolis: Indiana Historical Bureau, 1933). Courtesy Indiana Historical Bureau.*

Who's Your Hoosier Ancestor?

GENEALOGY FOR BEGINNERS

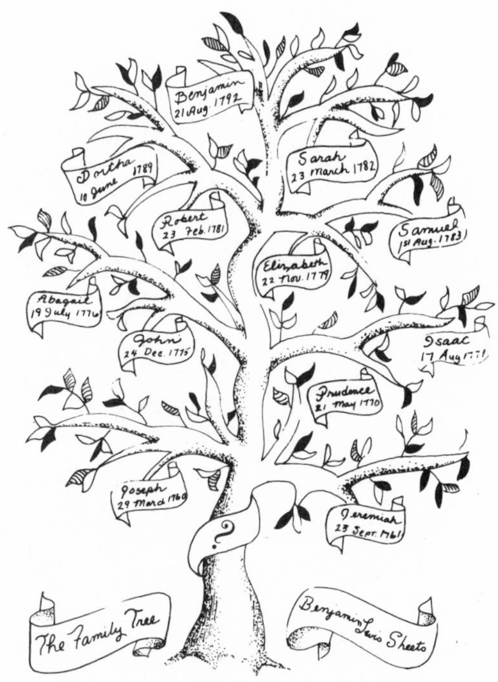

MONA ROBINSON

INDIANA UNIVERSITY PRESS
Bloomington and Indianapolis

The paper used in this publication meets the minimum requirements of American National Standard for Information Sciences—Permanence of Paper for Printed Library Materials, ANSI Z39.48-1984.

Manufactured in the United States of America

Library of Congress Cataloging-in-Publication Data

Robinson, Mona, date.
Who's your hoosier ancestor? : genealogy for beginners / Mona Robinson.
p. cm.
Includes bibliographical references and index.
ISBN 0-253-34996-6 (cloth). — ISBN 0-253-20731-2 (paper)
1. Indiana—Genealogy—Handbooks, manuals, etc. I. Title F525.R63 1992
929'.1—dc20 91-39969

1 2 3 4 5 96 95 94 93 92

Contents

PREFACE

Genealogy, once the hobby of maiden aunts, social climbers, and ancestry snobs, is now the third most popular hobby in the United States, topped only by stamp and coin collecting. Fueled by our nation's Bicentennial celebration and by renewed interest in things historic, genealogy finally came out of the closet and into the parlor just a few short years ago. Today's family researcher is not a snob, nor necessarily an older person or a fuddy-duddy. Most genealogists are "with it" people, no matter what their ages or backgrounds might be. Today's genealogists seldom care whether their families were illustrious, wealthy, titled, or famous. The new genealogists are more interested in learning about themselves by learning about their families and the past. They seldom sweep anything regarding the family "under the rug," prefering a horse thief in the lineage to not knowing anything about the family. Genealogy has thus become a friendlier and less stressful hobby which appeals to a broader group of people.

The genealogist who begins research today also has access to a much wider variety of genealogical resources than ever before. The number of publishing firms specializing in genealogical books has expanded and the number of books being published or reprinted is vast and constantly growing. All sorts of records—vital, church, government, military—are also being printed for the use of genealogists. Discoveries of long lost records keep occurring, and such records are being rushed into print to meet the increased demand by genealogists. Libraries are now catering to, rather than ignoring, the family researcher. These facilities are buying more genealogical books, providing separate genealogical sections, and training personnel specifically to assist genealogists. This is a fine time for anyone to begin to conduct family research. You can still reap the benefits of today's increased interest in genealogy, however, even if you began your genealogical research many years ago. And, people with an interest in Indiana can benefit from learning about this interesting state, its people, its historical background, when the various kinds of records were first kept, where they are now kept, and about the other sources which they might be able to use.

Indiana is not a hard state in which to conduct family research, but it does take a knowledge of the land, the people who came there, and why they came.

People from other states generally have no idea about conducting family research outside their own state. This isn't surprising because over the years each locality has kept different records and kept them differently than in other areas. Indiana, as a part of the Old Northwest Territory, was a "trough" which funneled settlers from the south, the southeast, the east and the northeast into the Old Northwest after the Revolution. Indiana was a "feeder," by which I mean that the Indiana Country was a natural channel to the west, with most settlers passing through it on their journey westward. While quite a few of the early settlers stayed in Indiana, as it became a territory and then a state, many more merely passed through it to lands beyond. Many settlers came to Indiana, liked the area and stayed, but others remained only a few years or a few generations and then moved on into newly opened land in Illinois, Missouri, Iowa, and Michigan, and later, into Kansas, Wisconsin, the Dakotas, Arkansas, Texas, and farther west. Some disenchanted settlers even migrated back east or south to their former homes. It seems that nearly everyone has at least one ancestor who was born in, came from, or lived sometime in Indiana. A great many of our ancestors claimed Indiana as home at one time or another.

The earliest Indiana settlers found a wild country which was frequented by equally wild and inhospitable Indians who did not welcome white settlers or settlements. Those first intrepid settlers had to be of hardy stock to endure the long, hard journey to Indiana, let alone settle there. The journey was rugged and roundabout, and the pioneers often met terrible obstacles on their way to Indiana Country. There were high mountains, deep gorges, swift rivers, and often treacherous and indistinct trails to follow. The Indians fought the entry of whites into their lands, and many would-be settlers were slain before they could even reach Indiana.

Once those hardy souls arrived in Indiana, they had to build a temporary lean-to shelter and clear the land of huge trees. Underbrush had to be cut and burned, some land had to be drained, and then it had to be cultivated before a crop could be planted. In order to get there before the spring planting season, the pioneers had to make the arduous journey in fall or winter when traveling conditions were extremely harsh. Most of Indiana was marshy, and the settlers were often felled by illnesses they had not previously encountered. It's no wonder many did not stay but moved on to other, less daunting lands. The people who stayed were the hardiest of the hardy, and the people who live in the state of Indiana now seem to be just as hardy, although the marshes and bogs have long been drained, and the land and climate are kinder to the inhabitants than they once were.

It is because Indiana was a "feeder" to states west of it that so many family researchers want information about the state, its history, and its records. People whose ancestors once lived in Indiana, or merely passed through it, need to know what records are available to them and where they can find those records. They also need to know about the background and history of the state so that their research can be as fruitful and as uncomplicated as possible. Because records began with the establishment of the counties and the counties began relatively early in its history, Indiana is not a difficult state to research in. Knox County, Indiana's first, was established in 1790 as a part of the Northwest Territory, and many other counties were then carved from it. Thus, many county records begin before Indiana became a state.

Indiana is a state generally composed of conservatives, and the land, the climate, and the people are all on the conservative side. If Missourians say "Show me," then Indiana's Hoosiers might say "Show me—then I'll think on it." Natives of Indiana are generally content with the status quo and don't often "rock the boat." Hoosiers vote conservatively and have a state government which is seldom in debt. They are rock-solid people who reflect a pioneer ancestry of which they are rightly proud. These "pioneers" may have come late in the eighteenth century or late in the twentieth century, but they share a common respect for the state and its pioneer roots. The people of Indiana have made the state a prosperous one, with fine farms and livestock and a few large cities which support varied industries. Over the years, so many people reported being "born in Indiana" on the federal censuses that one wonders how the state could have held them all.

If you are searching for an ancestor who was born in Indiana and you have no other information to help in your search, you will need some guidance about finding data about him or her. The purpose of this book is to present the means and methods for locating elusive ancestors who once lived in Indiana. The first few chapters contain a brief overview of the history of Indiana from earliest times, including background on the Indians who inhabited the area at various times; a brief discussion of the land and climate of the state, its boundaries and land distribution; descriptions of the migration paths that the settlers used; the backgrounds of the settlers at various periods in Indiana's history, their nationalities, religious preferences, and state or country of origin, and where they settled in the state. The book is arranged by resource groups rather than by a chronological history of the state in order to make information about certain records clearer and easier to find and use. Thus some historical information is repeated throughout as it relates to the subject of the chapter at hand.

Subsequent chapters discuss the basic types of Indiana records available to the family researcher, as well as the contents of the records, where they are located, how to find and use them, and the value of each type of record to the genealogist. These records include the various governmental records, such as birth, death, and marriage records; probate records, such as wills, administrations, estate settlements, and so forth; federal records, such as censuses, military records, bounty land records, and ships' passenger lists; church and cemetery records; county histories; records found in the home; and other miscellaneous records.

Hints about using some less well known kinds of records should also prove useful to the reader.

Genealogy has long been considered an inexact science and, although it still cannot be classified as an exact one, the current use of approved scientific method in genealogical research has made it more widely accepted as such. By following good genealogical principles, by documenting evidence, and by verifying every bit of information in your genealogical research, you can help to increase this growing respect for genealogy.

Genealogists, as a whole, are usually extremely serious about their hobby and spend a great deal of time and energy on it. This is not to suggest that genealogists are always prim and serious, because we have a great deal of fun with our hobby! No one who has read through very many census schedules and early wills will dispute the fact that much of our research can turn up items and incidents that are amusing, if not downright hilarious. It had to be a genealogist who remarked that "old genealogists never die, they just lose their census." This book will try to introduce you to both the serious and the entertaining sides of Indiana genealogy. A hobby should be fun as well as enlightening for those afflicted with the "genealogy bug." The more you learn about the state, its history, and its people, the more you will learn about yourself—which should be the true goal of the genealogist.

Who's Your
Hoosier Ancestor?

Indiana, a Varied Land

CHAPTER

1

Before there were people in Indiana there was the land. The climate, the terrain, the soil, the minerals, and the waterways were all there, waiting for the people to come and use them. The environment of Indiana, the way the land lay, the rivers that ran by and through it directed the settlers into certain parts of the state before leading them into other sections. As is true in most places, the land then shaped the people just as the people shaped the land.

Indiana's boundaries were originally laid out by the provisions of the Northwest Ordinance of 1787 when present-day Indiana was part of the newly created Northwest Territory of the United States. This was the large area located north and west of the Ohio River. The Northwest Ordinance established laws which were largely English in nature to govern the territory and later the states that were carved out of the Northwest Territory. These states were Indiana, Illinois, Michigan, and most of Wisconsin.[1]

When Ohio and Kentucky became states, their boundaries determined Indiana's southern and eastern borders. The western border of Ohio became the eastern boundary of Indiana, and the 1792 low-water mark on the northern shore of the Ohio River became Indiana's southern boundary. An enabling act set the western boundary thus: a line drawn up the middle of the Wabash River from its mouth, through the center of Vincennes and northward to the northern boundary. The northern boundary was an east-to-west line running ten miles north of the southernmost part of Lake Michigan. The northern boundary was later moved south about ten miles.[2]

Indiana has been called an "indifferent state," which is perhaps an unfair estimate. Irvin S. Cobb, humorist of the 1920s and 1930s and a Kentuckian, wrote that he considered Indiana to be the most typical and most average of the states in America.[3] It is an extremely varied state geographically. The scenery is pleasant in all parts of the state and beautiful in most of it. Farmlands of the northern section gradually blend into the rolling hills of central Indiana south of Indianapolis. The hills then continue to roll southward to the Ohio River. The wooded hills of Owen, Monroe, Greene, and Brown counties have been compared favorably to those of New England for the beauty of their spring and fall foliage. From the northern lake region along Lake Michigan in extreme northwestern Indiana to the "knobs" of southeastern Indiana, the changes are more startling than in nearby Illinois or Ohio.

The land of Indiana was pushed and scraped into its present form by the glaciers that long ago moved into the region from the north. The glaciers extended far into the state, bringing with them a great deal of sand, gravel, rocks, clay, and silt. When the glaciers finally began to melt and recede northward, those materials were left behind. The glaciers scraped the northern and central parts of the state to a flat or gently rolling topography, and land in the southern part was sculpted into the hilly uplands characteristic of the area. The glaciers left huge chunks of ice behind as they retreated, and those great blocks of ice melted to form the many lakes of northern Indiana. The largest blocks formed the Great Lakes, and the smaller ones became the thousands of small lakes in the north.[4] The lakes and swamps were so numerous that the first inhabitants, the Indians, could travel by canoe almost anywhere in northern Indiana.

Northeastern Indiana is considered a morainal lake area, where sand and gravel were deposited by the retreating glaciers. This region lies north of the junction of the Eel and the Wabash rivers and extends to north of Fort Wayne. Most of central Indiana, which lies south of the east-to-west flowing Upper Wabash, is flatland or rolling hilly plain. This land is mainly agricultural and is generally very fertile. In the southwestern corner of Indiana is the Wabash lowland, formed by the erosion of the land by the river. To the east of this lowland are numerous uplands, of which the Norman and the Dearborn are the most important, running diagonally from midstate to the southeast. The Scotsburg lowland joins the Dearborn upland and is near the Muscatatuck regional slope. Indiana's topography is extremely varied, although the variations are all very gradual except for the "knobs" area in Floyd County.[5]

Elevations in the state vary from less than four hundred feet to over twelve hundred feet above sea level. In most of southwestern Indiana the elevation is from four hundred to six hundred feet above sea level. On both sides of the Wabash River the land rises to elevations of six to eight hundred feet and stays at that elevation all the way to Fort Wayne and on into Ohio. The land in central Indiana varies from eight hundred to one thousand feet above sea level, with some land around Richmond gradually rising to twelve hundred feet. These higher spots are the only "peaks" in the state, but because of the gradual rise they don't seem much higher than the land around them. Much of this highest land in east central Indiana actually seems flat because of the gradual rise in elevation.[6]

The southeastern part of the state is actually not nearly so high as the rest of the state but it seems much higher because of the extremes in elevation found there. From the four hundred feet measured at the low-water mark of the Ohio in Harrison County to the nearby hills, which measure about six hundred and ten feet, the rise is very abrupt. This rapid change in elevation makes the higher parts seem even higher than they actually are. The greater relief seen in southeastern Indiana is the result of erosion and the subsequent reshaping of the bedrock over the ages. The land has not "risen," as one would think, but actually has "fallen" to elevations lower than those in nearby central Indiana.[7] Unglaciated bedrock is found in southern Indiana between the southwestern point in Posey County and New Albany in Floyd County. This land, untouched by glaciers, extends up into northern Monroe County above Bloomington. Surrounding this area is a drift area where the glaciers dropped small boulders and other drift materials. The least topographical variation is found in Tipton County in north central Indiana. This is the area scraped flat by the retreating glaciers. Most of northern Indiana is outwash-lake and river sedimentary or end morainal in nature.[8]

The major drainage systems of the state are the St. Lawrence, the Maumee Basin, the St. Joseph Basin, the Calumet Basin, the Mississippi Drainage, the Kankakee Basin, the Ohio River Basin, and the Continental Divide in Whitley County.[9] From the Continental Divide the waters flow eastward on the eastern side and westward on the western side. The principal rivers of Indiana are the Wabash and the White rivers, and the mighty Ohio, which forms its southern boundary. The East and West forks of the White River empty into the lower Wabash near Princeton in Gibson County. The Wabash then joins the Ohio below Evansville in southwestern Indiana. The Whitewater River flows through east central Indiana and empties into the Ohio in Dearborn County. In the northeast part of the state the Kankakee River flows westward into Illinois. In northern Indiana the St. Mary's and the St. Joseph's rivers flow into the Maumee River, which then empties into Lake Erie. The diversion of the rivers by the Continental Divide can be seen by noting the direction in which the rivers flow out of the state.

Not only are the land features varied, but the seasons in Indiana are not at all "half-way." Humidity is generally high because of fairly heavy rainfall in the spring and fall. Infrequent dry spells during the summer are, nonetheless, also accompanied by extremely high humidity. The Rocky Mountains block the passage of moist Pacific air from the interior of America, including Indiana. Thus, the midsection of the country is exposed to either warm, tropical air from the Gulf of Mexico or cold, dry air from Canada. This explains the hot, humid summers and the cold, dry winters that are common in Indiana. In July the temperature can reach one hundred degrees, and in the winter the temperature often goes below zero. The average rainfall in the state is about forty inches, which accounts for the high humidity.[10]

Indiana is subject to rather violent weather patterns and severe thunderstorms, and tornadoes often occur there. About twenty-two tornadoes and two hundred thunderstorms hit the state every year. Our ancestors called tornadoes "cyclones," and many people built "cyclone cellars" near their homes for protection from these violent storms. Lightning, high winds, and damaging hail also cause a great deal of damage during the summer months. March through July is generally the worst period for severe weather in Indiana.[11]

Flooding of the major and minor rivers has been a problem since pioneer days, but flood-control lakes and dams have reduced the problem in recent years. A severe flood, however, caused hundreds of people to leave their homes in the winter of 1990 and 1991. The worst recorded flood was in the spring of 1937 when towns along the Ohio and Wabash rivers had to be evacuated because of dangerously high waters. Before settlement days, flooding may have prevented the Indians from living in Indiana except during the dry seasons. Travel by water was, however, easier for our pioneer ancestors when streams were high.

Indiana lies in two distinct climate zones. The southern one-fourth of the state is in the humid subtropical zone. The coldest month in this zone averages above thirty-two degrees, and the warmest month averages at least seventy-one degrees. In this zone rainfall is distributed fairly evenly throughout the year. The rest of the state lies in the humid continental zone where the coldest month averages below thirty-two degrees. No other differences exist between this zone and the slightly warmer zone to the south.[12] "Lake-effect snow" helps to give northwestern Indiana much heavier snowfall than that in the rest of the state because of moisture blown off Lake Michigan by cold winter winds.

The original native trees which once grew in Indiana are not found there now. When the settlers came in the early 1800s they cut down most of the forest and burned off most of the ground vegetation. Natural tree growth before settlement was mostly broadleaf deciduous trees such as beech and maple. Oak and hickory were also very common, as were sugar maple, white ash, white pine, tulip poplar, and other forest trees with an average height of about one hundred feet. The largest trees towered from one hundred-fifty to two hundred feet in the air and grew to as much as twelve to sixteen feet in diameter. The stump of one huge tree near Corydon is said to have been so large that it was used as a dance floor by the pioneers. According to legend, it was over sixteen feet across. Only a few virgin trees remain in the state today.

The only prairie land was in northwestern Indiana, where rainfall was too scant to grow trees. The blue grasses of the prairie were large and reedlike and grew from eight to ten feet in height. This tall, coarse, tough grass made traveling through it difficult and unpleasant. Buffaloes walking through such grasslands were often buried to their shoulders in the tall reeds.[13] Because of this difficulty, the Indians who traveled in the area preferred to use the rivers and streams instead of fighting the grasses. Settlers could not easily pull up this reedy grass and had to resort to grubbing it out laboriously with hoes and hatchets. They sometimes burned the grass off the land and then dug out the roots by hand. The land was quite fertile despite, or perhaps because of, the prairie grasses. Today, remnants of the original prairie still exist in the northwest corner of the state.

North of the original prairie, lying along and around Lake Michigan, are the sand hills, dunes, and marshes of northwest Indiana. Nearby the prairies are abloom with wildflowers unique to the area. The wildflowers seem to be the original kinds of plants which grew there when the first white men arrived in the late seventeenth century.[14] Plant life in this area is extremely varied, with cactuses growing in the sand dunes and orchids blooming in the marshes. Lichens and moss of the far north, and pawpaw, tulip trees, and sassafras of the semitropics all grow in this small area of the state.[15] Likewise, magnolias and mimosas grow in southern Indiana, although both are generally found growing in much warmer southern climates. A hard freeze may cause magnolias to drop their blooms, and mimosas to die back, but they seem to sprout again the next year.

There were many swamps and marshes in the lowlands when the first settlers came to Indiana. The only cleared land was where lightning had started fires that burned the forests and where thin topsoil could not support the growth of trees in southern Indiana. The land near the marshes proved to be terribly unhealthy places, although many settlers tried to live there. Malaria, known as "the ague," plagued the pioneers, and many people even died from its effects. The summer of 1827 was a particularly bad year for malaria. Typhoid epidemics also took their toll, and the doctors' only answer seemed to be bloodletting.[16] Other settlers, weakened by the ague, moved farther west to healthier, drier land. Efforts to drain the marshes were begun fairly early by the settlers, and today Indiana has few marshy spots. The unwholesome living conditions near those swamps may have been another reason that the Indians did not live in Indiana during most of the seventeenth century.

If you have a tradition that your pioneer ancestors died in Indiana during the early settlement period or even up into the 1840s, the reason may have been either "the ague" or cholera. Cholera epidemics (*cholera morbus*) swept through the state in 1832, when Madison, Indiana, had forty-two cases and twenty-two deaths by November 8.[17] Cholera struck again in the late 1840s, when many Hoosiers died from the disease. Because so many people died during an epidemic, not everyone has a tombstone. Men, women, and children died from these illnesses, and many families lost all of their able-bodied men to cholera. Milk sickness, caused by a poisonous plant eaten by milk cattle, killed many people, especially women and children, who drank most of the milk.[18]

The glaciers which scraped the surface of the state left behind them many minerals which would later be important to the economy of the state. These minerals included clay and clay products, gravel, sand, limestone, sandstone, marl, and other minerals which have been and are still being removed from the ground to be sold. Indiana also mines bituminous coal, petroleum, and natural gas. Most coal is extracted by surface strip mining rather than by deep shaft mining, principally in southwestern Indiana.[19] Gold has even been found and mined in Brown and Morgan counties in central Indiana, although not too profitably.[20] The climate and the fertile land of Indiana are also conducive to agriculture. Corn, wheat, and other kinds of grain, soy beans, livestock, vegetables, fruits, and dairy products are all produced in the state.

Indiana is culturally different in the northern and southern sections of the state. The southern part was settled first by people from the uplands of southeastern America. Settlement in Indiana then moved in gradual steps from the south to the central part, and from the central to the northern section. The central section was settled by people from both the southeast and the east, as well as by people from southern Indiana. The northern two-thirds of the state was then settled by people who had come largely from the mid-Atlantic, northern, and northeastern states. Because the settlers came from different areas and had dissimilar origins, their cultural backgrounds were also very different. Differing nationalities also added to the cultural differences. Even today, these differences remain between the northern and the southern sections of Indiana.

The economic makeup of the northern two-thirds of the state is largely industrial in and around the cities and agricultural in between those cities. The largest northern Indiana cities are Gary, Hammond, South Bend, Elkhart, and Fort Wayne. Central Indiana is a mixture of the industrial and the agricultural, having the capital and largest city, Indianapolis, and several other fairly large cities—Kokomo, Lafayette, Muncie, Anderson, Terre Haute, and Richmond. The southern part of the state is more rural, with fewer large cities, which are less industrial than those in the north. Evansville, New Albany, Bloomington, and Columbus are the largest cities in southern Indiana.

Because of the diversity of economic and cultural backgrounds, regionalism is very pronounced in the state. It is rooted in the kinds of people who originally settled each region and in the kinds of people who later came to live there over the years. Regionalism has been a strong deterrent to the economic growth of the state in many ways, but it has also strongly influenced its development. As long as ethnic and cultural differences exist, regionalism will continue to exert forces in Indiana. In recent years, however, Indiana's population has gradually become more homogeneous, and the effects of regionalism less obvious. Whether this change is advantageous for Hoosiers remains to be seen.

The Indians of Indiana

CHAPTER

2

The first inhabitants of Indiana were the people called "Indians" by Christopher Columbus, who believed he had sailed to India when he actually had landed on the North American continent. Indiana, "the land of Indians," was named for those people even though few Indians lived there when the state was named. Six Indiana counties carry Indian names: Delaware, Miami, Ohio, Tippecanoe, Vermillion, and Wabash. Indians are often called "native Americans" but they were not natives of this continent.

The first Indians were a nomadic people who probably came to the North American continent from Asia by way of the Bering Strait between 12,000 and 14,000 years ago. They began to come here after the last Ice Age and gradually spread out from Alaska, down the Pacific coast, and then across the entire continent.[1] At first, they came in small groups about the size of large families. Because they came during different periods over thousands of years, the early arrivals looked very different from later ones. As these people spread across America they adapted to the different climates of the various places where they lived, further changing their appearance, customs, and even their language. The earliest Indians were hunters and gatherers who roamed about in a fairly large area. They used tools but did not grow crops or live in one place for a very long time.[2] Only a few artifacts, such as spear points, remain as evidence that these early Indians ever lived in Indiana. Spear points, found along with bones of extinct mammoth and bison that also lived there, have given them the name "spear point" people. They belong to the Paleo-Indian Tradition.

THE GROWTH OF TRIBES

The next group of Indians, who lived in Indiana between 8000 B.C. and 1000 B.C., may have been descendants of the earlier "spear point" people or may have been an entirely different group. These later Indians lived in larger groups or tribes instead of in the small family groups of the earlier period. They were also nomadic hunters and gatherers who grew no crops of any kind, but they made and used tools.[3] They went on long trading journeys across the country and sometimes migrated to other parts of the country to live. These people considered themselves the guardians of the land, not its owners, and often moved out of an area when they felt it was overused. They observed simple rituals, among them ceremonial burials. Their burial mounds are found in many places in Indiana. These early tribal people of the Archaic Tradition lived in the area for about 7,000 years.[4]

THE WOODLAND INDIANS

The next group of Indians who lived in Indiana were people known today as the Woodland people. They are better known than the two earlier cultures because they left artifacts of their lives here, but all three early groups were prehistoric, meaning that they lived before their history was written by Europeans. The Woodland people spread over most of eastern America between 1000 B.C. and A.D. 900. Most of the archaeological "finds" in Indiana represent the Woodland period. Still hunters and foragers, the Woodland people were beginning to practice rudimentary agriculture. Their first crop was maize (corn), which the women planted. They grew squash and sunflowers for the seeds.[5] They also ate wild game, roots, and berries. During this period the Indians learned to use the bow and arrow and made distinctively decorated cooking pots representative of the particular tribe. Broken bits of these pots have been found and used to determine which cultures lived in a place at a certain time. The style of pot, the kind of clay used, and the type of decoration all help to identify the particular group of Indians as they moved about the land.[6] Archaeologists can also determine the approximate date the utensil was made by carbon-dating the shards, or pieces, of pottery.

The characteristic burial mounds of the Ohio Valley were built during the Woodland period, and the people are often called the "Mound Builders." At first the mounds were primitive but later they became more complex. People buried in the mounds were probably important tribal persons, who were buried surrounded by exotic materials from faraway places. Among the materials found in the burial mounds are copper from Lake Superior, shells from the Gulf Coast, obsidian from Wyoming, sheet mica from the Appalachians, and flint from Illinois and Ohio, all obtained on trading expeditions.[7] The mounds seem not to have been built or used after about A.D. 400, at about the same time the trading networks disappeared. Examples of the burial mounds can be seen in various places in the state. The most outstanding are those at Mounds State Park near Anderson and at Angel Mounds near Evansville.[8] These mounds are evidence that the people cooperated for the good of the tribe and suggest that the tribe had become more important than the family. The Woodland Indians have been determined to have been tall, slim, and very attractive people with straight black hair and black eyes, light copper-colored skin, and prominent cheekbones.[9]

THE MISSISSIPPIAN INDIANS

The last of the prehistoric cultures is known as the Mississippian Tradition. These Indian people lived in Indiana from about A.D. 900 until the early 1600s. They left the area just a short time before the first white men, French explorers and missionaries, traveled through northwestern Indiana. These later Indians may have been descendants of the Woodland people, but they didn't use the tools, weapons, or the elaborate burial ceremonies and burial mounds used by the Woodland people. People of the Mississippian culture lived mostly in southwestern Indiana, along the lower Ohio River, and a few lived in northwestern Indiana.[10] They cultivated crops of maize, squash, pumpkins, beans, and tobacco. They learned to plant seeds from wild plants and from plants cultivated by Indians in other parts of America. In order to grow such varied crops, the Indians had to live in one place semipermanently, and, thus, they became less nomadic.

These later Indians built homes, villages, and farms, and built forts for protection from enemies. The tribe had grown even larger than those of the earlier cultures, and the chief and the shaman became extremely influential persons in the tribe. The mounds they built were meant to raise their temples above the surrounding village and were not intended for ceremonial burials.[11]

Even though these later Indians lived semipermanently in an area, they were chiefly hunters and fishermen. And even though the elaborate trading networks had collapsed, their trading journeys to other areas continued. Artifacts of this period include arrowheads, spear points, club and hatchet heads, pottery, and tools for everyday use. For some unexplained reason, these seemingly very successful Indians left the area in about 1600. Why they left and where they went is a mystery. It is not known whether they left in small groups, departed in a great migration, or were wiped out by illness. Perhaps game was less plentiful in Indiana or they decided to move on to new land. Indians reported in the early 1800s that most of the bison had frozen to death one winter in the 1600s. At any rate, the Indians who met the French explorers as they first crossed Indiana were not members of the Mississippian tribes. There do not seem to have been any Indians living in Indiana from about 1600 until the time the French came.

FRENCH EXPLORERS AND MISSIONARIES

When La Salle crossed Indiana between 1679 and 1681, the Miami Indians were the principal tribe in the area. The Indians then living in Indiana had been driven out of land farther east by fierce Sioux and Iroquois tribes and by advancing white settlers. The largest Indian towns in Indiana were at Kekeonga near present-day Fort Wayne, at Ouiatanon on the site of modern-day Lafayette, and at the large Osage village near Peru. Eventually, the Potawatomi moved in from Michigan, the Kickapoo from Wisconsin, and the Shawnee from Kentucky, and in the late 1700s, the Delawares were "invited in" from Ohio to increase tribal strength.[12] Because the tools and weapons of these tribes are different from those of the earlier cultures which lived in Indiana, it seems almost certain that they had not lived here before. The only way we know about the Indians who were in this area when the French came is from documents written by the French explorers and missionaries. The Indians had no written language but did have oral traditions about their tribal history. Records about the Indians were also made by the English and Americans who later came to Indiana.

The French came into Indiana from Detroit to explore "the Ohio Country" northwest of the Ohio River. These first expeditions from Canada showed the French the value of the area which would later become the Northwest Territory. Indiana waterways especially impressed the French because the rivers flowed in a direct line, with only one short portage from Fort Wayne into the Wabash and then into the Ohio River at the southern tip of Indiana. There the Ohio joined the Mississippi River, offering fast transportation to the French settlement at New Orleans and to the Gulf of Mexico. This fairly easy and fast means of reaching the Mississippi would prove valuable to the French, and they readily realized its importance. They also recognized the potential for trade with the Indians and wisely cultivated their friendship and they became allies. The French lived with, and like, the Indians, adopting Indian ways and marrying Indian wives. The French generally dealt fairly with the Indians, unlike the British, who often exploited the Indians. French missionaries introduced Christianity to the Indians and taught their children.

FRENCH TRADING POSTS AND FORTS

The French set up a string of trading post-forts between Detroit and the Mississippi River to protect their claim on the land. Trading stations were set up at Post Miami, now Fort Wayne, in 1715; at Ouiatanon on the Upper Wabash near Lafayette in 1719; and early in 1733 at Vincennes on the Lower Wabash.[13] Some scholars believe that Vincennes was settled as early as 1715. Only the French settlement which grew up around the fort at Vincennes was destined to become permanent. Later, the French government encouraged the families of soldiers and other French civilians to come to live in and around the posts in Indiana. This move was made to enlarge the French population in the area and to strengthen and enforce French claims to the land.

A French trader as depicted by Frederic Remington. From Charles Moore, *The Northwest under Three Flags, 1635–1796* (New York: Harper and Brothers, 1900).

The French also encouraged the Indians to settle around the trading posts and forts, partly for protection and partly to secure the Indians' trading allegiance. The Indians who traded with the French began to live near the forts, where they could strike better fur-trading deals. They liked living "close to the market" and felt safer at the forts under the protection of the French soldiers. This change in their lives robbed the Indians of their tribal identity and made them dependent upon the French for goods and supplies. The braves began to neglect their families and tribal duties in favor of fur trapping or loitering around the trading posts. They began to drink liquor and fight among themselves instead of hunting, fishing, and tending to their tribal responsibilities. All of these actions led to the weakening of the tribal unit as smaller groups began to live apart from the tribe. The longer the Indians lived near the Europeans, the more their culture changed and the more they lost in the arrangement.

Records of the early French forts are scant. Some official correspondence between the commandant at Vincennes and French headquarters at New Orleans exists, as do a few early censuses taken of settlers there which give no names. The 1767 French census taken at Vincennes lists 232 white men, women, and children, 10 Negro and 17 Indian slaves, and 168 "strangers." The "strangers" were the hunters, traders, and wanderers called "voyageurs" who were passing through the area.[14] Some of these early French records have been printed in various publications over the years, many by the Indiana Historical Society, but they have not been collected into one comprehensive volume.

BRITAIN ENTERS THE NORTHWEST

France's success in middle America was evident to the British, who controlled all of eastern America. Once the British realized that France had claimed the center of the continent and was enjoying a prosperous fur trade, they began to covet the area themselves. Where the English had been keeping traders back behind the frontier, they soon began to let them enter the upper Ohio River Valley. By 1749 over three-hundred English and American traders were operating in that area.[15] Angered by the threat to their trading monopoly with the Indians, the French began to build forts along the main trails to Detroit and Quebec. This move was made to safeguard the fur-trading trails and to ensure their supremacy over the area. As a countermeasure, the English began to give the Indians more trading goods, hardware, tools, and dry goods than did the French, as well as handsome presents as "bonuses." The Indians had become over dependant on the French goods, and when Britain blocked French shipments in the 1740s, during the War of the Austrian Succession, France's hold on the Indians was severely damaged.[16] Because the French couldn't pay them with trading goods, many Indians began to trade with the British and Americans, considering the goods a necessity. The lesser tribes' fear of the fierce Iroquois, allied with the British, was also used by the British to force the Indians to deal with English traders. All of these acts served to undermine the French hold on their Indian allies, as well as their claim on the country, although most of the Indians remained loyal to the French. Realizing that the greatest threat was the unchecked entry of British and American traders, France was determined to strengthen its position in Illinois and Indiana.[17]

France decided that more French settlers would secure their hold on middle America, and more French civilians from Canada and France were encouraged to come to settle there. Only about 1,500 French people were living in the "Illinois Country," which included Indiana, in 1752. The Indians had also come to an important decision. They did not want more white settlers—not Frenchmen, not Englishmen, and certainly not Americans! Meanwhile, more and more English and Anglo-Americans were moving into the Ohio Country, and soon both France and Britain claimed the area. It was during this time that the Delaware Indians were asked by the other Indian bands to move into Indiana in an effort to discourage further white settlement. The Delawares settled in east central Indiana in what is now Delaware County.

THE FRENCH AND INDIAN WAR

Conflicts between the British and the French between 1689 and 1763 led to the French and Indian War, known in Europe as the Seven Years War. France, aided by the Potawatomi tribes, raided frontier settlements in Virginia, Pennsylvania, and New York. The Miamis, although still allied with the French, were not as active in this campaign because they had been ravaged by smallpox. There was also much dissension among the tribes over loyalties. Britain won most of these conflicts, and France eventually lost its hold on North America. In 1763 the Treaty of Paris gave control of America to Britain, and English troops occupied the former French forts. In 1763, in Pontiac's Rebellion, the Miamis and the Potawatomis captured Fort Miami and Fort Ouiatanon and surrounded Detroit in an attempt to oust the British from America. With Britain's victory, France lost its hold on American land. After the Treaty of Paris and France's loss of power, the Indians finally lost hope of French aid and gave up overt hostility toward the British. The Indians had grown so dependent on European trade goods that they eventually turned to the British for aid and became their reluctant allies. The Indians liked the Americans less than they liked the British, and the British less than the French.[18]

Where the French had not deliberately disturbed the land and holdings of the Indians or purposely changed their culture, the British managed to do both. The French were more interested in trade than in farming, and the French missionaries emphasized religion within the framework of the tribe. France's hold had been through a paternalistic policy which also emphasized Christianity, whereas Britain's hold was more militaristic and dictatorial. When France had lost power in America, the Indians had lost an ally and a friend, but they still preferred the British soldiers to American settlers. It is interesting to note that Britain controlled America for only twenty years, between the close of the French and Indian War and the beginning of the Revolutionary War. During that time, the English system of law was implemented in the Illinois Country, and it was that system which would be used when the area became the Northwest Territory of the United States.

The British, aware of the Indians' strength and potential for mischief, decided to placate them by prohibiting American settlement beyond the Appalachian Mountains. The Proclamation of 1763 reserved this land exclusively for the Indians and for licensed fur traders. Britain hoped to benefit from increased trade with the Indians, but many Indians still preferred the French, especially the Indians along the Wabash River, where Britain had not built or fortified new forts. The former French fort at Vincennes, however, was manned and maintained by the British. The English, unlike the French, did not treat the Indians as friends, and their hold on them was largely maintained by force or bribes. It was the English who began the barbaric "Indian custom" of scalping settlers, which the Indians continued for many years. Admittedly, some American settlers also resorted to scalping, but the fact is that many Indian atrocities in the Old Northwest had their origins in the English bounty payments for scalps. Detroit Lieutenant Governor Henry Hamilton got his nickname, "Hair-Buyer," because he, in full war paint and Indian dress, supplied the tribes with guns and knives and urged them "to take up the hatchet."[19]

Indiana was not involved in the Revolutionary War until 1778, when a group of Virginians and Kentuckians marched with young George Rogers Clark into the Ohio Country and took it from the British. The Indians and their loyalty were the key to dominance in "the west," and both the Americans and the British worked to gain their loyalty. Clark's small group of Americans first captured the former French posts on the Mississippi River in western Illinois and then twice took Fort Sackville from the British at Vincennes. After first taking the fort, Clark was forced to leave it in the hands of a small American garrison, which the British easily overpowered. His second attempt, the famed trek through flood-swollen southern Illinois to British-held Vincennes was successful, and this time the Americans held the fort. That victory won the Northwest for the United States and effectively signaled the "beginning of the end" of the Revolutionary War—or so Hoosiers like to think.

Clark and several wealthy and influential French civilians had to foot the bills for that venture, for which they were never repaid. Later, Virginia granted to Clark and his men 150,000 acres of land in southeastern Indiana as payment for their brave service.[20] This land, called "Clark's Grant," is located in Harrison County "at the Falls of the Ohio" across the Ohio from Louisville. The town of Clarksville was founded by George Rogers Clark.

In 1778 the area north of the Ohio River and west of Ohio Territory was organized as Illinois County, Virginia. At that time a traveler named William Wilson described the three principal tribes in Indiana as the "Wabash Tribes," made up of the Kickapoo, Mascoutins, Wea, and Piankashaw; the Twightwees, or Pitts (named for Fort Pickawillany in Ohio); and the Ottawa and Potawatomi, who lived on the Maumee River in northern Indiana.[21]

At the close of the French and Indian War in 1783, French officials and the more influential French families had left Indiana and Illinois. They had either moved back to Canada, to the Spanish settlement across the Mississippi River, or to French Louisiana. The French community and the Piankashaw village at Vincennes remained, however. An influential Piankashaw chief, Tobacco's Son, lived in a fairly large Indian village near Vincennes in 1778 and was considered a friend of the Americans. Within about ten years most of the Piankashaws had left Indiana for Illinois and Iowa. The last Piankashaws left in 1786 after selling their land to white settlers, Scotch-Irish Presbyterians from Pennsylvania, the Carolinas, and Kentucky, who had built on the Indian lots before 1783.[22]

Despite their loss in the Revolution, the British still controlled Fort Ouiatanon on the Upper Wabash. They hoped to regain control of the continent and urged the Indians to harrass white settlers whenever possible. The Wea Indians lived in the area between the Vermillion and the Tippecanoe rivers, and the Miamis near the junction of the Wabash and the Miami rivers. The Piankashaws, most of whom had left Indiana, occasionally swept down from northeastern Illinois to harrass settlers around Vincennes, and other tribes also attacked settlers from time to time. The Shawnees, the fiercest of the Indiana tribes, were led by Tecumseh, his brother, The Prophet, and Blue Jacket. They raided along the Ohio River and were reported to have ceremonially sacrificed their war captives before raids. The Shawnee had come to the midwest from Georgia and northern Florida and got their name from the Suwanee River there. The fierce Shawnee warriors exerted strong influence on the lesser tribes, the Kickapoos, Potawatomis, Delawares, and Miamis.

The few scant French Catholic church records dating from 1749 which remain at Vincennes give only the names of persons involved in church rites and church events. The local archives there also have a few early land grants records. No early marriages, wills, inventories, appraisals, public sales, or other such records remain. Official records made by the French government may have been taken by French officials when they left in 1763 after the French and Indian War. The records also might have been sent to Kaskaskia in the Illinois Country, to Canada, or to France, or they may have been destroyed.[23] The English and Americans who came to Vincennes after the French left considered the remaining French settlers "indolent, apathetic, and poverty-stricken." In 1796 there were about two hundred houses in Vincennes, one-fourth of which were empty. The houses were very small and badly furnished, but Virginia miner Moses Austin found the village "quite charming."[24]

THE NORTHWEST TERRITORY

At the end of the Revolutionary War, Massachusetts, New York, Connecticut, and Virginia released their claims to land north of the Ohio River and west of Ohio Territory and ceded it to the new United States of America. In 1787 Congress organized this area, containing the current states of Indiana, Illinois, and

Michigan, as the new Northwest Territory. At about this same time some of the Indians who lived in southern Indiana were beginning to leave the area for land farther west. Settlement in this new territory proceeded much more slowly than in the areas to the south because of a very real Indian threat. Thus, settlement was almost completely prevented until the 1795 victory of American troops under General "Mad Anthony" Wayne at the Battle of Fallen Timbers. (See below, chapter 6.)

INDIANA TERRITORY

Indiana Territory, organized in 1800, encompassed all of the area from the western border of Ohio to the Mississippi River. Excepted from this area was a small part of lower Michigan and the triangular "gore" in southeastern Indiana, which then belonged to Ohio. Although the Northwest Territory had more than 50,000 settlers by 1800, most of them were living in the comparative safety of Ohio, where Indian attacks were less severe. Indian raids north of the Ohio River were thought to be incited by Britain and Spain. Even though Great Britain had lost her claim to America, it still had trading posts in the heart of the continent. Naturally, the Americans wanted Britain ousted from the fur-trading posts, suspecting correctly that the British were supplying arms to the Indians of the Northwest Territory.[25]

INDIAN CLAIMS NULLIFIED

The claims of Indian tribes to land in Indiana were gradually nullified by fifty-four cessions starting with the 1795 Treaty of Greenville following the Battle of Fallen Timbers. The tribe most closely identified with Indiana was the Miami, which had come there from Ohio by the late 1600s. Led by their chief, Little Turtle, the Miamis claimed land which made up most of present-day Indiana. Although the Indians lost a great deal of land to white settlers by the Greenville Treaty, the settlers were not content and wanted still more Indian land. By the late 1700s quite a few settlers and squatters had already entered southern Indiana, mostly along the Ohio and the Wabash rivers, where few Indians were then living. Some Delaware Indians had come to east central Indiana during the late eighteenth century and lived in the Muncie and Anderson areas near the Shawnees. Some other tribes had also been allowed to come into northern Indiana, possibly at the invitation of the Miamis, and had moved as far south as the Upper Wabash by 1800. The Piankashaw, the Potawatomi, and the Ouiatanon had also come down from the Great Lakes to live in villages along the Wabash and the Vermillion rivers.

The Indiana tribes were persuaded to give up more and more of their land by government treaties, by force, and sometimes by outright deception. Indian treaties which opened land to settlers were those made at Fort Wayne in 1803, which took parts of Daviess, Martin, Dubois, Pike, Orange, Sullivan, and Gibson counties and all of Knox county; at Vincennes in 1804, which took all of the counties bordering the Ohio River from Clark County westward to Posey and the rest of Gibson county; and at Grouseland in 1805, which ceded a wedge of land in southeastern Indiana between the "gore" and the Fort Wayne cession. A cession was made by the Miami, the Delaware, and the Potawatomi Indians by another treaty in 1809, which ceded all of Vigo, Clay, Owen, half of Monroe and Jackson, and all of Sullivan, Greene, and Lawrence counties.[26] The 1809 treaty infuriated the Indians, especially the Shawnees, who contested the cession of Indian lands by only a few tribes. They felt that all of the tribes should have consented to this action for it to be valid. Under a remarkable leader named Tecumseh, the tribes then tried unsuccessfully to unite to drive out white settlers. Tecumseh tried to organize a strong confederation, but the tribes did not seem able to cooperate to accomplish their goal. William Henry Harrison led troops north from Vincennes to Tippecanoe, where the first of several battles were fought. In 1811 the Battle of Tippecanoe was won by American forces, but it did not break the Indian resistance. Shortly afterward, Indians were once again raiding American settlements on the frontier.[27]

The outbreak of the War of 1812 found the Indians allied with the British, with the exception of the Miamis, who remained neutral because of apathy and illness. Several vicious massacres took place in southern Indiana during this second war with Britain. In August 1812 the Pigeon Roost settlement in Scott County was largely wiped out by Shawnee Indians, whom the settlers had considered friendly. In this massacre nine related adults and fifteen children were murdered in a raid on several cabins. It seems that the incentive for the raid was the five-dollar reward offered for each American scalp. The Shawnees' resentment of the earlier land-grabbing treaties may have been the real reason behind this brutal attack.

As the Indian crisis grew increasingly worse, General William Henry Harrison and some five thousand Kentucky volunteers marched north to rescue the besieged garrison at Fort Wayne. Then, joined by Indiana militiamen, they began to destroy the villages of the Miamis, the Potawatomis, and the allied tribes. A final confrontation north of Lake Erie defeated the Indians and British in the Battle of the Thames, where Tecumseh was killed in battle. This victory destroyed the Indian confederacy and ended the Indian threat in the Northwest Territory. The 1814 treaty ending this war with Great Britain also put an end to the British-incited scalpings and other atrocities and allowed settlers to safely enter Indiana Territory.[28] In 1818 the Miami and Delaware Indians ceded yet another tract of land to the United States. This cession, the New Purchase, was for land just north of the 1809 central Indiana cession, which had so infuriated the Shawnees.

An excellent source of records made by the territorial government of the Northwest Territory is the set of books called *Territorial Papers of the United*

States, compiled largely by Clarence Edwin Carter. Records of the men who were in Indiana during those early, prestatehood days are found in the volumes devoted to Indiana. Included are voters' lists, petitions to the government for various causes and reasons, lists of public officials, and the names of the Indians who deeded land to the "Wabash Company." These Indians reserved twelve leagues above Vincennes "to be to, and for, the use of the said inhabitants," that is, the Piankashaw Indians. Because these Indians were gone long before Indiana became a state, it is probable that the grudge surrounding use of this land actually caused several scattered attacks on white settlers in the area around Vincennes. After the close of the War of 1812, Indian threats to settlers had more or less ceased, and only a few scattered incidents occurred. Some Piankashaws who had once lived near Vincennes came down from northern Illinois to capture and kill several members of a family of settlers, the Cannons, who were my ancestors. This brutal attack took place across the river from Gibson County and might have been caused by the unpopular treaties which forced the Indians to leave Indiana.

Despite the many treaties with the government and the many promises made to them, almost all of the Indians were required to leave Indiana in 1838 during the "great Indian removal." The tribes were relocated in territories west of the Mississippi River, mainly in Arkansas and Oklahoma territories. The Potawatomis were the first of the two major tribes be forced to leave; they were relocated in Kansas. The Miamis followed a short time later. At that time, most mixed-blood marriages were dissolved, unless the white partner chose to go west with his or her Indian mate. Most children of Indian-white marriages went with the Indian parent, although a few were allowed to stay in Indiana with the white parent. Only a few Indians were allowed to remain in the state, among them the Miami leader Jean Baptiste Richardville, who received huge amounts of land and was allowed to live in luxury in his Fort Wayne home, and Frances Slocum, red-haired wife of a Miami war chief. She had been captured at the age of five in Pennsylvania and in 1837 refused to leave her Indian family.

The sad Indian removal is remembered as "The Trail of Death."[29] The Indians had lost their last tentative hold on land promised to them "forever" by the United States government. At present some members of the Miami tribe live in Miami County in northern Indiana, and some others live near the Indiana-Michigan border. Records of the 1838 Indian removal are found at the National Archives in Washington, D.C., in the records of the Bureau of Indian Affairs. To inquire about Indian records, contact the Bureau of Indian Affairs at 1951 Constitution Avenue, N.W., Washington, D.C. 20240.

The early history of Indiana is entwined with that of the Indians who lived there when the first white settlers came. This ended only when the United States government sent the tribes out of the state in 1838. Members of the Indiana tribes gradually disappeared after the removal, and many probably blended into the western tribes. Most people in Indiana who claim Indian ancestry are descended from Indian-white marriages made in the southeastern states, mainly in western North Carolina. There, many white settlers married members of the Cherokee tribe, and they or their descendants later migrated to Indiana. The proportion of these mixed marriages was rather high and accounts for many part-Indian people who came to live in southern Indiana.

Six volumes of Indian records, *Cherokee by Blood*, have been compiled by Jerry Wright Jordan. They deal with the removals of tribal members by the United States government between 1817 and about 1835. A fund was later set up to repay Indians who could prove that they or their ancestors had been removed by the U.S. government from land east of the Mississippi. These Indians were relocated to lands west of the Mississippi River, but many descendants who lived elsewhere are accounted for in the second and later volumes. Volume two contains the *Guion Miller Report*, which gives complete genealogies for many descendants, including known Cherokees and those "accepted" by both Cherokees and whites as being Cherokee, white and black families with family traditions of Indian ancestry, and even many Creeks, who misunderstood eligibility to participate in the fund. It also contains records of payment to authenticated descendants by the government prior to 1910. Guion Miller was Special Commissioner to the United States Court of Claims from 1906 until 1910, and his report was actually a summary of all the information gathered for the 46,000 applicants to the fund. Microfilms of the *Report* are available at the National Archives in Washington, D.C. Unfortunately, they are difficult to read and decipher.[30]

Two new Indian museums have been opened in Indiana, the Eiteljorg Museum in Indianapolis and the Lesueur American Indian Museum in New Harmony. Charles-Alexandre Lesueur, a former curator of the Philadelphia Academy of Natural Sciences, came to New Harmony on the "Boatload of Knowledge" and lived there from 1826 to 1837. He excavated the Indian mounds in the Harmonist cemetery and the Bone Bank, located ten miles southwest of New Harmony and ten miles above the mouth of the Wabash River. There the river had eroded the river bank, exposing artifacts of the Mississippian culture. Pottery and arrow heads from that site are on display in the museum in New Harmony.

Indiana Boundaries

CHAPTER 3

THE NORTHWEST TERRITORY

Indiana, once part of Illinois County, Virginia, was therefore under the control of the Commonwealth of Virginia for a time. Following the Revolutionary War the Northwest Territory was established, with Indiana becoming a part of that territory. The Northwest Territory encompassed land lying north and west of the Ohio River and included Indiana, Illinois, and parts of Michigan and Wisconsin. The Ordinance of 1785 provided, among other things, for the survey of the land in the Northwest Territory. Indiana was the first territory which was completely surveyed using the new rectangular survey system instead of the older system of "metes and bounds." The old system used existing topographical features, such as rocks, trees, and streams as boundary points to identify land and boundaries.[1]

At that time courts were established by the territorial government at Vincennes, and these courts remained in operation at Vincennes after the formation of Knox County on June 20, 1790. The court at Vincennes granted 400 acres of land to just about every American who wanted land. For a list of some of the people who bought land, see House Document 198, 23rd Congress of the United States. For a list of militia donations of 100 acres at Vincennes in 1790, see House Document 455, 25th Congress. *The Vincennes Donation Lands*, by Leonard Lux, was published in the Indiana Historical Society Publications, volume 15, in 1949, and covers this subject, as does *The American State Papers*, which contains documents relating to the Vincennes district lands. *Grass Roots of America*, 1972, is an alphabetical surname index to eight volumes of public lands records and the volume of claims. *Land Records of Indiana*, abstracted by Immogene B. Brown, is a series of five volumes of land descriptions prepared from the surveyors' notes. Included are the counties of Brown,

Delaware, Jackson, Madison, and Martin. Some Jeffersonville and Vincennes land office records are found in Clifford Neal Smith's *Federal Land Series*, volume 1, *1788–1810*, volume 2, *1799–1835* and volume 3, *1810–1840*.[2]

At first, when there were few inhabitants, there was only a provisional government for Indiana Territory, with a governor and three judges chosen by Congress. The territorial government was to continue in effect until the time when a new state government could be formed. Provisions of the Ordinance of 1785 allowed the male inhabitants of Indiana Territory to elect an assembly when the adult male population reached 5,000. Once that happened, a delegate could be elected to the United States Congress, where he could support legislation but could not vote. When the population reached 60,000 free inhabitants, the people (males over age twenty-one) could draw up a constitution and petition Congress for statehood. The Ordinance stipulated that the area comprising the Northwest Territory could be carved into not more than five states nor fewer than three.

INDIANA BOUNDARIES

The eastern border of Indiana was laid out along a line called the first principal meridian. The line governs Indiana land east of the Greenville treaty line, which was agreed upon in the 1795 Greenville Treaty with the Indians. The second principal meridian was then placed on the range line that begins where the Little Blue River meets the Ohio River and runs up to the northern boundary of Indiana. It governs the surveys of all public lands in Indiana except those previously laid out by the French at Vincennes, by the government at Clark's Grant in Clark and Scott counties, and by the Greenville treaty line. The base line crosses this line at right angles at 38° 28′ 20″ north latitude. From these two lines all of the later rectangular surveys in Indiana were made, and from them the land descriptions take their names and numbers.[3] The deputy surveyors were given complete instructions and were told to "note in your field book . . . all rivers, creeks, springs and smaller streams of water . . . all swamps, ponds, stone quarries, coal beds, peat or turf grounds . . . the quality of the soil . . . mines, salt-licks, salt-springs and mill seats. . . . "[4] The state field notes and maps are in the office of the Auditor of the State of Indiana in Indianapolis. By using these field notes researchers can sometimes locate the land of their ancestors on a current map.

Indiana Territory was established in 1800. At that time, Knox County covered a part of western Ohio, all of Indiana, about three-fifths of Illinois, and part of lower Michigan. The first counties in Indiana Territory were established by proclamation of the governors of the Northwest Territory and Indiana Territory after Indiana in 1805 had gained enough population to reach the second step toward statehood. At that time the Indiana legislature could begin to set up new counties.[5]

The first land surveys were generally small and, for the most part, private land grants. These included the French tracts at Vincennes and Clark's Grant in Clark and Scott counties. The "Vincennes Tract" was given to the French in 1742 by means of a "Gift Deed." The tract lay at right angles to the trend of the Wabash River at Vincennes and contained about 1,600,000 acres.[6] These were old surveys made before the Indians' title to the land was removed by government treaty or purchase. The old surveys were not rectangular and straggled off haphazardly on diagonals or perpendicular to the nearby rivers. A grant of land was generally laid out at right angles to a stream or river, and thus, the boundary lines of Clark's Grant followed the trend of the Ohio River at Eighteen-Mile-Island northeast of Louisville.[7]

When the federal government obtained title to the land in Indiana, the new rectangular system of surveys began to be used. The rectangular system was a blessing which saved endless litigation and also assured settlers of true ownership of the land. In Kentucky, which followed the old metes and bounds system, many settlers lost their land because of faulty land titles. Daniel Boone, Thomas Lincoln, and hundreds of other Kentucky pioneers were the victims of defective land titles and lost land there.[8] Many people left Kentucky and came north to Indiana in hopes of obtaining valid land titles provided by the rectangular survey system. In the early 1800s, the survey of land in Indiana was made according to instructions issued by the surveyor-general of the United States. The land was all laid out from the intersection of the second principal meridian and the base line in southern Indiana. Land in "the gore," a wedge-shaped strip along the Ohio River in southeastern Indiana, was laid out from the first principal meridian and its corresponding base line. The intersection of the second principal meridian and the base line is called the "initial point," and all of the land in Indiana was laid out north, south, east, and west from this point.[9] There are thirty-one principal meridians and base lines in the contiguous United States, and four in Alaska. At the intersection of these two lines is the initial point of each of the survey areas, some of which are numbered, as in Indiana, and others which have proper names.[10]

As the surveys moved toward the north and south from the first survey lines, settlement moved with them. The rectangular system had been developed and used partially in Ohio, where it was tested and refined. The system was adopted May 20, 1785, but was not used in Clark's Grant to the Virginia and Kentucky volunteers. The Indiana State Library has the *Official Plat Book of Clark's Grant in Clark County, Indiana, 1789–1810*, by William Clark.[11] The earlier private land grants in Indiana were allowed to remain in effect, and the new surveys ran up to meet the old surveys. Because the survey system was ordered by Congress, the Indiana townships are often called "congressional townships."

The north-south columns of townships are called "Ranges" and the east-west rows of townships are called "Townships." The ranges are numbered north and

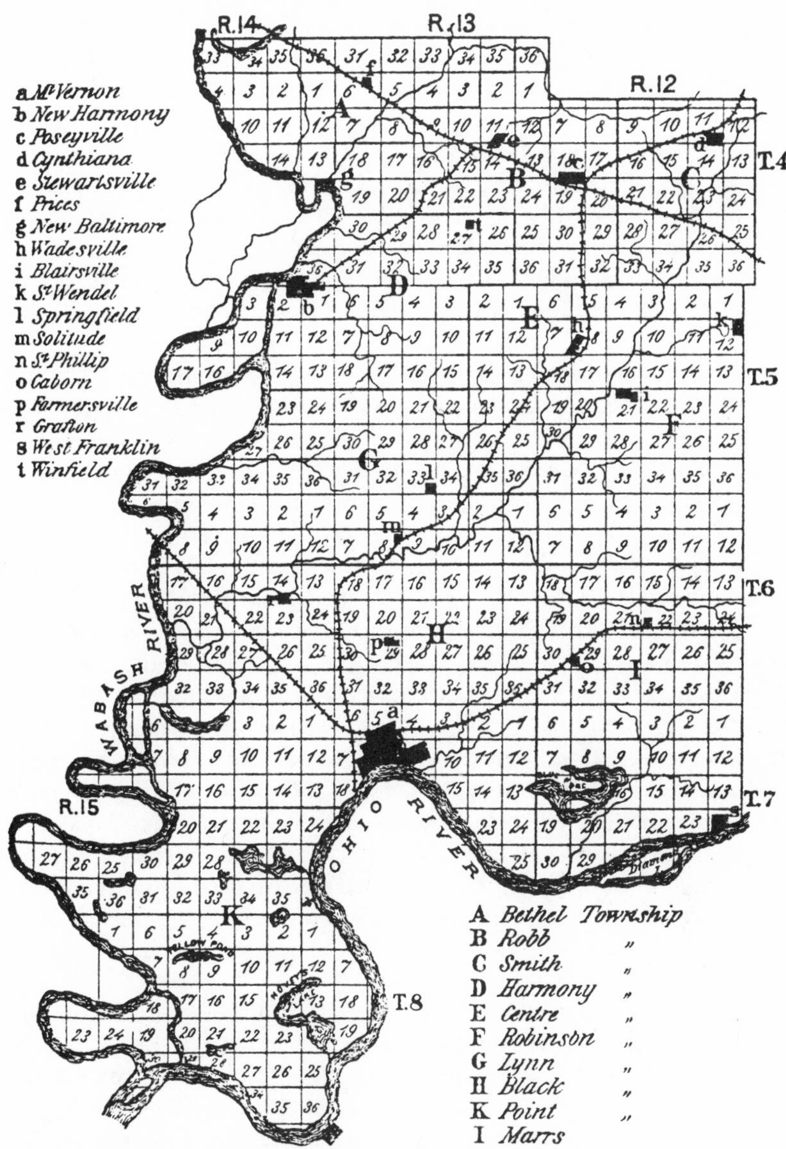

Outline map of Posey County, Indiana, showing irregular numbering of sections caused by irregular terrain. From Goodspeed Publishing Company, *History of Posey County* (Chicago, 1886).

south from the base line, and the townships are numbered east and west from the principal meridian. Each six-mile-square township has a corresponding designation based on its position in the grid.[12] For example, the township that is the second one north of the initial point and the second one east of the initial point is called "Township 2 North, Range 2 East" and is often abbreviated to "T 2 N, R 2 E." Each township was about six miles on a side and was further divided into 36 sections. Each section was about one mile on a side and contained about 640 acres. Sections in a township are numbered starting with number one usually in the northeast corner and going back and forth across the township until number 36 is located in the opposite, or southeast, corner of the township, although numbering can begin in any place.[13] Section 15 in the description above would be listed as "Section 15, Township 2 North, Range 2 East." Where the boundary of a county is irregular because of the presence of a river, there may be irregularities in the sectioning of the townships.[14]

Thomas Freeman, the government surveyor, produced by an amazing survey the description of the old Vincennes Tract, which had originally been made by metes and bounds. This survey was used when a new treaty was made with the Indians at Fort Wayne in 1803.[15] As soon as this treaty was signed, settlers began to come to the Vincennes area, and surveyors began to survey the Tract into townships and sections. Once the land was surveyed, a land office was established at Vincennes in 1804 and officially opened in 1805 when land was opened for entry.[16] Records of the Vincennes land office can be found in the Genealogy Department of the Indiana State Library in Indianapolis. The two-volume set *Indiana Land Entries*, by Margaret Waters, 1948 and 1949, reprinted in 1977, includes volume 1, *The Cincinnati District, 1801–1840*, for the counties of Dearborn, Fayette, Franklin, Jay, Ohio, Randolph, Switzerland, Union, and Wayne, and volume 2, *The Vincennes District, 1807–1877*, for the counties of Daviess, Gibson, Knox, Lawrence, Martin, Monroe, and Pike. These records are for only the first purchasers of the land, not for later buyers. The records are incomplete. Later land transactions are recorded in the appropriate county courthouse.

Later treaties opened new lands for settlement, and land offices were opened at Jeffersonville in 1807, Brookville in 1819, Terre Haute in 1820, Fort Wayne in 1823, and LaPorte in 1833. Many entries from the land office at Jeffersonville are recorded in the Ball State University publication *Original Returns: Federal Land Sales in Indiana*, in two volumes with a surname index. Included are lands in Brown, Bartholomew, Decatur, Ripley, Franklin, and Jennings counties. The office at Brookville was moved to Indianapolis in 1825. Ball State University abstracted from the microfilm the *Original Federal Land Sales, Township 21 North, Sold at Indianapolis and Original Federal Land Sales, Township 20 North, Sold at Indianapolis*. The counties included are Clinton, Tipton, Madison, Delaware, Boone, Hamilton, and Randolph. The Genealogy Division at the Indiana State Library indexed both compilations by surname.[17] The Terre

Haute office was moved to Crawfordsville before 1828, and the LaPorte office was moved to Winamac in 1839, as land sales moved to those areas.[18]

In Indiana the first settlers had to cross Indian land in order to get to the first land opened at Vincennes. Because the Indian threat was a definite deterrent to settlement, General Harrison negotiated with the Indians to purchase the land between the Vincennes Tract and the Ohio River. In 1804 the Indians ceded land south of the Buffalo Trace and the Vincennes Tract to the United States. At that time, the second principal meridian was moved twelve miles east of its original position to where it is located today.[19] It now extends from the Ohio river northward to the state of Michigan, although it originally began twelve miles east of the southeast corner of the Vincennes Tract. From the base line and the second principal meridian, this newly purchased land was divided into townships and sections.

The early Indiana counties had unlimited boundaries and were largely unmapped. Their governmental organization was as vague and unlimited as their boundaries. Boundaries were determined primarily by executive and legislative acts, but county boundaries were juggled around again and again, nearly always to the advantage of the already established towns. Despite the efforts of dedicated surveyors such as Thomas Freeman, errors and ambiguities often existed in county boundaries. Thus, overlapping boundaries and errors in the survey of boundaries had to be corrected continually for many years after the first land was purchased. Jurisdictions of courts often did not follow the boundaries fixed by law. Some county lines were not surveyed at all and remained ambiguous until they were eventually corrected. Much reshuffling of county boundaries also occurred as new counties were formed from parts of nearby counties.[20]

Knox County, the first county in Indiana Territory, was established in 1790 as a part of the Northwest Territory. The next county, St. Clair, was laid out along the Mississippi River in 1795 in what is now Illinois. Randolph County was established in 1803 immediately above St. Clair County. Another large county, Wayne, was located in northern Indiana. It formed a wedge which extended south from the southern tip of Lake Michigan to the portage at Fort Wayne and then southeast along the river into Ohio and included land now in the state of Michigan. Another wedge-shaped area, "the gore," was taken from southeastern Indiana and given to Hamilton County, Ohio. Included were present-day Dearborn, Switzerland, half of Franklin, most of Union, half of Wayne, and parts of Randolph and Jay counties. Land lying within the gore was sold with land in western Ohio, not with land in Indiana. Thus, if your ancestors purchased land in this area during the days of early settlement, records of that land purchase will be found in Ohio records.

Early Ohio Settlers, Purchasers of Land in Southwestern Ohio, 1800–1840, by Ellen T. Berry and David A. Berry, lists the original purchasers of federal land, including land in the gore, from the Cincinnati Land Office in Cincinnati, Ohio. In addition to the name of the purchaser, you will find the date of purchase, place of residence at the time of purchase, and the range, township, and section where the purchased land was located. Most of the land was sold in 40- to 160-acre parcels and cost the purchaser from $1.25 to $4.00 per acre.[21] With the data given in this book, you can then obtain further information by writing to the Land Office of the Ohio State Auditor, 88 East Broad Street, P.O. Box 1140, Columbus, Ohio 43216, or to the U.S. Department of the Interior, Bureau of Land Management, Eastern States Office, 350 South Pickett Street, Alexandria, Virginia 22304.

INDIANA COUNTIES

Indiana Territory was formed in 1800 and included what is now the state of Illinois. Knox County was the first and only county in Indiana from 1790 until after Indiana became a territory in its own right. Clark County was formed next in 1801 from the southern part of Knox County. Clark County lay west of the White and the Blue rivers in southern Indiana and extended from Fort Recovery on the Wabash River to the point where the Blue River meets the Ohio River. Knox County made up all of the rest of Indiana. Knox County also extended into Illinois in another wedge which ran from the Gary, Indiana, area southward to Great Cave (Cave-in-Rock) in Illinois, where it met St. Clair and Randolph counties. This area later was included in Illinois Territory when it was formed in 1809. The Ohio Enabling Act of 1802 gave "the gore of Indiana" to Indiana, although the citizens of the gore remained partial to Ohio. Many had originally come to the gore from nearby Ohio. In 1808, Wayne County, a part of Indiana Territory since 1803, was removed from Indiana Territory and given to Michigan to become part of the newly formed Michigan Territory. Counties could only be formed on territory ceded to the United States by the Indians, and in 1804 most of Indiana, including Knox and Clark counties, was still claimed by them. County formation was, therefore, limited by the boundaries of Indian lands.[22] Indian cessions preceded formations of counties by only a short time.

Indiana had advanced to the second stage of its journey toward statehood in 1805, and the power to set up new counties passed to the territorial legislature. After Clark County was formed in 1801, it was followed by Dearborn County in 1803. In 1808 Harrison County was formed with the Second Principal Meridian as its west boundary line and Clark County as the eastern boundary. The rest of Indiana was all Knox County, Indiana Territory. The first Indiana settlers chose land along the Ohio and Wabash rivers, and settlement moved inland and northward from these and other nearby rivers. The first counties to be settled were Knox, on the Wabash River, and Harrison, Switzerland, and Clark, along the Ohio River. When Illinois Territory was formed in 1809, the present Indiana boundary was adopted on the west, with the exception of a small wedge in the Gary area near Lake Michigan.[23]

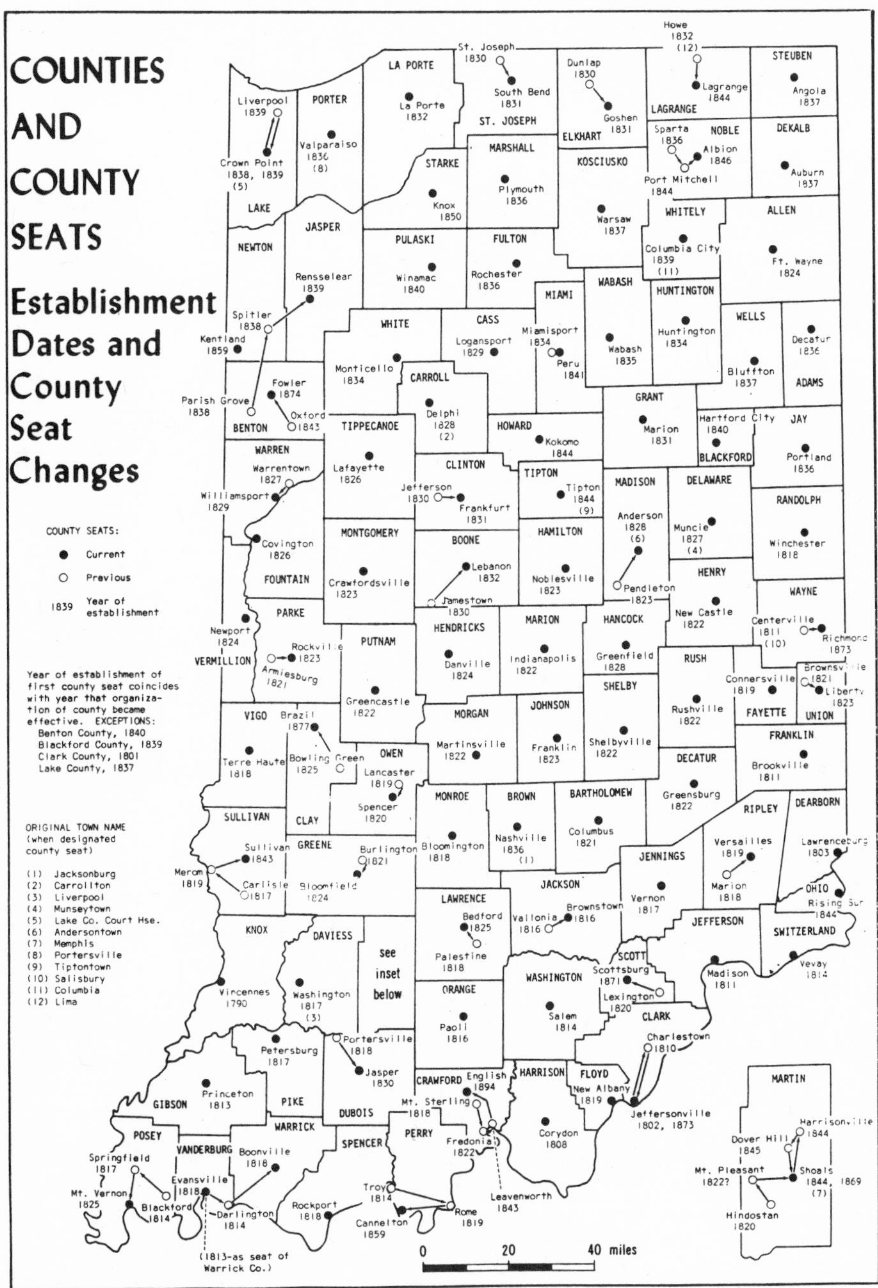

From Robert C. Kingsbury, *An Atlas of Indiana* (Bloomington: Department of Geography, Indiana University, 1970). Courtesy Robert C. Kingsbury and Department of Geography, Indiana University.

In 1811 Franklin, Jefferson, and Wayne counties were established. Gibson and Warrick became new counties in 1813, followed by Perry, Posey, Switzerland, and Washington counties the next year. This made a total of eleven counties in Indiana Territory. Jackson, Orange, and Ripley were added in 1816, the year when Indiana finally became a state. At the time of statehood there were fifteen organized counties: Knox, Gibson, Posey, Warrick, Perry, Orange, Jackson, Washington, Harrison, Clark, Jefferson, Switzerland, Dearborn, Franklin, and Wayne.[24]

The first state capital was established at Corydon in Harrison County, a few miles west of New Albany. Corydon had been laid out in 1808 by General William Henry Harrison, who had originally owned its site and named it for a shepherd in the song "Pastoral Elegy." Corydon served as the state capital for only about five years. A more centrally located capital was needed, and on June 7, 1820, the Fall Creek Settlement, begun in the previous February, was chosen. The settlement, in what would soon be Marion County, was renamed Indianapolis by the legislature. The pseudo-Greek name was formed by adding the Greek ending "-polis," or "city," to the state's name. The new capital was laid out in 1821, and Corydon, the first state capital, became merely the county seat of Harrison County.[25]

Daviess, Jennings, Pike, and Sullivan counties were added to the new state in 1817. New counties established in 1818 were Crawford, Dubois, Lawrence, Monroe, Randolph, Spencer, Vanderburgh, and Vigo. That same year, Indiana was granted territory called the "New Purchase" through the Treaty of St. Mary's, which was made with the Indians. The New Purchase was divided by expanding the boundaries of Randolph, Franklin, and Jennings counties.[26] Randolph County was then a long north-to-south county with no actual northern boundary. Wabash and Delaware counties lay across the central part of the state and blended into the large area of unorganized territory which made up all of northern Indiana. Delaware and Wabash counties were not the current Delaware and Wabash counties. By this time, Indiana had been a state for four years, and the increasing population was causing the continual formation of new counties. Fayette and Floyd were newcomers in 1819, followed by Martin and Scott counties in 1820. In January 1821 four new counties, Bartholomew, Greene, Parke, and Union, were added to the state. In December 1821 Decatur, Henry, Marion, Morgan, Putnam, Rush, and Shelby counties were established. Two new counties were formed in 1823, namely, Allen and Hendricks, and in 1825 Clay and Fountain became Indiana counties.[27]

Tippecanoe joined the ranks in January 1826, and in 1827 Warren and Delaware counties were added. This later Delaware County had no connection in organization to the earlier (1820) county of the same name, although it lay within the boundaries of the earlier county. Carroll and Cass counties were set up in 1828, and in 1830 Boone, Clinton, Elkhart, and St. Joseph counties were added. Grant was the only new county in 1831.[28]

County boundaries were shifted around as the new counties were formed, and a particular spot may have been located in several different counties over the years. As the population spread northward, the formation of counties also moved to the north. LaPorte, Huntington, and Lagrange counties were formed in 1832, Miami and Wabash in 1833, and White County in 1834. A great many new counties were established in 1835: Adams, Dekalb, Fulton, Jasper, Jay, Kosciusko, Marshall, Newton, Noble, Porter, Pulaski, Starke, Steuben, Wells, and Whitley. Lake County, in extreme northwestern Indiana, and Brown County, in an already established south-central area, appeared in 1836.[29] Blackford was formed in February 1838, and Benton County was established two years later. Additions and transfers of land among counties were taking place during all of that time. In 1844 Ohio, Tipton, and Richardville (now Howard) were formed. The next new county was Newton, formed in a reorganization, in December 1859.[30] The present counties of Indiana have remained the same since 1909. There are ninety-two counties in the state.

Most land in Indiana was bought in individual purchases from the original buyer, not from the federal government. Records of such land transactions are in the office of the county recorder in the county where the land was purchased. Many grantor and grantee records of those individual land transactions in Indiana counties are on microfilm in the Genealogy Division of the Indiana State Library in Indianapolis. *Land Claims in the Vincennes Land District in the State of Indiana*, House Document No. 198, was published by the Indiana Historical Society in 1983. It deals with the claims made in the said district in March 1806 (under an 1804 act of Congress) for grants made under the French and British governments; claims founded on such supposed grants, from the courts; donations of 400 acres to heads of families made on or before 1783; and claims to the donation of 100 acres to militiamen who were enrolled on August 1, 1790, and who served militia duty. The names of men and women who filed such claims, evidence and witnesses to the validity of the claims, and the disposition of the matter are all reported in this booklet, which is available from the Indiana Historical Society. (For complete details regarding land records in Indiana, see below, chapter 8.)

Many varied materials regarding the 92 counties of Indiana are filed in the Genealogy Division of the Indiana State Library, and materials for the individual counties are generally housed in the public library in the county seat of each Indiana county.

Emigrant Trails

CHAPTER 4

People who do family research learn early on that there is more than one way to do research and more than one type of record to use. Each genealogical problem will probably require a different approach, and some of the avenues of research are not the standard, tried-and-true ones. One of the methods which can sometimes be useful in genealogy is the study of emigration trails. You may be able to determine how your ancestors came to Indiana by learning about the paths and trails then in use. You may also find clues as to how they arrived there by learning where your ancestors first settled.

Not all settlers followed the standard routes into Indiana. Not all pioneers came from Kentucky, and not all of them came down the Ohio River by flatboat, although a great many of them did. The time period during which your ancestors came to Indiana can offer some clues, however. Where and when your ancestors settled in Indiana can probably give the best clue as to where they had come from. Other helpful clues might be church affiliation, since large groups of church members often tended to migrate together; nationality, because ethnic groups also tended to migrate together; economic conditions in America, since moves were common during very good and very bad times and particularly after a war; occupation, because they may have moved to a place where their talents were in demand; and whether new land had recently been opened in the area, because new, cheap land always beckoned on the frontier.

Records made by your ancestors as they crossed the country can be useful in plotting their migration path. They might have come from Lancaster County, Pennsylvania, on the Great Warrior Path to Virginia. This path led from the Quaker State southward into the Carolinas and then back toward the north and into the new land of "Indiana Country." Contrary to what you might think, settlers did not dash across the country from one spot to another. Instead, a family might have stayed in one area, say in Virginia, for a generation or two before moving on to new land, perhaps in Kentucky. It may have taken your ancestors quite a few years or even generations to get from Pennsylvania to Kentucky and then on into Indiana.

If you already know where your ancestors lived at various times, then their migration path may be fairly obvious. But, if you know nothing about their previous homes, from family traditions or from family records, you will need to use other means to determine where your ancestors had formerly lived. These "means" might be land records, census records, church entries and removals, court records, and many other miscellaneous records, and for the very early days, the territorial records. It will help if you possess good common sense and a detective's knack for uncovering clues. A "sixth sense" and a whole lot of serendipity are also useful when searching for your Indiana ancestry. Luckily, both clues and actual records can be found in Indiana. The emigrant paths and trails used by the emigrants to get to Indiana were many and varied. By learning about these trails, you may gain some insight into how your ancestors came to Indiana.

THE INDIAN TRAILS

At the end of the Revolutionary War there was a large movement westward, first by the hunters and traders and then, later, by the pioneer settlers. People who entered Indiana in the late eighteenth century came on trails that the Indians had used before them. The Indian trails were originally animal paths made by wild animals as they traveled across the land in search of food, water, and shelter. These paths followed the streams and ran through the valleys and over the ridges. They followed "the path of least resistance," or the quickest and easiest means of getting from one place to another.[1] The Indians used the animal paths because they led to the things that the Indians also needed—food, shelter, water, and transportation from one place to another. The wild animals had learned to cross streams where the water was shallow and the current less swift, and the Indians followed the animal paths across the fording places. The animal paths also led to salt pools and deposits, where the Indians got salt to flavor their food and to preserve their meat. The animals frequenting the trails were, of course, meat for the Indians. Thus, the trails provided the Indians with most of the things they needed, including animal pelts and plant fibers for their clothing and teepees. Mainly, the animal paths were the quickest and easiest way to cross the land.[2]

We seldom realize how much the Indians traveled about the country in prehistoric America. Indian trails stretched from coast to coast and from Canada southward into Central and South America. The trails were not only numerous but many were also extremely long. The trails ran along rivers and streams, where they avoided dense underbrush, rough ground, and marshy areas and followed the safest, easiest path to their destination. Because the animal paths were very narrow, only one person could use them at a time. Therefore, the Indians traveled in single file when they used the trails. The traditional use of single file by American Indians was not a military strategy, as often reported, but was merely an adaptation to environmental conditions. The narrow trails widened only where heavier traffic caused them to grow wider, such as near the larger Indian villages, the salt pools, and sugar maple groves.[3]

Many different Indian tribes probably used the same trails as they hunted, fished, traveled, or migrated from one area to another. The shorter trails connected to longer ones which then met even longer ones. Trails criss-crossed the land, and many of them extended for extremely long distances. The Indian tribes often traveled long distances, as much as one to two thousand miles, to visit and trade with other tribes or to wage war on them. Such a use for hostile ventures probably accounts for the name given to one important trail known as "The Great Warpath."

The Indians traded with tribes on the ocean shores, in the mountains, and even in the desert. Metals, beads, and tools not native to the midwest have been found buried in Indian mounds in Indiana. These materials were probably trading goods obtained on trading expeditions to faraway tribes. Some extensive Indian trading networks are thought to have existed in the Americas.[4] Sign language and picture drawings were used to communicate with tribes whose language was different, because there were many languages and variations of tongues among the Indians of America. There were a great many Indian trails in use long before Europeans came to America.

THE WATERWAYS

Nearly all of the Indian trails east of the Mississippi River ran along waterways, and the Indians used both land trails and waterways as they traveled. When the land travel became too difficult, the Indians took to their canoes and traveled on the streams and rivers. And, when the rivers became too shallow or too turbulent, they concealed their canoes and continued their journey on land. The canoes were retrieved to use on their return trip. The main concerns of the Indians were speed, safety, and ease of travel.

The principal rivers used by settlers coming to the Old Northwest were the Kanawha and the Ohio, and to a lesser extent, the Potomac, the New River, the Kentucky, and the Tennessee. When they traveled across the country, white settlers used the rivers and streams far less than the land trails because they generally carried more household goods than could easily fit into a small boat or a canoe. They also couldn't easily switch from land to water travel when encumbered by a loaded wagon and horses. Once the settlers reached their destination, however, the rivers and streams became their "roads." When they entered new land, the settlers found that no roads of any kind existed, only virgin forest and heavy underbrush. Thus, the settlers were glad to use the Indian trails and animal paths for travel on foot or horseback, but they generally used the waterways where no trails existed.

The principal rivers of eastern America connected with many smaller rivers and streams to form a network of "roads" across the country. Because most eastern rivers were navigable in only one direction, downstream, the return trip generally could not be made on the waterway Emigrants who traveled to the northwest from Virginia, the Carolinas, Tennessee, and Kentucky used the Indian trails much more often than they used the rivers and streams.[5] In Indiana the principal waterways were the Ohio River, the Wabash River, the East and West forks of the White River, and the Whitewater River.

So important were the waterways that in 1820 the Indiana General Assembly declared the West Fork of the White River "from its junction with the East Fork to the Delaware Indian towns in Delaware County . . . to be a public highway." Designating a river or a stream a "public highway" kept it free from mill dams and other obstructions and therefore open to rafts and boats.[6] Numerous other rivers and streams were also declared highways and were used for travel and transporting goods until roads could be built. The first roads were, at best, loblollies in wet weather and dusty and rutted during the dry times. Indiana rivers were generally shallower and slower-moving than rivers in the east and were usually navigable in both directions. Being able to travel upstream as well as downstream appealed to the early pioneers, who were used to one-way river travel. Therefore, most of the early Indiana settlers chose land along a waterway so that they could have an easy means of travel and transportation right at their door. During pioneer days navigable Indiana rivers were well used for travel and for moving produce to markets downriver.

THE IMPORTANT EMIGRANT TRAILS

The most important land trails used by the emigrants on their journey to Indiana were the Great Indian Warpath, the Old Pennsylvania Trading Path, the Occaneechi Path of Virginia, the Lower Creek Trading Path of the South, and the National Road, a later extension and improvement of the Old Trading Path.[7] Of those trails only the National Road was man-made, although the early eastern sections of the road were built on top of the old Indian trading path. All of the other emigrant routes were essentially old Indian trails that had been widened by the settlers' wagons as they traveled toward new land in the south, the southwest, and the west.

Many settlers who came to Indiana began their westward journey in Pennsylvania using the Great Indian Warpath. This trail, known more often as the

Warrior's Path, led from eastern Pennsylvania near Philadelphia, across the Susquehanna River near Harrisburg, and then southwest through the Shenandoah Valley to the upper tributaries of the Tennessee River. The Warrior's Path then ran through Tennessee to Chattanooga, where it turned northward toward Kentucky. The Warrior's Path ran for nearly eight-hundred miles from eastern Pennsylvania to the interior of Kentucky.[8] The reason for this long and roundabout route into Kentucky can be readily seen when you look at the topography of the southeastern United States.

The high mountain ranges running between the coastal region and inland America were a huge deterrent to settlement beyond them, even more of a deterrent than the threat of Indian attack. The Alleghenies, the Appalachians, and the Blue Ridge Mountains not only prevented the settlers from entering the interior but also served to contain the Indians, who had been hostile since the French and Indian War. Would-be settlers were prevented from entering the land beyond the high mountains because they could find no easy way to cross them. The mountains served as a big chute which channeled the emigrants southward into the Tennessee Valley instead of leading them directly across. This explains why most emigrants traveled so far to the south before veering northward again, through the opening in the mountains called the Cumberland Gap.[9] The only way to enter Kentucky was overland from the south by way of the Cumberland Gap, which was not discovered until the 1760s and not improved until 1769 by Daniel Boone. The importance of the Cumberland Gap to westward settlement can be seen when standing atop the 1,440-foot-high overlook. The Gap truly was the only way to enter Kentucky from the south and southeast.

Many settlers used the Warrior's Path immediately after the Revolutionary War when nearly everyone seemed to be moving to new places. Mass migrations often occurred after major social and political upheavals such as wars, depressions, famines, and natural disasters. After the Revolutionary War, people from New York, Pennsylvania, Maryland, Delaware, Virginia, and the New England states began to move into the newly opened land in southeastern America. The Warrior's Path, which had been used extensively during the earlier, Indian migrations, was one of the most important of the emigrant trails that led settlers toward Indiana. A great many early settlers used this particular trail in their search for better, cheaper land in the "West."

The shortcut provided by the Cumberland Gap allowed Daniel Boone to cross the mountains and to blaze the Wilderness Road into eastern Kentucky. Pioneers gladly used this easier and shorter route to get to Kentucky, and the Gap allowed them to avoid the fearsome Ohio River trip with its Indian raids. More than seventy thousand people followed the Wilderness Road into the Mississippi Valley in the fifteen years between 1774 and 1790.[10] Not only was rich new land available, but also the federal government and several of the states had begun to give bounty land to veterans in lieu of cash payments for their military service. This extra inducement caused even more veterans to file for bounty land and head for the new Northwest Territory.

THE OCCANEECHI PATH OF VIRGINIA

Another famous Indian trail used by the settlers was the Occaneechi Path of Virginia. It led from near Old Fort Henry on the James River to the important Indian trading town of Occaneechi on the Roanoke River, near where it crosses the present Virginia and North Carolina state line. From there the trail passed through the Carolinas to the site of Augusta, Georgia, where it connected with other major trails of the southeast. The Occaneechi Path was more than five hundred miles long, but it was not a very important trail until traders and settlers began using it in about 1675. Early settlers followed it into the fertile valleys of Virginia, and it also became a well-used turnpike leading into the south.[11] Many pioneers used this trail to come from the upland south to Indiana in early settlement days.

THE LOWER CREEK TRADING PATH

The Lower Creek Trading Path was another great connecting trail which later became a permanent road. It ran from Greenville on the Mississippi River, on through Mississippi, Alabama, Georgia, and South Carolina. It connected directly with the Occaneechi Path and also with the Warrior's Path of Virginia and Kentucky. The Lower Creek Trading Path was used by many settlers as they moved across the southeastern part of America, up the Warrior's Path of Kentucky, and on to land in Indiana.[12]

THE GREAT WARPATH

Another much used branch of the main Warrior's Path, or Warpath, led from near Staunton, Virginia, through the land between the tributaries of the Shenandoah and Roanoke rivers. It then ran westward through the valleys of the New River and the swift Kanawha to meet the Ohio River near present-day Gallipolis, Ohio. Westward migration moved into the wilderness through another important gap in the mountains at the New River.[13] Here civilization left off and the wild and truly dangerous part of the journey began. This vast and wild country was uninhabited, mountainous, and covered by dense forests. Many people followed this treacherous route into northern Kentucky. During the late 1700s many German, Scottish, Irish, and English people from the east swarmed into Kentucky using this branch of the famous Warpath. It has been estimated that more settlers entered the midsection of the country by way of the Kanawha and the Cumberland Gap than by Braddock's Road in Maryland and Pennsylvania, or by the Ohio River, or even later by the National Road.[14] Some settlers dropped off along the way to settle along the rivers and streams, but the majority pushed on toward Kentucky and the newly opened land in the Northwest Territory after 1787.

THE WARRIOR'S PATH OF KENTUCKY

In Kentucky the Warrior's Path was the continuation of several other trails which led up from Georgia and the Carolinas through eastern Tennessee, where it crossed the main trail, the Great Warpath. The Warrior's Path then ran through the Cumberland Gap into Kentucky, where it was known as the Warrior's Path of Kentucky. It ran up through Kentucky to the Ohio River, opposite the place where the Scioto River joins the Ohio. Another branch of the Warrior's Path led from Boonesboro in eastern Kentucky to Louisville on the Ohio River.[15] The Warrior's Path of Kentucky was used by Indians from Ohio when they raided the first small Kentucky settlements. The Indians did not then live in Kentucky, but they considered it their hunting grounds. They were enraged when American settlers moved there, cleared the land, planted crops, and began to build homes. When the settlers began to act as if they planned to stay, the Indians began raids from across the Ohio River. The Indians attacked the Kentucky settlements and carried captives, including Daniel Boone, back to Ohio on the Warrior's Path.[16] The Indians kept white settlers as slaves in the Indian villages of southern Ohio or sold them to Canadian tribes. It has been estimated that more than 2,000 men, women, and children were carried off by the Indians from Kentucky and the Northwest Territory between 1785 and 1812, and not one out of ten was ever heard of again.[17] Some captives were cruelly tortured to death, but others were eventually ransomed back. The Warrior's Path was used, in turn, by American forces when they fought and finally subdued the Indians in northwestern Ohio. Both of these branches of the Warrior's Path were used heavily in the settlement of Indiana after 1800 and are very important to the Hoosier family researcher.

THE OLD TRADING PATH

As early as 1750 the first traders and settlers were beginning to cross the Allegheny Mountains and settle in the Ohio River basin. To get there, the emigrants used the Old Trading Path, the main east-to-west trail which ran from Philadelphia westward to the site of present-day Pittsburgh, called Fort Duquesne by the French and, later, Fort Pitt by the British. This important Indian path followed no waterways, crossed only the Susquehanna River, and was a direct route from the Atlantic coast to the Ohio River. Because the Susquehanna River was generally shallow and easily forded, this trail could be used at all times of the year and was a particularly important route for migration from the east.[18]

The early settlers moved westward along the Old Trading Path, or the Great State Road of Pennsylvania, and its northern branches. They moved in short bursts from one section of the country to the next, from eastern to central Pennsylvania and then into eastern Ohio. As land wore out or as new people came to buy it, the original settlers often sold out and moved westward. The younger sons of German farmers, having lost land to their eldest brother in the European system of primogeniture (first-born inherits all), were forced to move west in order to have land of their own. By the late 1700s pioneers were venturing across the Ohio River into the Ohio frontier. Some people were forced to return to Pennsylvania because of fierce Indian attacks, but they did not give up, and eventually the frontier moved further into Ohio. These adventurous pioneers kept up this hop-skip-and-jump activity across southern Ohio and down into Kentucky, and, eventually, some moved into Indiana Territory. It seemed that "West is best!" and the farther west, the better!

People who started out in Pennsylvania or Maryland might have gotten to Indiana by traveling down into Virginia, then into the Carolinas and up into Tennessee or Kentucky. Don't be surprised if your ancestors who said they were "from Virginia" took this roundabout route to get there. They may have been born in Ireland, Scotland, or England, immigrated to Pennsylvania, and then moved on to Virginia on this meandering route. Many immigrants landed in Philadelphia and very soon began the southerly migration which took them, by turns, into Maryland, Virginia, and North and South Carolina. Virginia may have been the place they stayed the longest or merely the last place they lived before coming to Indiana. From the south, it was a fairly short trip up to Kentucky, where some families stayed for a few years or even a generation or two. After the Revolution many people moved into central and western Kentucky from areas farther south and east. Some had entered eastern Kentucky very early when it was Kentucky County, Virginia. But, by the late 1700s, the mismanaged and confused Kentucky land grants situation caused many settlers to forfeit land they thought they had owned in Kentucky.[19] This is the reason many Kentuckians moved across the Ohio River into southern Indiana in the early years of the nineteenth century. Some other groups of pioneers merely crossed Kentucky with the aim of settling in Indiana, once the area was deemed safe for settlement.

INDIANA TRAILS AND ROADS

Indiana was not actually considered safe for settlement until after the War of 1812, although quite a few settlers came to the area long before that time. People first settled in the area along the Ohio River, moving into Indiana at

Clarksville, Corydon, Madison, and all of the southern counties. Some traveled up the Wabash River by boat, raft, or flatboat and settled along the river both above and below the old French town of Vincennes. Others came in from the east fairly early, through the state of Ohio, and settled along the Ohio border in central Indiana. The principal old Indian trails which ran through Indiana in the early days of settlement were the Old Buffalo Trace, the Rome Trace, the Yellow Banks Trace, the Red Banks Trace, and the Shawnee Trace in Illinois. Others were the Blue River Trace, the Saline, or Salt Route, Trace, and Whetzel's Trace through the New Purchase territory. As a trace widened and became more road-like, it was called a "trail."

The Old Buffalo Trace

The earliest and most important trail in Indiana was the Old Buffalo Trace, which was used by about two-thirds of all the early settlers who came into southern Indiana west of Louisville, Kentucky. People from the mid-Atlantic states of Maryland, Delaware, Pennsylvania, New Jersey, and New York booked passage on steamboats at Pittsburgh, steamed down the Ohio River, and landed at the Falls of the Ohio. From there the Buffalo Trace led westward to newly opened land. The trail was named the Buffalo Trace because it had been a buffalo run across southern Indiana even before the Indians came. The buffalos' hooves had widened and deepened the path until it was nearly as wide as a narrow road, over twenty feet wide in places, and was worn down below the surrounding ground.[20] Two wagons could travel abreast over much of the trail. Even today, remnants of the Old Buffalo Trace can still be seen running through the fields of southern Indiana.

The Buffalo Trace ran on a northwesterly diagonal through the southern quarter of Indiana from the Falls of the Ohio at New Albany to Vincennes, where it exited Indiana. The Buffalo Trace was called by many other names, depending on who used it and where they were traveling. The Indians had called it "Lan-an-zo-ki-mi-wi," meaning "buffalo road." People going to Vincennes generally called it the "Vincennes Trace." Those coming from Kentucky called it the "Kentucky Road," and those going to Clarksville called it the "Clarksville Trace." "Harrison's Road" was still another name given to the Trace, in honor of William Henry Harrison, who secured the land from the Indians. The line of the 1804 treaty with the Indians ceding this land to the United States ran along the Buffalo Trace.[21] Travelers entered the old French tract at Vincennes by way of the Buffalo Trace from Louisville, by the Rome Trace, or Rome Road, from Rome in Perry County, by the Yellow Banks Trace through the present towns of Selvin and Rockport, by the Red Banks Trace from Evansville and Princeton, and by the Shawnee Trace from Illinois.[22]

The Buffalo Trace entered Indiana at the site of present-day New Albany, opposite Louisville, Kentucky, and led in a northwesterly direction toward Vincennes. It crossed the "knobs," those high, rounded hills of southeastern Indiana, then passed through the current towns of Paoli, Shoals, and Washington, and ran on to Vincennes, then the principal town of Indiana. Today's U.S. Route 150 generally follows the path of the Buffalo Trace. Because the settlers in southern Indiana came mainly from the upland south, they found this hilly, wooded section similar to land they had left behind in Kentucky, the Carolinas, and Virginia. They liked its looks and settled there, unaware that the soil was not always fertile enough to grow the kinds of crops they wanted. This may have been one of the reasons many of the early settlers soon moved on into other areas.

Because of its location, its width, and its relatively easy path, the Buffalo Trace became the most important overland roadway across early Indiana. And, because it connected directly with the western extension of the Warrior's Path of Kentucky, it was used more extensively than any other trail entering southern Indiana. The first Indiana stagecoach line began in 1820 and ran on the Old Buffalo Trace from New Albany to Vincennes for many years. Rangers patrolled the Trace to protect travelers, first on foot and, by 1812, mounted on horses. There were also rangers' camps along the Trace, one at Milburn's Springs in Dubois County, at Cuzco, and one at Blue River where the Trace crossed the river. Pioneer forts built along the Buffalo Trace were at Petersburg, Fort McDonald at the Mudholes, and Fort Butler and Fort Farris, both in Dubois County.

The Yellow Banks Trail

Many people entered Indiana from western Kentucky using one of several Indian trails and pioneer traces. The Yellow Banks Trail, named for the color of the river banks there, led north from Rockport on the Ohio River, through Chrisney and Gentryville, joining the Rome Trace near the present Pike County line. It ran from the Ohio River to a Delaware Indian summer camp located at the forks of White River. Although this was Piankashaw territory, the Delawares had been permitted to camp there. A fork of the Yellow Banks Trail entered Dubois County north of Dale, extended north to Portersville and on into Daviess County. The trail from Rockport to the Indian camp was patrolled weekly by three soldiers and one scout. Many pioneers who settled in Dubois County had come to Rockport on the river and then followed the Yellow Banks Trail to the Freeman line and on to their new homes in Indiana.[23]

The Red Banks Trail

The southern bank of the Ohio River at Henderson, Kentucky, was called the "red banks," and the trail across from these banks was also called by this name. The Red Banks Trail ran almost due north and south from the banks of the Ohio River opposite Henderson, through Evansville and Princeton to Vincennes. The

Red Banks Trail was also patrolled by rangers to protect pioneers coming to Indiana. The people of Vincennes had petitioned the state legislature for a good road there and for forts and taverns ("houses of entertainment") to be set up no farther than twenty miles apart on this trail. Many people who settled in western Gibson County and northern Vanderburgh County came there on the Red Banks Trail.[24]

The Blue River Trace

The Blue River Trace began near the mouth of the Blue River at Fredònia and ran from the Ohio River northward to join the main Buffalo Trace. It had been an Indian trail before the settlers came and was cut from the main trace to the river in September 1807. An established trail on the south bank of the Ohio, opposite the mouth of the Blue River, ran far to the south into Kentucky. Many people who came into this part of Indiana and other sections of the Indiana Territory came via this route in the early years of the nineteenth century. The Fredonia Road ran westward from that place.[25]

The Saline Trace

At the same time the Indians ceded the Vincennes Tract to the United States, they also ceded "the great salt spring" on the Saline River, which joined the Ohio below the mouth of the Wabash.[26] This salt spring was in what is now Illinois and near Old Shawneetown. The Saline, or Salt River, Trace began across the Ohio from the mouth of the Salt River, where a small fort had been built in 1750 by Kentuckians. Because salt was such a useful and valued commodity, the road to the spring was known as the "Salt Route." The trace ran from north of Princeton southwest to where the Little Wabash meets the Wabash River fairly close to Shawneetown. Guards were posted around the spring and salt works and along the route north to protect the salt from the Indians, who had previously been able to use it freely. The Indians received 150 pounds of salt each year as royalty, but this evidently wasn't enough to satisfy them. The salt works, which produced 200,000 to 300,000 bushels of salt annually, was called the "United States Saline" in 1807. Many pioneers came to Indiana using the Salt River Trace.[27]

Other smaller and shorter trails joined the longer, larger trails and traces, and all were used by settlers coming into the land which would become Indiana.

MAN-MADE ROADS IN INDIANA

The Old Michigan Road, the National Road, the Old Chicago Road, the Vincennes and Indianapolis Road, and the Lafayette Road were man-made roads which supplemented or supplanted the older trails. An important emigrant trail,

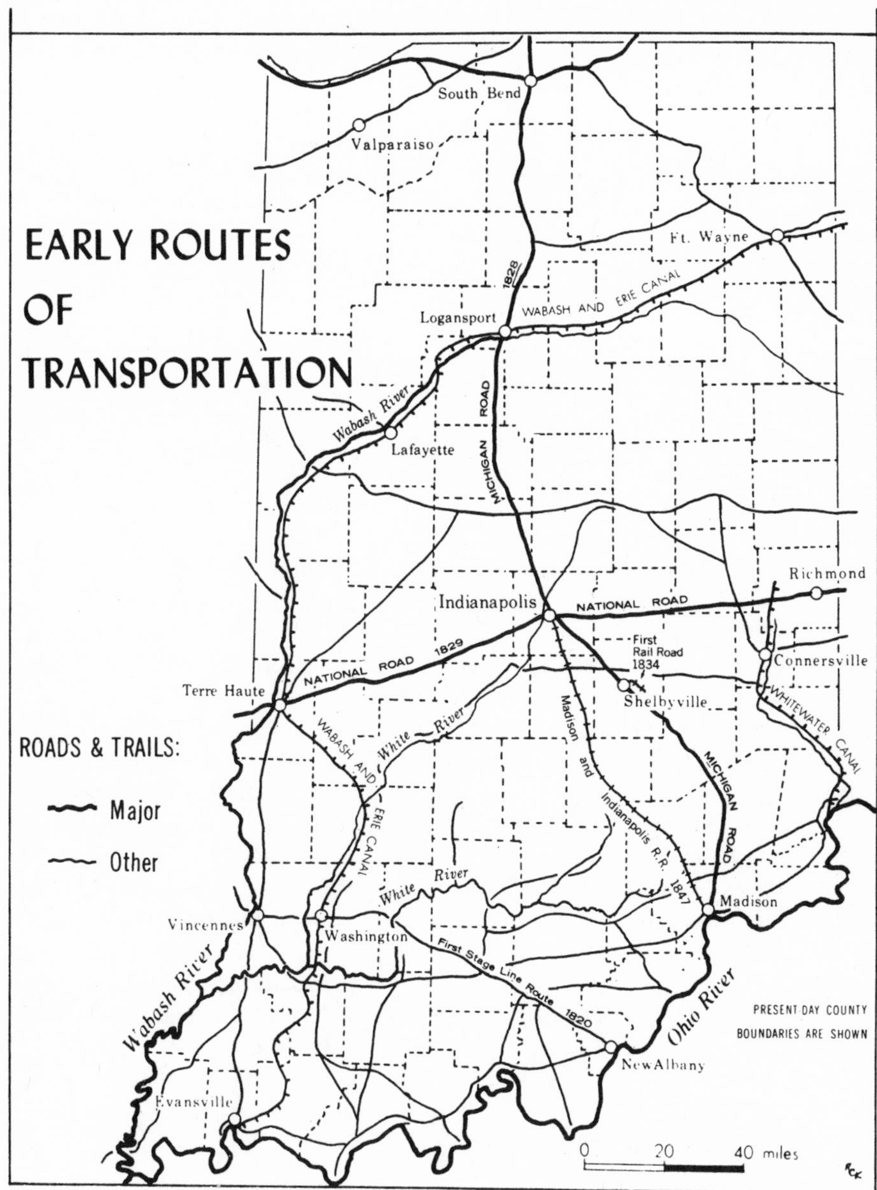

From Robert C. Kingsbury, *An Atlas of Indiana* (Bloomington: Department of Geography, Indiana University, 1970). Courtesy Robert C. Kingsbury and Department of Geography, Indiana University.

originally an Indian path, was improved and extended to become the National Road, which eventually extended from Philadelphia, Pennsylvania, almost to St. Louis, Missouri.

One of the earliest man-made roads in Indiana was "Kibbey's Road," which originally ran from Milan toward Cincinnati and may have originally been an Indian trail. Kibbey's Road was laid out in about 1801, by "Captain E. Kibbey," and was the first road to cross the state from east to west.[28]

The National Road

The eastern section of the National Road was originally the Old Indian Trading Path of Pennsylvania, which then became the State Road. An east-to-west national road had first been suggested by the young George Washington after a surveying trip through the Western Country in the 1750s.[29] Later, by order of the U.S. Congress and at the urging of then President Washington, the National Road was extended in sections from Philadelphia toward the west. It was built largely by local labor with federal funds over its entire length and was the first federally financed road in America. Built between 1811 and 1839, it eventually passed through Baltimore, Frederick, and Cumberland, Maryland, through Wheeling, West Virginia, and Columbus, Ohio, and then through Indiana and Illinois to St. Louis, Missouri. It became a very busy emigrant road in the mid-nineteenth century and was one of the most extensively traveled roads in the country for many years.[30]

The Indiana part of the National Road was built between 1829 and 1839. Emigrant use of the National Road was heaviest in Indiana during the 1850s when it brought many settlers from Europe and the eastern United States. In each section of the country, men were recruited to survey, lay out, and build the road. Lists of the men who helped to build the National Road can often be found in the old county histories of the central Indiana counties the road passed through. In Indiana the road crossed the state from Richmond, on the eastern border, through Indianapolis, and on to Terre Haute on the western edge. Today's U.S. Route 40 largely follows the original path of the National Road through Indiana. In recent years U.S. Route 40 has been replaced in importance by the newer Interstate 70, which still follows the basic path of the old National Road.

The Old Chicago Road

A lesser road in Indiana was the Old Chicago Road, which ran from Indianapolis northwest to Chicago, then a small town on the shore of Lake Michigan. This historic roadway led many emigrants from Virginia, Kentucky, and Ohio up into the new and unsettled regions of northern Indiana after 1840. The Chicago Road was the main channel of travel from Vincennes to Indianapolis and from there to Chicago. It became extremely wide in places because of the great number of emigrants who traveled on it. It went through Crawfordsville to Williamsport, on the Wabash River, and then ran northward to Chicago.[31]

The Lafayette Road

Another secondary road, the Lafayette Road, ran from Vincennes through Sullivan to Terre Haute, then on through Covington to Lafayette. It was heavily traveled by pioneers as they sought newly opened land in the counties of northern Indiana between 1840 and 1860. This road may have been the basis for Indiana Route 41, which now runs from Evansville, on the Ohio River, through Terre Haute, and then on to Lafayette. People who used this route had often come to Indiana by way of the Ohio and Wabash rivers.[32] Settlers found the land in central and northern Indiana more fertile than in the southern part of the state, and, thus, more settlers chose to stay in the northern counties.

The Michigan Road

The first north-south route through the state was the Michigan Road, which was begun in 1828. It was needed to connect northern Indiana and the state of Michigan with the new state capital at Indianapolis. The rapid growth of the northern counties also warranted an improved north-south roadway for better travel and transportation. The Michigan Road road was the first Indiana road to be financed by the state government. Indiana received three percent of the proceeds of the sale of public lands along the right of way of the road. Because this land happened to be in the middle of Potawatomi lands its acquisition divided those lands and weakened the Potawatomis' hold on the country.[33] The road extended from the northern Indiana harbor town of Michigan City eastward to the south bend of the St. Joseph River, southward to Logansport, and on to Indianapolis, where it ended "in front of the governor's house." The other half of the Michigan Road began at Madison on the Ohio River and extended to the northwest to meet the northern extension.[34] The road was completed in 1836. The National Road crossed the Michigan Road at Indianapolis. Interstate 65 generally follows this old roadway.

All of these paths, trails, and roads brought settlers to Indiana over the years. The early ones were merely narrow paths; later trails were wider but still rutted. The early roads were filled with tree stumps that were cut to regulation height, which was just below the axles of a wagon. None of these rutty, bumpy, dusty or muddy roads, including the National Road and the Michigan Road, had a bit of rock or gravel on them. Traveling on them was an experience never to be forgotten. The only times the early roads were useful was during the summer, when they were dry but exceedingly dusty, and during the winter, when they were frozen solid. And the only time the rivers and streams were truly navigable was during the spring and fall, when they were full. Otherwise, they were either too shallow in the summer or frozen too solid in winter for boats to use.[35] When canals were proposed, the citizens of Indiana were definitely interested.

INDIANA CANALS

The success of the Erie Canal had a great effect on the states west of it, and the extension of the Erie Canal into Indiana made canal building the "thing to do." Canal building was the fad of the mid-1800s, in Indiana as well as in the states east of it. Between 1832 and 1870 a great many canals were built in the state, and even more were proposed but not built.

The Louisville and Portland Canal

The first Indiana canal was proposed in 1805 and begun in 1819 at the Falls of the Ohio at Louisville. The project was a complete failure, but a later, short canal less than ten miles long, the Louisville and Portland Canal, was built around the then treacherous Falls of the Ohio near Louisville.[36] This canal was used until 1825 to cover the few miles from Jeffersonville to New Albany on the Kentucky side of the river. The canal was vital to the Ohio River steamboat travel and to the development of the Old Northwest. With the removal of the Falls this short canal was no longer needed; it fell into disrepair and all traces of it eventually disappeared.

The Wabash and Erie Canal

The Wabash and Erie Canal, begun in 1832, was an extension of the main Erie Canal. It joined the Ohio portion of the Erie Canal at Toledo and followed the Wabash River from there, crossing the summit at Fort Wayne between the Maumee and the Wabash, and then running on southwest to Terre Haute, passing through Logansport and Lafayette. It was begun at Fort Wayne in 1832, reached Peru in 1837, Lafayette in 1843, and Terre Haute in 1848. From Terre Haute it veered southward to meet the proposed Central Canal near Worthington and reached the growing river town of Evansville in 1848. It was the longest canal in the early nation, stretching 468 miles diagonally across the state. The cost of the canal was over eight million dollars. Private operators ran the canal from 1859 until 1874.[37]

The Central Canal

The Central Canal was proposed to leave the Wabash and Erie at Peru and run southeast to Marion, then south to Indianapolis, and on through Martinsville and Spencer to meet the southern leg of the Wabash and Erie Canal near Worthington. An eastern extension of the Central Canal was proposed to run from

Anderson to Muncie to link up with the Whitewater Canal. As a result of financial difficulties caused by the Panic of 1837, followed by the depression of 1839 to 1843 and by a decline in interest in canal building, only a short portion of the Central Canal was built.[38]

The White Water Canal

The White Water Canal in east central Indiana was in operation between 1832 and 1865 and ran from Lawrenceburg in Dearborn County to Cincinnati, Ohio, and then on up through Connersville to Cambridge City and Hagerstown. A steep drop of almost five hundred feet along the seventy-six-mile canal necessitated fifty-six locks and several dams and aqueducts.[39] Thirty-six miles of the canal were completed from Lawrenceburg northward before the state suspended construction because of the financial crisis in 1839. A private company bought the canal property and completed the construction in 1848. The canal operated for about twenty years and proved useful to residents of southeastern Indiana.[40] It was supposed to extend to Muncie and was then to follow the west fork of the White River to above Noblesville, where it would have met the proposed Central Canal. It ceased operating in 1865.[41] Like that of the Central Canal, the extension of the White Water Canal was never built. The towpath of the canal was used for a railroad track bed in 1867. A part of the old White Water Canal has been restored and is now a tourist attraction near Metamora in Franklin County.

Several other legs of the Wabash and Erie Canal were also proposed, but the financial backing for canal building was withdrawn with the coming of the railroads to Indiana. Building and operating railroads was less expensive than building and operating canals. Thus, when the first railroad came to Indiana in 1834, the days of the canals were numbered, just as the days of the railroad later were numbered. Available money was redirected to railroad building and the days of the canals were nearly over.[42] Existing canals, however, continued to be used in the state for a few years longer.

RAILROADS IN INDIANA

The first railroad in Indiana was built near Shelbyville in Shelby County in 1834. It was followed by the Madison and Indianapolis Railroad in 1847, and by 1869 most of the important cities in Indiana were linked by rails. The longest pioneer railroad was the New Albany and Salem (later the Monon), which stretched 288 miles from the Ohio River to Lake Michigan.[43] Railroads were largely instrumental in bringing the southern Indiana counties out of the pioneer stage. The railroads brought improved transportation of goods and people, and they also brought many emigrants to Indiana after 1840. The growth of agriculture and manufacturing in the state would not have been possible without the advanced transportation offered by the railroads.[44] In 1850 there were only 225 miles of railroad tracks in Indiana, but by 1880 there were 46 separate railway lines in the state. Many of these lines converged in Indianapolis, Kokomo, Terre Haute, Crawfordsville, Fort Wayne, Anderson, and Lafayette.[45]

Railroads remained the single most important form of transportation until well after World War I. By 1920 Indiana had rail connections to every state in the United States and had 7,812 miles of track running throughout the state. More than two hundred passenger trains stopped every day at Indianapolis's Union Station.[46] But by the 1940s, the days of the railroads were coming to an end. Trains were replaced by private automobiles, semitrailer trucks, and airplanes after World War II. By 1969 only twenty-two railroad lines served Indiana, and in 1987 only four long-distance lines were still in service.[47] Occasionally chartered excursion trains operate out of Indianapolis today. An interesting offshoot of the railways were the interurban railway lines of the late nineteenth and early twentieth centuries.

THE INTERURBAN RAILWAYS

Electric and interurban railroad lines sprang up in Indiana in the 1890s and early 1900s and were heavily used until as late as 1947. In their heyday the interurban lines carried a great many people over comparatively short distances for a small fee. There were 678 miles of electric lines in the state by 1900 and 1,825 miles by 1914, second only to the number in Ohio.[48] Interurbans were most popular for travel from one town to the next and for a small fee. The interurbans were more prevalent in eastern and east central Indiana than in other parts of the state. The only interurbans running south of Terre Haute were five short lines which converged at Evansville. Another interurban line ran from Indianapolis through Columbus, Seymour, and Scottsburg to Jeffersonville and New Albany. Several lines also circled the lower part of Lake Michigan from Chicago to Michigan City, LaPorte, South Bend, and Elkhart. Between 1890 and 1915 over 250 companies incorporated and had plans to build interurban railway lines.[49] The interurban trains were used by families and groups to take outings, to visit relatives, or to shop in nearby towns. Salesmen and businessmen also took advantage of the low-cost interurban trains for short business trips. But, as more people bought automobiles and as roads were improved, the interurbans were used less and less. Automobiles let people travel anywhere at any time, and the people of Indiana along with the rest of the nation liked that convenience. Most of the interurban lines had been abandoned by the 1940s because more families had purchased automobiles.[50] Thus, interurbans also lost ground to railroads, automobiles, buses, and trucks just as the canals had been supplanted by the railroads. A vestige of the old southern interurban was still used for freight between Scottsburg and New Albany and Jeffersonville as late as 1970.[51] Today the interurban is just a fond memory of the older generation. Interurbans were not a great factor in emigration to Indiana but were a part of its history.

THE VALUE OF EMIGRANT TRAILS

All of the early emigrant trails and the great waterways provided routes for pioneers entering the Northwest Territory and the states of Indiana, Illinois, and Michigan, which were carved from that Territory. Emigrant trails were vital to the settlement of Indiana because there were virtually no roads there in the early days. Settlers could enter the land only by using the navigable waterways or the Indian trails which had once been animal paths.

If your ancestors came to Indiana before 1830, they had to use those primitive paths and trails or the existing waterways to get to the area. Studying the emigrant trails that led toward your ancestors' Indiana home might help you to determine which trails your ancestors used as they traveled to Indiana and then to new land in the territory or state. Once you have determined the pathway, you may be able to determine the place from which they emigrated. The first emigrants came on foot, on horseback, and in horsedrawn wagons as they crossed the high mountains and forded the rivers to get to "Indiany." Other pioneers chose to come to the area in canoes, boats, flatboats, or steamboats on one of the many waterways.

Most of the later emigrants came to Indiana on the roads that were built on the beds of the old emigrant trails and roadways, which lay, in turn, on top of the still older Indian paths and animal trails. Flatboats and steamboats brought early emigrants from the eastern states to the river towns along the Ohio River. From there they traveled overland to new homes in the wilderness. Steamships full of settlers were puffing up the Wabash River to Vincennes by 1816, just a few short years after the Wabash had carried only Indian canoes. After 1840 many emigrants came to Indiana using the plank roads, the canals, and the railroads. Some came in heavily loaded covered wagons on the National Road, others came on barges on the Wabash and Erie Canal, and still others floated down the Ohio River to Indiana on rafts or flatboats. Recent emigrants have come to Indiana from other parts of the United States and from foreign lands using airplanes and jet planes.

In researching your family history you will use a great many kinds of records and a variety of methods to learn about your ancestors. Often, one of the most interesting and most fruitful methods is the study of the migration paths used by pioneer settlers when they came to Indiana. Study the history of the state from territorial days onward, pore over the maps from the time when your ancestors came, and put yourself into their shoes for awhile, and you may be able to determine a great deal about their journey to "Indiany."

Who Came to Indiana?

CHAPTER

5

People have always had good reasons for deciding to leave a beloved and familiar homeland, for packing up and moving to a new and unfamiliar place. Immigrants came to America for various reasons, among them their desire for religious freedom, better living conditions, and abundant, free, or inexpensive land. They also came here to escape religious and political persecution, poverty, and famine. The people who immigrated, or migrated, to Indiana came for many of those same reasons. Of course, people came for differing reasons depending on conditions which existed in the country and the world when they came. Reasons for migration have varied at different times in the state's history.

THE INDIANS

The first people who lived in Indiana were the American Indians, who lived here only when conditions were favorable and left when they were not. The Indians returned to the area again when hunting, fishing, and forage were good. Different groups of Indians had lived in Indiana from about A.D. 800 until the early 1600s. The last group of Indians had left the area and they, or other Indians, were just beginning to return when the French explorers came there in the late 1670s.

SOUTHERN INDIANA SETTLERS

The French

The next people to come to the area were French soldiers and explorers who came as representatives of the French government. France planned to gain control of the land and, at the same time, enrich its treasury from the fur trade. The first Europeans who actually lived in Indiana were the Frenchmen who came as hunters and trappers, and the French missionaries who came to teach the Indians. Like the French soldiers, the French civilians were semipermanent residents who probably did not intend to stay. They were later joined by other civilians from France and French Canada, who were farmers seeking land in Indiana. French people first settled around the fort at Vincennes in southwestern Indiana in about 1733.[1] They also settled at the sites of Fort Wayne and Lafayette, where other French trading post-forts were located. The French government had increasingly encouraged more French citizens to settle in the area to strengthen its claim in the Indiana Country. Britain also sought to gain control of the land, and was ultimately successful. Following Britain's success in the French and Indian War, many French civilians remained in Indiana after French officials and military personnel left. These French civilians were the first white citizens of Indiana.[2]

Pioneers emigrating to the western country. Courtesy Indiana Historical Society Library.

Later, in the 1830s and 1840s, some French people also entered southeastern, west central, and northwestern Indiana, some coming directly from France and others from Canada. The British deported many French-speaking Canadians during this period, and some exiled French Canadians came to Indiana. There were 2,279 people of French birth living in Indiana in 1850.[3] Today many people of French descent still live in the area around Vincennes and along the

Lower Wabash River, in Switzerland County, and in large and small towns throughout the state.

The Swiss

In 1802 French-speaking Swiss immigrants from the Vevay district in Switzerland came to Indiana Territory to found the town of Vevay. John James Dufour, founder of the settlement, had come to America in 1796 in search of land suitable for vineyards. After unsuccessfully trying to grow grapes in Kentucky, Dufour chose for his settlement the southeastern Indiana area that would become Switzerland County. Once the Swiss settlers arrived, they planted vineyards, which later became a fairly successfuly venture. The Swiss settlers built brick homes instead of the log cabins usually built by early settlers.[4] Quite a few people of Swiss descent still live in Switzerland County in and around Vevay.

The Scots-Irish

It has been noted that the first people to challenge the frontier, wherever it existed, were either the Scots, the Irish, or that stubborn combination of the two, the Scots-Irish. They seemed to like the excitement of the frontier and to thrive on the challenge it presented. Many came from the British Isles early in the 1720s and went to live beyond the earlier German settlements on the frontier of south central and western Pennsylvania. Others settled all along the Atlantic coast. Many of the Scots-Irish settled at the edge of or beyond the frontier, partly because of derring-do and partly because the Quakers weren't overfond of these Presbyterians. They did make an effective barrier against the Indians, however.[5] The Scots-Irish soon began to move on beyond permanent settlement into the wilds west and south of the established frontier. Some had begun to emigrate south into Maryland, Virginia, and the Carolinas by the middle 1700s. In the late 1730s the Scots-Irish were the majority in the valley beyond the Blue Ridge Mountains. In the 1780s, following the Revolution, others came directly from Pennsylvania into Ohio, where they again settled beyond the frontier. Some Scots-Irish also left the relative safety of Pennsylvania in the 1780s and traveled by flatboat down the Ohio River to Kentucky.

After a few years, many Scots, Scots-Irish, and Irish moved north from Kentucky into "Indiana Country" and, later, into Indiana Territory. The Scots-Irish, Germans, and English Quakers made up the largest number of Indiana's earliest settlers. These upland southerners were the first settlers in inland Virginia, the Carolinas, Tennessee, and Kentucky, and they were also the first Americans to enter Indiana Country after about 1785.

Scots-Irish and Scottish emigrants from the upland south entered the southern part of Indiana very early and settled all along the Ohio and the Lower Wabash rivers. A number of Scots-Irish also came from Pennsylvania to live in and around Vincennes just a few years after the Revolutionary War. Many of those settlers were "squatters" who entered the area illegally before it was opened to settlement and before it was truly safe to live there. Another small Scottish Presbyterian settlement in Jefferson County was begun between 1815 and 1820.

The Germans

Some German people came to America very early, landing in New York or on Long Island in the 1630s, and shortly afterward moved on into western New York. By the early 1700s they had moved into Pennsylvania and New Jersey. The early German settlers were joined by the English, the Dutch, and a few Scottish and Irish people. In the early 1700s, there was another large German immigration, from the Palatinate.[6] These German immigrants landed in Philadelphia and in the other eastern ports and then fanned out to settle in the nearby eastern Pennsylvania countryside. After living there for a time, many moved on into the central counties of Pennsylvania, and then, as the Scotch began to enter the state, some Germans moved down into Virginia, Maryland, and Delaware and, eventually, into the southern United States. After living awhile in southwestern Virginia, the Carolinas, Tennessee, and later in Kentucky, these German people began to move into southern Indiana.

In 1814 Father George Rapp and a group of German Lutheran dissenters established the utopian Harmony Society at Harmonie (now New Harmony in Posey County) on the Lower Wabash River. The first kindergarten in America was held at New Harmony by the Rappites.[7] The Harmony Society, composed of about one thousand German Americans and based on Christian communalism and strict celibacy, eventually failed. In 1824 Father Rapp and his followers left Indiana and sold the community to Robert Owen, a Scotsman, who instituted an intellectual community there in about 1825.[8] This idealistic venture did not succeed, lasting only about two years, but the community itself has lasted into the twentieth century.

Germans also moved from the eastern states into Ohio and then crossed the border to live in southern and central Indiana. There are communities named Germantown in both Dearborn and Wayne counties and a German township in Vanderburgh County. After about 1840, northern Indiana had a heavy influx of German settlers from the northern tier of eastern states. A particularly heavy immigration of people who came directly from Germany began in 1836 and grew even heavier by the late 1840s. This particular German immigration was due in part to the effects of the Napoleonic Wars and to adverse economic and political conditions in the Germanic states.

The largest German immigration took place during the 1850s and up to the start of the Civil War. These people often came directly from the ports of New

York, Philadelphia, and Baltimore to Indiana and other midwestern states. German immigrants also docked at New Orleans and journeyed up the Mississippi River to settle in the Ohio River towns of Evansville, Jeffersonville, Madison, and Lawrenceburg. German immigration into Franklin, Dearborn, and Wayne counties is covered in a series of articles about the Whitewater Valley written by Chelsea Lawlis in volumes 43–44 of the *Indiana Magazine of History*, published by the Indiana Historical Society.

German families moved to Dubois County between 1836 and 1841, and a majority of the present-day residents there have German surnames. Elfrieda Lang tells the story of the German immigration to Dubois County in volume 41 of the *Indiana Magazine of History*. She tells about the immigrants' residence in Germany and their preparations for the voyage, the voyage itself, the immigrants' arrival in America and their journey to Indiana, and their lives in Dubois County, where they founded a number of Catholic churches. German cabinetmakers also came to the area in the mid-nineteenth century to build furniture. Ferdinand, a German-Catholic community, was founded in 1840 on the Troy-Jasper road by the Reverend Joseph Kundik, and some German immigrants also settled Bethlehem, now Freelandville, in Daviess County, in the 1830s.[9]

A few German families settled in Richmond beginning in the mid-1830s, and their numbers grew throughout the period prior to the onset of the Civil War. Many German Catholic emigrants settled in Oldenburg, a German Catholic community in east central Indiana. There were also large and influential German settlements in Indianapolis, Terre Haute, and Fort Wayne, to name only a few of the many towns and cities populated by Germans. Making up the largest percentage of foreign-born persons in the 1850 Indiana federal census were 28,584 German-born residents. The Germans who settled in Allen County were Lutherans from Würtemberg who came in the late 1830s. These immigrants, "the most industrious and temperate," came to Indiana from New York on the Erie Canal and the Wabash and Erie Canal. Later, all parts of the Germanic states were represented in Allen County.[10]

After 1850 many immigrants came directly from Germany and moved into southern, central, and northern Indiana. There was a mass exodus of Germans from their homeland from 1848 until the start of the Civil War. Most of these people moved into Ohio, Indiana, Illinois, and, later, into the states north and west of them. Political and economic problems in Germany caused many Germans to emigrate, beginning with the intellectuals in about 1848 and followed by the general public later on in the movement. Large German communities are found in the southern part of the state—around Evansville, in Dubois County, clustered around Cincinnati, at Terre Haute and Indianapolis, and widely spread across northern Indiana. There were probably German families in nearly every village, town, and city of the state. In the southern Indiana counties where German immigrants had already come to live, other Germans came in the mid-nineteenth century to join the earlier settlers. The Indiana State Library has many records of German immigrants, including forty-eight pages of genealogical records for German families in Fort Wayne.

The Quakers

Not only did many people come to America for religious reasons, but once here, whole congregations often emigrated together from one area to another. Among the sects who migrated together were the Society of Friends, or Quakers, who had left England to escape both religious and political persecution. Many of the people who settled in Indiana were Quakers of British extraction who came to the Orange County area from Virginia and the Carolinas. They had begun their journey in Pennsylvania and then traveled down through Maryland and into southern Virginia and the Carolinas. During the 1820s and 1830s, many Quakers left South Carolina and came to Indiana to escape the hated institution of slavery. They had bought, and freed, slaves in the south and brought them to the free state of Indiana, where they helped the blacks establish themselves as free persons. Indiana Quakers were actively involved in the abolition movement and in the "underground railroad" in Indiana before the Civil War. Quakers were largely of English extraction, but the sect also had converts from other nationalities and religions. There were even some German Quakers, who were recruited by William Penn before he founded the Colony of Pennsylvania.[11]

CENTRAL INDIANA SETTLERS

In pioneer days the southern third of Indiana was settled first, mostly by people from the upland south. The central part of the state was settled by some southerners but more often by people from the mid-Atlantic states. People from New Jersey, Maryland, and Delaware—most of them German, Scots-Irish, or English—came early to settle the counties along the Ohio border in east central and southeastern Indiana. The town of Lawrenceburg in Dearborn County attracted some elite business and clerical families from New Jersey, who found the rougher inhabitants less than desirable companions. The "rougher" people likewise disdained the elitist easterners. As land in the east central part of the state was quickly taken, other settlers moved beyond them to settle the area to the west. Settlers came from Pennsylvania, Maryland, Delaware, and Ohio to live in the central part of the state in the 1830s and 1840s. As new land was opened in stages farther north, people from southern Indiana also began gradually to move into central Indiana. After 1839, when the National Road was completed through the state, many people from the mid-Atlantic states used it to come to Indiana. The heaviest travel on this roadway was during the period between 1850 and 1860, just prior to the Civil War. People from Illinois settled in the Indiana counties bordering Illinois.

NORTHERN INDIANA SETTLERS

As you might suppose, the northern part of Indiana was settled last. It was settled principally by people from the northern tier of states east of Indiana, although people from the south and the mid-Atlantic states also came there to live. People from the New England states, New York, New Jersey, and Pennsylvania moved to Ohio and may have stayed there awhile before moving into northern Indiana. Settlement of Ohio was principally by northerners, as opposed to Indiana's mostly southern and southern-influenced settlement. New Englanders entered the northeastern part of Indiana between 1820 and 1830 and spread southward as far as Richmond. They also moved westward from Richmond in a narrow band stretching almost to the western border of Indiana. People from Canada and Michigan also entered northern Indiana in the 1840s and 1850s, as land was opened to settlement. There was also a fairly large entry of immigrants from northern Europe following the Civil War. Most of these were German, Irish, English, French, and Scottish.[12]

The emigration of people who were predominantly northerners into the northern counties of Indiana was probably due to the convenient emigrant tails which led there. It was natural to follow a trail that led to fertile land which had been newly opened for settlement. People from the northeastern states also may have liked northern Indiana because the land and the climate were similar to that in the northeast. All of these factors might have influenced their move to Indiana, but the main reason that northerners chose land in northern Indiana was because land was available there, whereas land in southern Indiana had already been taken. Today, evidence of their builders' northeastern origins can be seen in the quaint red and white barns dotting northern Indiana farmlands. These barns are very much like the nineteenth-century barns built in the eastern United States.

SETTLERS BROUGHT BY OCCUPATIONS

Emigrants from other areas who came to Indiana during the period of early settlement were mainly farmers interested in one thing—land—and land was both cheap and plentiful in the Hoosier state. Each pioneer settlement also needed people who followed other lines of work—doctors, blacksmiths, storekeepers, preachers, and, as the villages grew, lawyers, printers, newspapermen, merchants, innkeepers, casketmakers, stone carvers, drayers, wagonmakers, and other tradesmen. Some other occupations on the frontier included land speculators, surveyors, politicians (although usually not by trade), and, along the waterways, boat builders, riverboat and steamboat operators, and ferrymen. Women on the frontier were generally homemakers, but they were also employed as dressmakers, milliners, weavers, domestic servants, and midwives. Black women usually worked as domestics or washerwomen. During the nineteenth century most Indiana men were farmers, hired hands, or laborers. Many people emigrated to the frontier to try to find employment where their training and abilities were needed the most.

The Irish Laborers

Later immigrants to Indiana followed various trades according to the demands of the period. Some built roads, other built railroads, and still others dug canals. The canal-builders were mainly Irish and German immigrants who began working on the Erie Canal in New York State and stayed with the company as the canals were built westward. The potato famine of the 1830s, 1840s, and 1850s and the resulting hard times caused thousands of Irish to emigrate to America in hopes of a better life. At the bottom of the labor chain, where all newcomers seem to begin, the Irish arrived at a time when laborers were needed to build the canals and railroads that were beginning to cross America. These immigrants were met at the docks of New York City by canal men and were immediately recruited to work as laborers on the Erie canal. Many of these Irish laborers worked westward from Rome, New York, to the terminus of the canal at Lake Erie and then resumed building the canal near Toledo, Ohio.[13]

The Wabash and Erie Canal was the continuation of the Erie Canal in Indiana. It ran from Toledo into Indiana near Fort Wayne and then followed the Wabash River and the East Fork of the White River into southern Indiana. There it joined the Ohio River near Evansville. Two other canals, the Central Canal and the Whitewater Canal, were also begun in 1832, at the same time as the Wabash and Erie. The same Irish laborers, now experienced canal diggers, were joined by newcomers from Ireland, and together they built the Indiana canals. Because canal building ended rather abruptly in Indiana, many of these Irishmen stayed on to live in the state. Many settled along the canals and railroads they had helped to build.[14]

The Irish also passed through central Indiana as they built the transcontinental railroad. A great many railroads were built throughout the state after 1850, and the majority of the laborers were Irish, many of whom liked Indiana and decided to stay. Others returned to Indiana after the western railroads were built, bought land, married local girls or sent for their Irish sweethearts, and became Indiana residents.[15] The 1850 federal census for Indiana shows 12,787 Irish-born residents in Indiana, or about twenty-three percent of Indiana's foreign-born population. The Irish, nearly all Catholics, settled in Terre Haute, Fort Wayne, Indianapolis, and in almost every other smaller city and town in the state.

The English and Italian Stoneworkers

Men who were skilled stonecarvers and stoneworkers came to work in the stone quarries and mills of Lawrence and Monroe counties during the period immediately following the Civil War. Many of these people came from the British Isles, where they had followed similar occupations. Other stoneworkers immigrated from Italy to work in the quarries and stonemills of south central Indiana. Quarrymen from the northeastern states and from the southeastern part of the nation also moved into the stone country of Indiana to work.

When an occupation "dried up" in the east and jobs were no longer available, people who lost their employment often came west and took up new occupations. Coal mines in southwestern Indiana brought coal miners to the area from Pennsylvania, West Virginia, eastern Ohio, and Kentucky. The Indiana mines also converted quite a few Indiana farmers to coal miners as the need grew to meet the demands of coal-burning factories, power plants, and homes. Meatpacking plants in Hammond, Terre Haute, Madison, and many other cities drew many Germans, experts in the packing industry, to the state.

THE BELGIANS

Belgian settlers entered southern Indiana around Perry County in the 1820s and 1830s, and in the 1880s another group of Belgians came to the glass plants in northeastern and north central Indiana around Hartford City, Gas City, and Kokomo. The discovery of deposits of natural gas in central Indiana drew glass workers and glass blowers to the state from Ohio, West Virginia, and Pennsylvania. These glass workers had followed the gas wells from one place to the next, working at their trades in each spot. By the 1880s many glass plants were producing in Indiana. Once the gas deposits played out, the workers sought other jobs in the area. By the late nineteenth century, Belgians and their descendants lived in scattered locations throughout the central part of the state. There were also small pockets of Belgians living in St. Joseph County, especially at Mishawaka, by the late nineteenth century.[16]

DePauw University was named for Washington C. DePauw, a Salem lawyer who in 1883 gave money to Asbury College in Greencastle. DePauw was the son of a Belgian immigrant.

THE ITALIANS, SLAVS, AND JEWS

After 1870 several large groups of immigrants come into Indiana from Europe. They were Italians from southern Italy and Sicily, and Slavs and Jews from Austria-Hungary and Russia. Both the Italians and the Jews tended to settle in the industrial cities of northern Indiana even though they probably were farmers in the old country. They wanted to live with their countrymen, people who understood their culture and who spoke their language. Thus, they usually chose new occupations better suited to life in the cities.[17] These new Americans formed little groups of Italian and Jewish settlements in the cities where the mother tongue was spoken and familiar customs were kept. The second-generation members of immigrant families usually disdained the customs and language of the homeland, but the foreign-born members cherished them and kept them. Today ethnic customs, foods, songs, and dances are being revived by the descendants of immigrants, after many years and many generations of lack of interest.

THE SOUTHERN EUROPEANS

People from Poland came into northern Indiana after about 1870, moving into the cities of South Bend, Mishawaka, and Gary. Other Polish people settled in the smaller Indiana towns, including Elkhart, Logansport, and Calumet City. The Polish tended to retain their traditional customs, and today most descendants know of their Polish roots, foods, dances, and customs. Lithuanians, Hungarians, and Ukrainians from southern Russia and Austria-Hungary also seemed to gravitate to the cities in the northern half of Indiana, as did Slovaks, who settled in cities and in small towns in the northern third of the state. A few Greeks, Serbians, Macedonians, Croatians, French, and some Asians, mostly Chinese and Japanese, also entered northern Indiana during the latter part of the nineteenth century.[18] Almost every medium-sized town had a Greek family or two who traditionally operated a restaurant or candy kitchen.

THE WAVE OF IMMIGRATION AFTER 1900

Immigrants from northern and eastern Europe swarmed into Indiana in the early years of the twentieth century, when immigration to the United States swelled to mammoth proportions. Although Indiana never attracted quite so many European immigrants as did the industrial states of the northeast, northern Indiana counties still got their share. Most of these people moved into the cities in the northern counties, but others chose smaller towns and cities elsewhere in the state. These Europeans generally worked in the steel mills and other industries of northern Indiana. People representing nearly two dozen distinct nationalities were living in Gary during the period before World War I. They were Austrian, Croatian, Bulgarian, Czechoslovakian, German, Greek, Hungarian, Italian, Jewish (representing many nations), Lithuanian, Mexican, Polish, Romanian, Russian, Serbian, Spanish, and Yugoslavic.[19] Probably many other ethnic groups were also living in the northern Indiana counties at that time. More than ten percent of the total population of Lake County was foreign-born in 1950, when

Mexicans and southern and eastern Europeans made up the largest percentage of the foreign-born population there.[20]

THE MEXICANS

People from Mexico began to come north to work in the industrial cities of northern Indiana shortly after World War I when a strike in the steel industry drew lower-paid workers to steel mills in the Gary area. Generally, the men arrived first and were joined later by their wives and families. As they heard about the "better wages" there, other Mexicans also came to work the long, hard twelve-hour days for very low wages. Mexican mutual aid societies sprang up to provide social and cultural activities, burial insurance, and other benefits for these workers. Many people of Mexican descent now live in the industrial cities of northern Indiana.[21]

IMMIGRATION CURTAILED BY WAR

Emigration from northern and eastern Europe continued to be very heavy until it was slowed and finally curtailed by World War I. Isolationism and a strong distrust of immigrants developed in this country during the depression of the 1930s when there were few jobs for Americans, let alone jobs for newcomers. The isolationist feeling gradually eased and eventually faded after the 1930s. America's entry into World War II in late 1941 caused another big decline in immigration, although refugees from many European nations were given asylum in the United States before America entered the war. Since the end of World War II, many people have come into northern Indiana from the West Indies, Mexico, and the Far East. Following the Korean and Vietnam conflicts, many Asian people—Koreans, Vietnamese, and others—came to live in northern Indiana and in other parts of the Hoosier state.

THE BLACKS

Very few blacks lived in Indiana during early settlement and the period of the industrial revolution. Because the Northwest Ordinance prohibited slavery in the Territory, Indiana was considered the land of freedom to blacks from the slave states although they were not encouraged to live in the state. Blacks who wanted to settle in Indiana had to register with the county authorities and post bond lest they become wards of the county. Registers were begun in most counties but were not strictly enforced. The Indiana State Library has "Negro Registers" for the counties of Bartholomew, Clark (1805–1810), and Knox (1805–1807) and perhaps for a few others. Only a few freed blacks, called "free persons of color," or "freedmen" and "freedwomen," came to live in the state in the early days.

Over the next several decades many blacks migrated to Indiana, and, like the white settlers, they came from the upland south. The 1850 Indiana federal census shows that the largest number of blacks had come from North Carolina, Virginia, Kentucky, and Tennessee, which was the same proportion as for white residents. A few had come to Indiana from Ohio, and fewer still from the deep south states of South Carolina, Georgia, Mississippi, Alabama, and Louisiana. By 1860 the number of free blacks had grown to 11,428 in Indiana.

The 1851 state constitution expressly prohibited blacks from settling in Indiana and put many restrictions on them. Blacks could not vote, serve in the military forces, or testify against a white person, and black children could not attend white public schools. The state of Indiana actually helped to finance a movement to send American blacks "back" to Liberia in West Africa. Each person who emigrated was to receive one hundred acres of land and fifty dollars in cash.[22] It is not known whether any Indiana blacks took advantage of that "generous" offer.

Blacks who came to Indiana were either freed persons in their former states, were recently freed, or were runaway slaves. Freed slaves living in a slave state had only ninety days to leave the state, or they risked capture and enslavement again. Indiana was one of the closest free states and was, therefore, a favorite spot for escaped or freed blacks. Fortunately, there were some people in Indiana who were willing to help blacks travel north to freedom and safety. The "Underground Railroad" was the name given to a group of people who helped fugitives travel northward to freedom in Canada, Michigan, New York, and Pennsylvania. The freedom movement worked "underground," in secrecy, to provide food and shelter in "safe houses" along the escape route. The Underground Railroad was operated by Quakers, Covenanter Presbyterians, and others who detested slavery. The Covenanters believed that "no part of God's creation should be held in bondage."

The "president" of the Underground Railroad was Levi Coffin, a successful Fountain City merchant who had come to Indiana from North Carolina. The first "station" in Indiana was located at Walnut Ridge, a few miles south of Salem, where the Reverend J. J. McClurkin and Isaiah Reed often brought slaves to Bloomington, where many people sheltered them at great personal risk. Others who worked on the Underground Railroad were William Hawkins, a black from Daviess County, who brought slaves to Bloomington from the south; James Faris, whose Bloomington home was a way station; and Mrs. Myrears and Samuel Gordon, who also hid fugitives in their homes.[23] The next station north of Bloomington was at the Quaker settlement of Mooresville, and later at Morgantown, when some Covenanters moved there. In Mooresville John Cathcart hid the slaves and James Kelso took them on to another safe house. Activities of the Underground Railroad continued until the end of the Civil War.[24]

Increased northward migration by southern blacks took place between 1865 and 1900. In 1866 the exclusionary article intended to keep blacks out of Indiana was nullified by the State Supreme Court and black people could live there without restrictions. Black people organized their own churches, clubs, organizations, and recreational groups. For many years black people in Indiana worked mostly as domestics, farm hands, and general laborers. After 1869, when separate black schools were specified by an act of the Indiana legislature (where black population was large enough), most Indiana towns began to provide separate schools for black children. Blacks could attend white schools only if there was no separate black school. Since the law applied only to elementary schools, black teens could go to white high schools. In 1877, however, an act gave the school corporations the option of admitting black students to white high schools or establishing separate black high schools.[25]

Migration of blacks from the southern states was relatively light until the 1940s, when the economy of the south began to fail and blacks were needed to work in the heavy industry brought about by the war. At that time, many southern blacks migrated into the northern counties of Indiana to live and work in the large cities. Today, many cities in the state have large black populations, especially the northern industrial cities of Gary, Hobart, South Bend, and Fort Wayne. In central Indiana Anderson, Kokomo, Muncie, and Indianapolis have large black populations, as do Evansville, New Albany, and Jeffersonville in southern Indiana.[26]

The Ku Klux Klan was especially active in Indiana during the years after World War I when southern blacks were beginning to enter the state in large numbers. It is heartening to know, however, that an effort to revive the Klan in the 1960s failed miserably, even though the head of the Klan then lived in Indiana.

Military Records

CHAPTER

6

THE WESTERN CAMPAIGN

At the time of the Revolutionary War, Indiana did not exist as a state or territory but was then part of the "far west" claimed by Britain. In 1778, near the close of that conflict, George Rogers Clark led a band of about two hundred Virginians and Kentuckians down the Ohio River from the Falls of the Ohio, near Louisville, to take the land in southern Illinois from the British. They captured the French village of Kaskaskia and two British forts without firing a shot, and sent a small group of men to Vincennes to occupy the deserted French fort. The British, hearing of this, sent a force there and easily captured Fort Sackville.[1]

In February of the next year, 1779, Clark took one hundred and seventy men across flooded southern Illinois lowlands to surprise and recapture Fort Sackville from the British garrison. This extremely hazardous journey of nearly two hundred miles was made under terrible conditions and against tremendous odds. Clark had his men carry twenty American flags and march around to simulate a much larger force, fooling British commander, Colonel Henry Hamilton, into surrendering. With the recapture of the fort, Clark and his men were instrumental in winning the western campaign and securing for America the vast area of what would be called the Northwest Territory.[2] This was the only time during the Revolution that enemy territory was captured and retained by American forces.

Records of Clark's campaign, the Clark Papers, make up the largest single collection in the "Draper Papers," a vast compilation of pioneer materials gathered by Lyman C. Draper. The Draper Papers are housed at the State Historical Society of Wisconsin on the campus of the University of Wisconsin in Madison. Nearly twenty thousand items of Clark material, including his financial records and accounts, are housed in the Virginia State Archives at

Richmond. The Filson Club in Louisville, Kentucky, also has a sizable collection of papers related to Clark and the western campaign. The Missouri Historical Society, in St. Louis, and the Library of Congress in Washington, D.C., have Clark material. Lists of the men who were granted land for service in the western campaign have also been printed.[3]

Unable to repay George Rogers Clark for his expenses in the western campaign, Virginia instead granted 150,000 acres of land in southeastern Indiana to Clark and his men. The grant became known as "Clark's Grant." In the 1787 Treaty of Paris, which ended the Revolutionary War, Britain ceded all of the vast land between the Appalachians and the Mississippi River to America. In Indiana, George Rogers Clark is given credit for obtaining this land for the United States through his western campaign. It is the only campaign of the Revolution which was fought on Indiana soil. With the British cession of American land, the ground was prepared for the organization of the Northwest Territory in the land "north and west of the Ohio River."

REVOLUTIONARY WAR RECORDS

Many men who served in the army in the Northwest Territory between 1784 and 1811 had also served from 1775 to 1783 in the Revolutionary War. Some of them later served in the War of 1812 and even in the Indian Wars that began in 1817.[4] It is difficult to prove military service in the northwest until somewhat later than this period, but many men who had served elsewhere during the Revolution later moved to Indiana and lived and died there. The National Archives in Washington, D.C., has fourteen unnumbered manuscript volumes relating to the payment of Revolutionary War pensioners in the various states, including Indiana. These records are for payments made under various acts of Congress between 1818 and 1853. The volumes are arranged by state, then alphabetically by the first letter of the surname. Although there is not a great deal of useful information in these volumes, a typical entry shows name and rank of pensioner, state in which payment was made, and the amount paid in March and September of each year. If the pensioner died or moved to another state during the period recorded, that fact is indicated. In some cases, the date of death is also shown.[5] In the 1930s Estella O'Byrne compiled the two-volume *Roster of Soldiers and Patriots of the American Revolution Buried in Indiana.* The two volumes were published in 1938 by the Brookville, Indiana, D.A.R., and were reprinted in 1966 by the Genealogical Publishing Company, Inc. They are available at the Indiana State Library in Indianapolis.

MILITIA RECORDS

Between the end of the Revolution, in 1784, and 1789 the only existing military unit in the United States was the militia. The first need of settlers in the Old

Northwest was for a militia, and militia units were established as land was surveyed and settlers moved into Indiana. Not many of these records for county militia units survive, and those that do are generally found only at the local level, either in the state or the county, but principally in the county.[6] There may be militia lists hidden away in various places around the country, however. Douglas Clanin, director of the Harrison Papers project of the Indiana Historical Society, located, in the National Archives, an appeal from Harrison County settlers for rangers and militia to protect them. The partially legible document and the names of the members of the militia company were printed in the June 1987 issue of *The Hoosier Genealogist,* volume 27, number 2. The best source for records for this period is the set of books known as the *Territorial Papers of the United States,* compiled by Clarence Edwin Carter, which contains lists of petitioners and militiamen, and letters to and from territorial officials. Some county histories published for southern Indiana counties also contain militia lists and stories of their feats.

THE BATTLE OF FALLEN TIMBERS

People who tried to settle in Indiana were attacked by Indians from the earliest days of settlement, as the Indians tried to keep European settlers from entering and living on Indian land. These early conflicts grew until several major battles were fought in Indiana and Ohio between the Americans and the Indians, with the Indians generally winning. Late in 1790 the Indians defeated a military expedition led by General Josiah Harmar, shortly thereafter Major Hamtramck was also routed by them, and finally, in 1792, Ohio Governor Arthur St. Clair was forced to flee from Little Turtle's men.[7] In each case, American forces had been poorly trained and provisioned, and many Americans were killed. The Indians lost very few men, however, and were confident that they could eventually defeat the Americans. The tribes were determined to keep the white settlers back beyond the Ohio River and well out of Indian territory.

The turning point in these conflicts with the Indians took place in 1794 when General Anthony ("Mad Anthony") Wayne led a large expedition against the Indians in the Battle of Fallen Timbers near St. Mary's in northeastern Ohio. Wayne's army of 3,500 men was better trained and organized than the previous armies, and the Americans won a decisive victory. The British had promised to aid the Indians in this battle but the promised aid never came. The American victory at the Battle of Fallen Timbers led to the 1795 Treaty of Greenville, in which the Indians ceded away land that included the southern two-thirds of Ohio and a small part of southeastern Indiana, plus the Wabash-Maumee portage, Ouiatanon, Vincennes, and Clark's Grant. The British agreed to evacuate their American posts at this time but failed to do so. William Henry Harrison, then the governor of Indiana Territory, fought under General Wayne in this engagement.[8] Fort Wayne was built in northeast Indiana and named to honor General Wayne for his heroism in this engagement. The city of Fort Wayne now occupies the site of that fort, and a reconstructed fort has been erected there.

THE BATTLE OF TIPPECANOE

Tecumseh, the Shawnee chief, and his brother, The Prophet, became increasingly disturbed and angered as the Indian tribes were again and again persuaded to cede land to the United States government. In 1808 the two brothers established Prophet's Town on the Tippecanoe River near the site of present-day Lafayette. They tried to organize an Indian confederation to overthrow and drive out the whites. In 1811, when Tecumseh traveled to the south in an attempt to enlist the help of the southern bands, General Harrison led a force of about 1,000 Kentucky volunteers, Indiana militiamen, and a contingent of the Fourth U.S. Regiment up the Wabash toward Prophet's Town. On the way they built Fort Harrison near the site of present-day Terre Haute, and from there the army moved near Prophet's Town. Harrison knew that Tecumseh was not in the village but he had nevertheless expected to talk with, not fight, the Indians. Just before daybreak the Indians attacked and the battle began. Believing that The Prophet had made them invincible to bullets, the Indians were turned back after a short battle by the American forces.[9] Although there were heavy losses on both sides, the Americans believed that they had won the battle. This event, the Battle of Tippecanoe, was one of national significance because it is thought to have been "the first shot" fired in the War of 1812. The fame of this battle also helped Harrison to be elected the ninth president of the United States. *The Roll of the Army Commanded by William Henry Harrison from September 6 to November 24, 1811* was published by the Indiana Historical Society and is available in the *Indiana Source Book III,* pages 12–18.

THE WAR OF 1812

The War of 1812 ended a long series of Indian wars which began in about 1750 in the Ohio Country. After the close of this war, settlers finally were able to enter Indiana to live, free of Indian attack and the hated British influence. No territorial changes resulted from the War of 1812, but American control over the west was much stronger in 1815 than it had been previously. The war was also instrumental in promoting a movement for statehood which, in 1816, made Indiana the nineteenth state in the Union.[10]

THE BLACK HAWK WAR OF 1832

In 1832 Indiana residents living on the northwestern frontier bordering Illinois were alarmed by exaggerated reports of trouble developing between Black Hawk and his band of Sauk and Potawatomi Indians and the Illinois militia. People in Indiana were afraid of attack by the tribes of Illinois and northern Indiana. On May 27, 1832, Governor Noah Noble ordered Captain (later Major General) Joseph Orr to "repair to the Wabash and in your discretion take such steps as circumstances may require, as relates to the procuring of arms, provisions, and the calling of a sufficient force in the field, by entire companies, if increasing dangers demand it, or by requisition on each Regt. as pointed out by law if a stronger measure is not called for by the attitude and movements of the Indians."[11]

The militia companies of Captains David H. Brown, Jesse Davidson, Samuel McGeorge, John W. Odell, John Roberts, and Daniel Sigler were mustered into service on May 26 and 27 and attached to the 62nd Regiment under Colonel James Davis. After they entered Indian country and found no hostile Indians, the militiamen were disbanded on June 3, 1832, and were mustered out on that date. The muster rolls of these regiments are published in the *Indiana Source Book III.*

Residents of Elkhart and St. Joseph counties soon reported that several people had been murdered at Fort Dearborn (Chicago) and that the Michigan militia had been mobilized. To meet this threat, Governor Noble ordered Colonel Alexander W. Russell of the 40th Regiment to organize a force of 150 riflemen from the Marion County regiment to investigate threats on the northwest frontier. The men of the 40th met in Indianapolis on June 9 and were joined by companies from Johnson and Hendricks counties. Colonel John W. Wishard of the 57th Regiment from Johnson County and Colonel Thomas Nichols of the 61st Regiment from Hendricks County met with the 40th Regiment on June 9. The three companies went to South Bend and, meeting no hostile Indians, they returned to Indianapolis on July 3. The muster rolls of the five companies under Colonel Russell are also in the *Indiana Source Book III*, pages 346–349.

A congressional act of June 15, 1832, was to raise a force of six hundred mounted rangers, including two hundred from Indiana, to meet the reported Indian attack. Governor Noble, without waiting for further information, ordered General Orr to organize a company of rangers to serve for three months. Orr was to set up stations near existing settlements in order to keep in touch with the Chicago and Wabash settlements. He reported on July 5 that he had recruited men from the counties in his division and that they had met on July 2 at Attica, armed and outfitted for service and with ten days' provisions. Leaving Attica on July 3, they arrived in Iroquois, Illinois, two days later, set up a small camp, and prepared for battle. Instead of moving toward Indiana, the Indians moved northwest and were defeated on August 2 by the Illinois militia in the Battle of Bad Axe, Wisconsin. Noble ordered the men home on August 6, regretting "exceedingly" that the militia had "not had the chance to fight." The troops were mustered out of service on August 12 and marched to Parish's Grove, where they were relieved of their duties. The muster roll of General Joseph Orr's company of

Mounted Rangers, July 2–August 12, 1832, is found with the other muster rolls in the *Indiana Source Book III.*

Congress passed acts on July 14, 1832, February 19, 1833, and March 2, 1833, to pay the militia and reimburse them for lost equipment and horses. Some men were also paid expenses for rations and forage and eventually for horses lost. The pay per month was $8.00 for sergeants, $7.33 for corporals, and $6.66 for privates.[12] The Archives Division, Indiana State Library, has the muster rolls of the men who joined the Mounted Rangers provided by Congress on June 16, 1832. Included are men from Kentucky, Illinois, and Missouri as well as those from Indiana. Information given includes name, rank, unit, term of enlistment, and by whom enlisted.[13]

THE MEXICAN WAR

The Mexican War, which lasted from 1846 to 1848, added vast amounts of new territory to the United States. Although the Mexican border was situated far from the state of Indiana, many Hoosier men served in this war. Many little Indiana towns were given Mexican or Texan names by veterans of the war. The National Archives has a series of records as the result of an 1887 congressional act based on service performed between 1846 and 1848. Pensions were available to veterans who served sixty days and to their widows who had not remarried. A few death and disability files from the "Old Wars" Series are now included among these files. The files are arranged alphabetically, and a master index is on the microfilm *Index to Mexican War Pension Files, 1887–1926,* number T317, on fourteen rolls.[14]

Information in these files may include veteran's declaration with name of veteran; dates and places of birth, enlistment, and discharge; places of residence since service. A widow's declaration seeking a pension shows the same information about the service of the veteran; her name, age, and place of residence; the date and place of her marriage to the veteran, with the name of the person performing the ceremony; and the date and place of the veteran's death. A questionnaire shows the maiden name of the wife; the date and place of the marriage of the couple and the name of the person performing the ceremony; the name of a former wife, if any, and the date and place of her death or divorce; and the names and dates of birth of living children.[15] Such information can be helpful in family research and is well worth searching for if you suspect, or know, that your ancestor served in the Mexican War.

THE CIVIL WAR

Despite Indiana's strong southern heritage and its largely antiblack attitude, the state of Indiana was firmly behind the Union in the Civil War. Only a few diehard southern sympathizers refused to support the war effort, these largely from the southern third of the state. Indiana Governor Oliver P. Morton led the Indiana war drive, recruiting, training, and equipping large numbers of men. Because of Morton's efforts, nearly 200,000 men from Indiana served the Union in 129 infantry regiments and several cavalry and artillery units. Indiana, providing ten percent of the Northern troops, was second in number of Union men of military age who served in the war.[16] The Indiana State Archives has a card file of Indiana men who volunteered for service in the Civil War. Information on a card includes name, rank, company, regiment, period of original enlistment, place and date of birth, place and date of muster, age, physical description, occupation, date, place and manner of leaving service, and, in some cases, information on promotions and wounds received.[17]

Men from Indiana fought in every major battle of the war. The state also provided crucial supplies of food and goods to the Northern troops. Indianapolis was the center of Indiana war activities and was the site of an internment camp for Confederate prisoners during the war. Some Confederate soldiers who died while in this camp are buried in the old Greenlawn Cemetery in Indianapolis, along with many Union dead. In 1863, on one afternoon at Gettysburg, 210 of the 288 men of the "Iron Brigade," the Nineteenth Indiana Infantry, were lost. Many of these soldiers are buried in Greenlawn. By 1863 Greenlawn Cemetery was nearly full, and a commission was chosen to select a location for a new cemetery. An area known as Strawberry Hills was chosen for the site of a huge cemetery complex called Crown Hill Cemetery. Part of this area was designated a national cemetery because of the hundreds of Union casualties and the more than sixteen hundred Confederate war dead buried there.[18] The military section was long ago filled to capacity but the cemetery still buries military men in other areas.

An Indiana man called up for military service could pay another man to go to the service in his place. The State Archives has a file called *Civil War Substitutes.* Information on a card includes name of draftee, name of substitute, and unit to which substitute was assigned.[19] If your Indiana ancestor was of the right age to have served but did not serve, you might find that he bought the services of another man to go in his place.

Although no battles were fought in Indiana during the Civil War, in July 1863 the state was invaded by Confederate cavalry troops commanded by General John Hunt Morgan. In Morgan's Raid the Rebs swept through the southern Indiana towns of Corydon, Salem, Vernon, and several others, robbing and alarming the citizens. The primary reason for this raid was probably diversionary, although Morgan's Raiders took fresh horses and plundered larders in several towns. Morgan was chased into Ohio, where he was caught and imprisoned. He later escaped, returned to the war, and was later killed. Morgan's Raid brought the war closer to home and no doubt served to rouse the citizens to even more spirited support of the Union cause.[20]

2374

3—402.

Certificate No. 10708 **Department of the Interior,**

Name, Michael Myers BUREAU OF PENSIONS,

Washington, D. C., January 15, 1898.

SIR:

In forwarding to the pension agent the executed voucher for your next quarterly payment please favor me by returning this circular to him with replies to the questions enumerated below.

Very respectfully,

H. Clay Evans
Commissioner.

P. V. Rice
U.S. Pension Agent,
Indianapolis, Ind.

First. Are you married? If so, please state your wife's full name and her maiden name.

Answer. yes Nellie E. Myers Nellie E. Troutman

Second. When, where, and by whom were you married?

Answer. Feb 8/1894 Marion Ind Rev D. C. Darling

Third. What record of marriage exists?

Answer.

Fourth. Were you previously married? If so, please state the name of your former wife and the date and place of her death or divorce.

Answer. yes Josepha A Wingand died aug 10/1888 at Nashville Tenn

Fifth. Have you any children living? If so, please state their names and the dates of their birth.

Answer. Ellsworth and Elmer June 19 1868
Laura C January 29 1870 Charls C July 11 1876
Edwin June 7 1879 Maud and Myrtle Feb 21/1883

Michael Myers
(Signature.)

Date of reply, June 4, 1898 0-8 5301b750m1-98

A typical document from a Civil War veteran's pension file, giving information about the family of veteran Michael Myers. In the author's possession.

CIVIL WAR RECORDS

Civil War records are better in content and quantity than those of any of the wars before it. Military records for veterans of the "War of the Rebellion" are of two types: service records and benefits records. The pension applications have much more genealogical information than the service records have. For information about an ancestor's military service, however, you should investigate the service records also.

Veterans' Service Records

The Civil War service records at the National Archives include card abstracts and documents relating to individual soldiers. These might be voluntary enlistment papers, prisoner of war papers, hospital bed cards, and death reports. Jacket envelopes for men in Indiana State organizations are filed by the name of the state; by the arm of service (cavalry, artillery, infantry, and so forth); numerically by regiment; and then alphabetically by the surname of the soldier. Some of these files include cross-references to the names on regimental papers that are filed with the muster rolls. Unfortunately, there is no master index to the Civil War service records. To locate a service record for your ancestor, you must know the state, the complete name of the organization in which he served, and, if possible, his rank and places of residence before and after his military service.[21]

The service records contain the same sort of information on each soldier as the compiled service records of the earlier wars. In addition you will find the date his rank changed and the date, place, and nature of his discharge; in some cases, a voluntary enlistment paper or an abstract showing his age, county or town of his birth, his occupation, and his physical description. If he was hospitalized, a bed card shows his age, nativity, evidence of his marital status, his place of residence, and the date and occasion of his being wounded. If he died in service, a casualty sheet shows the place and date of his death.[22]

Veterans' Benefits Records

Civil War veterans' benefits were almost entirely pensions rather than bounty land warrants. Veterans, however, were given special consideration in Homestead legislation, generally for land in the western territories. To obtain a pension the veteran would first submit an application for pension, detailing his service and his need for a pension. Information, therefore, varies greatly from one application to another, but an applicant's file will contain some or all of the following information: applicant's name, military or naval unit, and place of residence; a summary of his military or naval record; his age or date of birth, or both; place of birth; date and place of his marriage; maiden name of his wife; date of his wife's death, if deceased; and the names of surviving minor children, with each child's birthdate and birthplace.[23] Even if the veteran was not granted a pension (although almost every veteran seemed to be granted one), his pension file should prove valuable because of the large amount of genealogical information found therein.

Widows' Pension Application Files

If a veteran died in the service or after being discharged, his widow would have been eligible to apply for a pension based on her husband's military service. The widow's pension application will contain much of the same information as the veteran's pension application, with additional information on surviving children, date and circumstances of the veteran's death, and, possibly, information about some of the widow's relatives. It is not unusual to find the name of the bride's father or mother or even some of her siblings in affidavits filed to substantiate the marriage in a widow's pension application. You need to know the name of the veteran, his branch of service, and the state from which he served.

There are two indexes to the veterans' benefits files. One is an *alphabetical index* under the name of the veteran, and the other is an *organization index* to use if you know the state and the outfit in which the soldier served. The latter index will get you the veteran's file much more quickly than the alphabetical surname index because there were so many soldiers who had the same names. Thus, the organization index is highly preferable to use if you can learn the name of the veteran's particular organization.[24]

In 1869 W. H. H. Terrell compiled the eight-volume *Report of the Adjutant General of the State of Indiana,* which can help to determine the organization in which your ancestor served. The genealogical library in your county of interest should have the volume of the *Report* for that county. The 1890 census of Civil War veterans, which was taken in conjunction with the 1890 federal population census, also listed the organization in which an Indiana veteran served. These schedules no longer exist for states beginning with the letters A through K, however. They, along with the 1890 census, were destroyed in a fire in Washington, D.C., so that none exist for Indiana. But, if your ancestor was living in another state at that time, he may be listed in the military census records for that state.[25]

You must use NATF Form 80 to request copies of veterans' service or pension files from the National Archives. To obtain this form, write to Services Branch (NNIR), National Archives Records Service (NARS), 8th and Pennsylvania Avenues, N.W., Washington, D.C. 20408. Upon receipt of the form, fill in all of the information you can and mail the form back to the NARS address given above.

Do not send payment with the form; wait until the NARS notifies you that records have been located and copied. A bill and instructions for payment will be included with this notification. Remit the payment, and the record copies will be sent to you. You must submit a separate NATF Form 80 for each file (pension, bounty-land, or compiled military service record) desired.[26] If you plan to request several files, ask for enough forms to cover those requests. Plan, too, on the entire process taking a considerable amount of time to complete.

Post–Civil War Records

Many Civil War veterans returned home disabled by wounds received during the war, and homes for these disabled men were established throughout the nation. One branch of the National Home for Disabled Volunteer Soldiers was established in 1888 at Marion, Indiana.[27] Records for the various homes, beginning in about 1865, are in the National Archives in Washington, D.C., and give military history, domestic history, home history, and general remarks. These records are part of the Records of the Veterans Administration, Record Group 15 in the National Archives.

You must know the state from which your ancestor served in order to use the Civil War service records, and the more you know about him, the easier it will be to get his records. The Military Division of the Indiana Historical Society and Indiana State Library also has a card file on microfilm of Civil War soldiers who were buried in Indiana. Called the *Veterans' Grave Registration File,* this file covers only 51 of the 92 Indiana counties. Given are the soldier's name, war, unit, the cemetery, location of the cemetery, lot or plot number, or both, and, possibly, dates of birth and death and name of next of kin.[28]

Men who had served in the Civil War on the Union side were eligible to join the Grand Army of the Republic (G.A.R.). Members held periodic "encampments," or conventions, one of which was held in Indianapolis September 4–9, 1893. The Indiana State Archives has the *Register of Visitors to the National Encampment of the G.A.R. at Indianapolis* in thirty-nine volumes, one for each Indiana Civil War volunteer regiment or battery. The information given includes veteran's name, company and regiment or battery, and usually town and state of residence in 1893.[29]

Veterans' Enrollments

The Indiana State Library and State Archives has individual books of veterans' enrollments for 1886, 1890, and 1894, arranged by county, with an individual book for each county. These records were kept by the county clerk in each county, and that official has (or did have) duplicate copies of the records. Information includes veteran's name, county and regiment, state from which he served, and number of children under age sixteen.[30]

THE SPANISH AMERICAN WAR

Relatively few men served in the limited engagements known as the Spanish American War (1898–99) and the Philippine Insurrection (1899–1902), but a few Indiana men did serve in them. The Indiana State Library has a microfilm of the registration cards called *Indiana Spanish American War Volunteers.* Information given includes name, unit, age, physical description, birthplace, occupation, and muster in and muster out dates.[31]

Enlistment registers for the Spanish American War are in the National Archives, arranged more or less alphabetically. There are index cards for pensions, arranged alphabetically by the surname of the veteran, which have been microfilmed as the *General Index to Pension Files, 1861–1934.* To request a copy ask for T288, which is on 544 rolls at the National Archives. The index card will show the name of the veteran; name and class of dependent, if any; service data; application number or file number; and, for an approved claim, certificate number or file number and the state from which the claim was filed.[32] In 1900 the Indiana Adjutant General's Office in Indianapolis published the *Record of Indiana Volunteers in the Spanish-American War, 1898–1899,* by James K. Gore. The book is available at the Indiana State Library in Indianapolis.

WORLD WAR I

American men were eligible for the draft at the beginning of World War I, and the Selective Service System (S.S.S.) was organized to handle the draft procedure. The S.S.S. kept the records of men called up for military service in World War I. It was previously impossible to see such records, but the Freedom of Information Act of 1967 and the Privacy Act of 1974 now allow you access to information in the World War I Selective Service draft records. You must know the address where your ancestor lived when he registered for the draft because this information determines the Selective Service board which served him. This is much easier in a small town than in a large city.[33] These draft records are located in the National Archives Field Branch, 1557 St. Joseph Avenue, East Point, Georgia 30044. They are part of the *Records of the Selective Service System (World War I),* Record Group 163.

The Selective Service records include mainly draft registration cards, docket books, and classification lists. The draft registration records contain information supplied by the registrant, including name, address, date of birth, age, race, citizenship status, birthplace, occupation, employer, dependent relative, marital status, father's birthplace, and name and address of nearest relative. The records are arranged alphabetically by state, thereunder by local board, and then by individual registrant.[34] Additional information regarding men in the armed forces after this time can be obtained by contacting the National Personnel Record Center (Military Records), NARA, 9700 Page Boulevard, St. Louis, Missouri 63132. You will need to use Standard Form 180, *Request Pertaining to Military Records,* which is available from any one of the following places: the St. Louis center; the Government Printing Office; any federal information center; local Veterans Administration offices; veterans service organizations; and the Reference Services Branch (NNIR), General Services Administration, Washington, D.C. 20408. Written consent of the veteran or his next of kin, if he is deceased, is required to obtain information of a personal nature.

Indiana Roll of Honor

The Indiana State Archives has bound volumes titled *Gold Star Roll of Honor, 1914–1918,* which record alphabetically the names of men and women who died during World War I. The *Roll of Honor* was originally published as *Gold Star Honor Roll, 1914–1918.*[35] If your ancestor or relative served from Indiana and died in World War I, his or her name should be recorded here.

WORLD WAR II

Access to records for men and women who served in the armed forces during the past seventy-five years is restricted to members of the immediate family. A living veteran can, of course, request data about his own service or give written permission for others to obtain it. Most of these later records are housed at the National Personnel Records Center, 9700 Page Boulevard, St. Louis, Missouri 63132. Such records can only be abstracted by the Records Center personnel because the privacy laws prevent viewing or copying by the public. Use Form 180 to request such information.[36] Millions of military records at the St. Louis center were destroyed in a fire on the top floor of the center on July 12, 1973, and millions more were damaged. James E. Cole, Jr., acting assistant archivist for federal records centers, estimates the following losses: 80 percent of the army records, 1912–1959; 60 percent of the air force records, 1947–1963; and 1 percent of army records for personnel discharged since January 1, 1973. Only the records of living military personnel have been reconstructed for pension and benefits purposes. Where no benefits are owing and for deceased personnel, there are no plans to reconstruct the destroyed records.[37]

DISCHARGE PAPERS

Information of a genealogical nature will generally be found in a veteran's discharge papers or in the death papers sent to a next of kin. The Freedom of Information Act allows the National Personnel Records Center to release the following information, if available: age or date of birth, salary, photographs, source of commission, duty status, office phone number, military and civilian education level, decorations and awards, with a copy of the citation, if available, present and past duty assignments and locations, records of nonclassified courts-martial, marital status, education, schooling, rank or grade, serial or service number, date of rank or grade, promotion sequence number, and dependants, including name, sex, and age. If identity must be verified, the center will add such items as names of father and mother, home address, and such.[38] The information retrieval service takes several weeks. You will be billed for the research, processing, and photocopying of the records.

Indiana counties were required to record the honorable discharge of soldiers and sailors who served in World War I. Some discharges from earlier wars, the Civil War and the Philippine Insurrection, may also be found at the courthouse in the county where the veteran lived when discharged, as well as some dishonorable and medical discharges. Records generally consist of typescript copies of the original documents received by each soldier when discharged. A few of these records have been microfilmed by the Genealogical Society of Utah, but most have not. Information includes name, race, rank, serial number, reason for discharge, birthplace, age when enlisted, occupation, and a personal description. The service record sometimes included with the discharge record gives length of service, prior service, marital status, arms and horsemanship qualifications, advancement, battles, decorations, honors, leaves of absence, physical condition, and character evaluation. World War II discharges were also required to be recorded at the courthouse, and the information is the same as for veterans of World War I.[39]

THE VALUE OF MILITARY RECORDS

You can see that a considerable amount of information can often be found in an ancestor's military service records and, especially, in his pension application or the pension application of his widow. Even though you have no concrete evidence that your ancestors served in a war, if they were the right age to have served, suspect that they did and search for that evidence. There is a strong possibility that they did serve and have left military records regarding that service. Look for a reference to any military service in the obituary, the county history, the tombstone, the family Bible, family records, church records, old letters, and on the death certificate. If, after a thorough search, you find no indications of military service for your ancestors, check to see if any of their close relatives served in the military and hunt for records for those persons. Family data may be given for relatives that will be helpful in your search.

Information found in military records not only can give you information about your ancestors, but it often suggests other sources to search. You can often extend your family pedigree a full generation or more by using a veteran's or his widow's pension application. Not only that, but you will begin to see your ancestors as real, flesh-and-blood persons instead of just names and some dates on your charts. Read the *Guide to Genealogical Research in the National Archives,* Section B, chapters 4–9, for further information about military records as a genealogical and family history source. Most genealogical libraries have this helpful book, or you can purchase the *Guide* from the National Archives Trust Fund Board, National Archives, Box 124, Washington, D.C. 20408. A free pamphlet, "Military Service Records in the National Archives of the United States" (General Information Leaflet F, revised edition, 1985) is also available from the National Archives.

PROBLEMS WITH USING MILITARY RECORDS

Few early Indiana military records, such as Revolutionary War and militia records, exist. Many were lost or destroyed, and others were evidently never made. Many eligible veterans also chose not to apply for pensions for service in the Revolutionary War and later wars. Thus, they will not be listed in the pension applications. Although there are a great many pension applications, few Revolutionary War service records remain. The United States did not exist until after the Revolution, and military records were kept according to the orders of each colonial government. Once the war was over, these records may not have seemed valuable and thus were disposed of.

The worst problem encountered when using the military records for the later wars is trying to find the correct name of the organization in which your ancestor served. The name of the particular unit is needed in order to get information on the person. Check for the outfit in the county history of the county from which you think he or she enlisted. Check in the area newspapers for the period, in the biography or obituary, and in the death notice. If your ancestor has a government headstone, the name of his or her military organization will be carved on it. And even if there is no military stone, the tombstone may still have the name of the military organization on it. Buttons, medals, a sword, or some other memorabilia may suggest the branch of service and even the organization to which your ancestor belonged.

The fire in the St. Louis Personnel Records Center created the biggest problem confronting researchers for World Wars I and II and later conflicts. A large proportion of the military records stored there was destroyed. To get around this problem, use the local newspapers from the time and place where your ancestor enlisted and perhaps the Selective Service draft records (if they still exist after the recent move to destroy them) to learn about your ancestor's enlistment and military service. If you have an old address book of your ancestor's, you might be able to contact some of his or her service buddies to learn the name of the organization in which your ancestor served and particulars of his or her service.

Indiana Church and Cemetery Records

CHAPTER

7

Indiana church records generally begin before the state began registration of vital records and are among the best kinds of genealogical records. You will find these records in books called the church registers. Church records were kept for the important events in the lives of our ancestors—the births, the marriages, and the deaths. But, where vital records are for the actual events, church records are for the rite involved with the particular event.[1] Rather than recording the date of birth, church registers record the date of baptism or christening. The baptism might have taken place a few days after the birth, several months after it, or even several years later, depending on the weather and the child's state of health. Instead of a marriage license, the church record will be the date of marriage banns or of the marriage ceremony. And, in most cases, the church record will be the date of burial instead of the date of death. Because the dates recorded in church records are usually fairly close to the dates of the actual events, they can be used when no vital records are available. And, because the church records will generally begin before the vital records do, church entries are particularly valuable for the period of early settlement. The records of christenings or baptisms, marriages, and burials are the most important and most used church records for genealogical purposes.[2]

ENTRY AND REMOVAL RECORDS

Another valuable record made by many of the early churches were the books which recorded the entry of members into or their removal from a congregation. Before moving to another place members would ask their home church for a letter or certificate of transfer, which they would take to the church in their new home. Various denominations called these letters by different names: the Society of Friends (Quakers) called them *certificates of removal,* the Baptists called them *letters of admission,* the Congregationalists called them *dismissions,* the Protestant Episcopal Church called them *letters of transfer,* and the Church of Latter-Day Saints called them *certificates of membership.*[3] These records of entry and dismissal are valuable, especially for the early days, because they can help you to trace the movement of your family from one congregation to another and, thus, from one part of the country to another. Not many of these records have survived, but the ones which do exist are very helpful to genealogists. Quaker records, which are uniformly excellent, still exist and have been published. To locate Quaker meeting houses see Index to Society of Friends Meeting Houses in the *Encyclopedia of American Quaker Genealogy,* volumes 1–6, by William Wade Hinshaw.

OTHER TYPES OF CHURCH RECORDS

Other kinds of church records which are useful to the family researcher are membership lists, tithing lists, lists of communicants, church minutes, financial reports, disciplinary actions, dismissals, and disownments (by Quakers). The early Baptist church minutes, for instance, recorded church actions involving the investigation of nonattendance, departure to join another church or another denomination, dismissal to form a new church, and the act of recanting, which was followed by the granting of a letter of dismissal by the congregation.

In the early days the actions of the church upon the membership were very strict and stringent. Church congregations dictated the lives and the actions of their membership and outlawed such things as "dancin', fiddlin', drinkin' whiskey, swearin', whorin', gamblin', and fightin'." By the 1830s church leaders had begun to attack drinking and drunkenness in Indiana, and temperance societies were organized in Charlestown, Indianapolis, Logansport, and Fort Wayne.[4] Sundays were strictly for Bible reading and religious meditation. An Indianapolis ordinance in 1837 levied a fine of one dollar against "any person who shall on the Sabbath day play at cricket, bandy, town ball, corner ball, or any other game of ball."[5]

THE ROMAN CATHOLIC CHURCH

The first churches in Indiana were established by the French Catholic missionaries early in the eighteenth century. By 1749 a Jesuit priest was living in Vincennes, where he ministered to the needs of the French soldiers and resident civilians. When France lost its claim to the land following the French and Indian War, most Frenchmen left the area, and the strength of the Catholic church was greatly reduced. When so many French Catholic people left Indiana, only the cathedral and the small French settlement at Vincennes survived. Very few of the early Catholic church records at Vincennes, dating from 1749, still exist. These give only the names of the persons involved in the various rites.[6]

The existing early Catholic records for the French post Vincent, as well as the later Catholic church records, are found at the Old Catholic Library in Vincennes. These early records were often kept in a mixture of bad Latin and old French and were written in a variety of handwritings. They can be very difficult to translate and to read. Following a decline in the strength and numbers of the Catholic faith in Indiana, a rebirth of its strength began in the 1830s. By that time Catholics had organized in Fort Wayne and were growing stronger elsewhere as more German Catholics came to the state. The influx of Irish and German Catholics brought Catholicism to more prominence by about 1850, although there were still only sixty-three Catholic churches in the state at that time.[7]

Catholic priests have been required to record baptisms and marriages taking place in their churches since the sixteenth century. Indiana parish records, generally in Latin, began in 1749. *Baptismal entries* give date of baptism, full name (the early entries in Latin), names of parents and godparents (sponsors), name of the priest who baptized, and, sometimes, the date and place where the individual later married. *Marriage records* give the date, name of the groom and maiden name of the bride, names of witnesses and the officiating cleric, and whether a church dispensation sanctioned the marriage. These Indiana Catholic records, from 1749 up to 1917, were microfilmed by the County Records of Indiana Microfilming Project (CRIMP). Records of any parishes established after 1917 were not filmed in the project.[8]

James J. Divita, a professor at Marion College in Indianapolis, in his paper "Using Catholic Records for Genealogical Research," printed in the September 1990 issue of *The Hoosier Genealogist,* reports that Indiana parish records filmed by CRIMP are available in the Genealogy Division of the Indiana State Library. The staff will not search through the records but will copy microfilm entries from specific written orders (film number, page number, and so forth) submitted by the person requesting materials. In order to use the parish registers, you must know the church and the diocese where an ancestor's baptism or marriage took place.[9] To help in this search, Divita has prepared a locator of Indiana Counties in Catholic dioceses:

(1) 1674–1784, Indiana was in the Diocese of Quebec.
(2) 1784–1808, Indiana was in the Prefecture-Apostolic (later Diocese) of Baltimore.
(3) 1804–1834, Indiana was in the Diocese of Bardstown (Louisville).
(4) 1834, the Diocese of Vincennes was established, including all of Indiana and the eastern third of Illinois.
(5) 1843, the Diocese of Vincennes was reduced to Indiana when the Diocese of Chicago was established.

(6) 1857, the Diocese of Fort Wayne was established in the northern half of Indiana.
(7) 1944, Indianapolis was raised to rank of archdiocese. The Dioceses of Evansville and Lafayette were established from Indianapolis and Fort Wayne areas, respectively.
(8) 1956, the Diocese of Gary was created from Fort Wayne territory.
(9) 1960, Fort Wayne was renamed the Diocese of Fort Wayne–South Bend.[10]

Divita suggests consulting Charles Blanchard's 1898 *History of the Catholic Church in Indiana* to learn the ethnic origins of ancestors who lived in a town having two Catholic parishes, since one might have been an English-speaking congregation and the other a German-speaking one.[11]

THE BAPTIST CHURCH

The first settlers who came to southern Indiana were Protestants, mainly Baptists, who came there from Kentucky and the upland south. And they came generally in the largest numbers. Their Baptist frontier religion was not a formal one because they did not like formality. Neither did they make use of the traveling preachers called "circuit riders," who were employed by the Methodists. Baptists generally distrusted the educated and paid clergy of other denominations. Therefore, Baptist preachers were usually poorly educated, part-time, unpaid lay preachers.[12] In fact, most Baptist ministers were full-time farmers who plowed on weekdays and preached on Sundays.

Baptist church records are called "minutes." The minutes kept in Indiana churches can include lists of members, lists of converts, financial accounts, and other diverse entries. Baptists established congregations in Clark County in 1798 and in 1803 built the Silver Creek Church, the first Protestant church in Indiana.[13] Baptists set up congregations in Jefferson County in 1806 and 1807, and a congregation also built a church near North Madison that same year. A congregation was also meeting in Harrison County by this time, and in 1813 the Old Goshen Church was built south of Corydon. The first Baptist church in Knox County was one on Maria Creek, which was established in 1809 with Isaac McCoy as pastor. In 1812 a brick church was built three miles southeast of Brookville by the Baptists. It is believed to be the oldest Indiana Protestant church still standing on the original site.[14]

Most Indiana Baptists were nominally of the "Regular" variety, as opposed to the "Separates" and the "Primitives." The "Regulars" were descended from the hybrid United Baptist origin and had prejudices arising from their Separatist heritage. They strongly opposed the education of their ministers.[15] The records of Indiana Baptist churches have been gathered together in the Franklin College

Library, in Franklin, Indiana. The records are extensive and should be helpful if you have Baptist ancestry in Indiana. The Indiana Historical Society has also printed some Baptist records in its various publications. The March 1989 issue of *The Hoosier Genealogist,* volume 29, number 1, contains the first few pages of *The Record of the 14 Mile Church,* a listing of members of a church located near Charlestown, then in the old Knox County and now in Clark County. William H. McCoy proclaimed it "the Oldest Baptist Church in Indiana" in his 1880 pamphlet, *History of the Oldest Baptist Church in Indiana Organized at Charlestown, Ind. 1798.* The name was changed to Silver Creek church in about 1803. Two handwritten volumes of this history were given to the Indiana State Library by McCoy. Volume 1 covers the years 1798–1806, and volume 2 covers 1807–1837. The few pages printed in *The Hoosier Genealogist* are an index and abstract of *The Record of the 14 Mile Church.*

The Separate Baptists

The "Great Awakening" of the early 1800s resulted in the "Separates," who supported the revival and who separated themselves from mainstream Baptists. The meetings of the Separates were characterized by exaggerated physical demonstrations. Adult baptism by immersion was the most important practice of the Separatist group, and the congregations were not overconcerned with denominational matters. The Separate Baptists were principally people from North Carolina and Virginia who came to Indiana shortly after 1800.[16]

The Primitive Baptists

There were two separate and distinct movements of "Primitive" Baptists in Indiana: One, called the "anti-means" Primitive Baptists, developed in east central Indiana and was led by elder Wilson Thompson of the Whitewater Valley Association. The other movement was called the "Two-Seed-in-the-Spirit-Predestinarian Baptists" and was centered in the Lower Wabash River valley.[17] The latter group was inspired by elder Daniel Parker of Illinois. Both movements had a radical emphasis on the doctrine of predestination as well as common social and religious backgrounds. Both groups began in about 1820 in Indiana, but they were totally unconnected.[18] Most Indiana Primitive Baptist churches have descended from one of the two organizations. The members oppose auxiliary temperance societies, temperance, missions, an educated professional ministry, Sunday schools, and the use of instrumental music in the church. The pastors are not paid a regular salary although members donate money toward the pastor's upkeep. Congregations meet once a month on Saturday and Sunday.[19] *Deaths Recorded in the Minutes of the White River Association of the Primitive Baptist Church, 1857–1878,* for the counties of Monroe, Greene, Lawrence, and Owen, is printed in the Indiana Historical Society's *Indiana Source Book III,* pages 307–308.

The major repository for the American Baptist Convention, formerly the Northern Baptist Convention, is at 1106 South Goodman Street, Rochester, New York 14620. One of the largest collections of original minutes of congregations, correspondence, annual reports, and missionary records is at the Historical Commission of the Southern Baptist Convention, 127 Ninth Avenue North, Nashville, Tennessee 37234, and Kentucky Baptist records are at the Southern Baptist Theological Seminary Library, Louisville, Kentucky 40206. For information about the various state Baptist repositories, contact the Samford University Library, Birmingham, Alabama 35209.[20]

THE INDIANA METHODISTS

In 1729, at Oxford University, John and Charles Wesley began the Methodist movement, so called because their lives were so regulated and methodical. Methodist ministers were preaching in the American colonies by 1766, and in 1784, at the close of the Revolutionary War, the Methodist Episcopal church was formally organized. Francis Asbury and Thomas Coke were named Methodist bishops.[21]

Methodists came into Indiana at the same time as the Baptists and came generally from the upland south. Methodists came in almost the same numbers or slightly fewer than the Baptists. The Methodist church on the Indiana frontier was a church of the people and, like the Baptist's, was not a formal church, although the aim of the movement was to bring culture to the frontier. Itinerant Methodist "circuit riders" traveled on horseback from one place to another to preach the Gospel to scattered congregations. At first, the homes of members served as makeshift churches visited by preachers as they made their rounds, or "circuits." The first circuit riders followed the settlers into the southern Indiana river valleys, and the churches there were named after the valleys. As the population grew and settlement moved northward, new circuits were added.[22] Gradually, each settlement erected a church building and hired a permanent preacher.

Methodism on the frontier was fueled by the energetic "revivals" that were held at week-long camp meetings. These meetings were combination revivals and social meetings that were a kind of vacation for the settlers. Many converts to Methodism were won at these tent revivals.[23] Methodist preachers came into Clark County in 1799 and into Dearborn County from Ohio early in the 1800s to begin establishing congregations. They spread out all across the southern third of the state in the early years of settlement and then gradually moved northward with the settlers.

In 1844 the question of slavery caused a split in the Methodist Church, which led to the formation of the Methodist Episcopal Church and the Methodist Episcopal Church South (Southern Methodists). Another group had previously broken away to become the Methodist Protestant Church. In 1939 the three groups joined again to become the Methodist Church.[24]

The records of the Methodist church in Indiana are kept in the Archives of DePauw University and Indiana United Methodism, Roy O. West Library, DePauw University, Greencastle, Indiana 46153. Founded by Methodists, DePauw is known for its extensive collection of Methodist records. Much of this collection has been microfilmed and can be viewed in the Genealogical Library in Salt Lake City, Utah, or at any LDS stake library. (A "stake" is a group of seven to twelve congregations with a combined total of two to five thousand members. There is only one library per stake, although many stakes have none.) Some local Methodist records are also housed in the New Harmony Workingmen's Institute Library in New Harmony, Indiana.[25]

On May 2, 1834, the Indiana Conference of the Methodist Church began publication of the *Western Christian Advocate,* a denominational newspaper which included obituaries, general news items, medical information, temperance and missionary news, reports of Methodist meetings, sermons, denominational concerns, and some marriages. In 1988 the Family History Section of the Indiana Historical Society published *Abstracts of Obituaries in the Western Christian Advocate, 1834–1850,* which deals principally with the obituaries of Indiana Methodists and people with Indiana connections, from surrounding states and from states far removed from Indiana.[26]

Evangelical United Brethren Church

Often called the "German Methodists," the Evangelical United Brethren Church merged with the United Methodist Church in 1968. Records for the Evangelical United Brethren Church are at the Historical Society, 1810 Harvard Building, Dayton, Ohio 45406.

The Free Methodist Church

The Free Methodist Church was the result of a split with the Methodists. For information about the history of this group, contact the Historical Center of the Free Methodist Church, Winona Lake, Indiana 46590.

The African Methodist Episcopal Church

Most Indiana blacks were members of the African Methodist Episcopal (A.M.E.) Church, and by 1860 there was an A.M.E. church in nearly every black community in the state. The church was the center of community life, meeting the religious, social, and moral needs of the people. An A.M.E. church was erected in Washington County in 1850.[27] An A.M.E. chapel at Lyles Station, in Gibson County, is the only existing rural A.M.E. church in the state.[28] The Terre Haute Allen Chapel A.M.E. Church, the oldest black congregation in the city, was organized by a group of freedmen in 1839.[29] The Beech Church in rural Rush County, begun by Quaker-aided free blacks, joined with the A.M.E. church in 1832, and the Indiana A.M.E. Conference was organized there in 1840.[30] The oldest black church in Indianapolis is the Bethel A.M.E. Church, which was organized in 1836.[31]

THE SOCIETY OF FRIENDS (QUAKERS)

The Society of Friends, or Quakers, were given their strange name when the founder, George Fox, warned an English magistrate to "tremble at the word of the Lord." The Friends soon began to be called "Quakers." Quakers refused to take an oath, even in court, refused to use force against anyone, and never fought in military conflicts. Quakers wore plain gray clothing, were opposed to amusements, and used *thee* and *thou* in ordinary speech. Members called each other by their full names and called the days of the week by numbers instead of by names.[32]

Quakers established their first Indiana monthly meeting in Wayne County in 1809. It was an offshoot of an Ohio monthly meeting and was called White Water Monthly Meeting. The White Water group had also begun a school there by 1811. Friends organized schools in Orange and Washington counties in Indiana. The Quakers were even asked by the Indian chief, Little Turtle, to teach his people how to till the soil and grow crops.[33] Quakers came into Indiana from the early 1800s until about the start of the Civil War. Initially settling in the southern part of Indiana, they gradually spread out into other parts of the state. Members of this sect had entered southern Indiana by way of the Buffalo Trace and its subordinate trails to settle in Orange, Martin, and Lawrence counties. Most of the Quakers in the Whitewater Valley came later and by way of the National Road, entering Indiana near Richmond, where they grew especially strong. Earlham College at Richmond was founded by Quakers.

Quaker records are consistently good and consistently kept, and the content is also consistent. The kinds of records kept are the minutes of the various "meetings." The Weekly Meeting recorded affairs of the local meeting, or "church," which met once each week. All business was conducted at the Monthly Meeting, which was composed of several Weekly Meeting groups. The records made at the Monthly Meetings are considered the most valuable to the genealogist.[34] Quaker records are uniformly excellent, still exist, and have been published. Quaker records for Indiana were gathered into seven volumes by Willard Heiss and were published by the Indiana Historical Society between 1962 and 1975. These seven volumes, *Abstracts of Records of the Society of Friends in Indiana,* contain a vast amount of Quaker information. Another seven volumes, *Encyclopedia of American Quaker Genealogy,* were compiled by William Wade Hinshaw, from 1936 onward. Volumes 1–6 were reprinted by the Genealogical Publishing

Company of Baltimore, and volume 7 is available from the Indiana Historical Society. Records of Indiana Quakers are also found at the Earlham College Library in Richmond, Indiana, and some local Quaker records are housed in the Henry County Historical Society Museum in Newcastle.

THE MENNONITES

The Mennonites, the Amish Mennonites, and the Hutterites were all offspring of the Anabaptists. Members of the Anabaptist (meaning "re-baptism") movement did not believe in infant baptism, baptized only believers, and advocated social and economic reforms and the complete separation of church and state. The Anabaptist movement began in Europe after 1520.[35] The Mennonites were persecuted for beliefs that were very different from other Christians. They acknowledged no authority except the Bible and what they called "enlightened human conscience." The sect, an offshoot of the Anabaptists, was opposed to war and the taking of oaths, and did not believe it was right or moral to be a lawyer or a soldier. They obeyed the law unless the Bible forbade a particular action. The Mennonites had no bishops or priests, and their elders and "exhorters" were chosen by members of the congregation from the church community.[36] Indiana Mennonite records are in the Archives of the Mennonite Church, 1700 South Main Street, Goshen, Indiana 46526. Goshen College is at present microfilming the Mennonite and Amish Mennonite records.

THE AMISH MENNONITES

The Amish sects, named after an early leader, Jacob Amen, form one division of the Mennonites. The Amish Mennonites believe in plain dress and use only hooks and eyes as fasteners. Many Amish do not use any kind of modern conveniences while others use some.[37] The Mennonites and Amish Mennonites came to Indiana from southeastern Pennsylvania and settled in north central, central, and southern Indiana. The most beautiful and productive farms in these areas are tilled by Amish farmers using nineteenth-century implements. Some Indiana Amish people have begun to cater to the tourist trade, utilizing their famous farm cooking and plain way of living. Records of the Mennonites and Amish Mennonites in Indiana are in the Archives of the Mennonite Church in Goshen, Indiana.

THE PRESBYTERIAN CHURCH

The denomination took the name Presbyterians from a Greek word "presbuteros," meaning "elder," because they elected the older men, or "elders," to represent them. Early leaders of the faith were the Swiss John Calvin and the Scot John Knox. The French Huguenots were also Presbyterians, but some features were changed when they migrated to Holland, and the church became the Dutch Reformed Church there.[38] The French Huguenots and the Scottish and Irish immigrants brought Presbyterianism to North America in the 1600s, and in 1706 the Presbyterian Church was formally organized in Philadelphia. Presbyterians observe only two sacraments, baptism and communion.[39]

The Presbyterian Church was a far more formal institution than either the Methodist or the Baptist churches. Its preachers were well educated and were paid to preach, and most of them came to Indiana from the east. These educated easterners were considered snobbish and ill-suited to frontier life by the rugged Indiana frontiersmen. The first Presbyterian church in Indiana was organized in 1805 in Knox County following a visit by missionaries from the Transylvania Presbytery in Kentucky the year before. The first minister of the Knox County church, the Reverend Samuel T. Scott, was also the first Presbyterian minister to live in Indiana Territory.[40] At first, the Presbyterian ministers were accepted only by other easterners who had come to Indiana. Eastern Presbyterians sent over three hundred "missionaries" to Indiana from eastern churches and seminaries to minister to the frontier flocks. The easterners were shocked by the backwardness of the west, but many of them stayed on to establish churches and schools. The Presbyterians who settled in Monroe County came from New Jersey, and they, as easterners, expected to be the most important and influential citizens. These people were instrumental in starting the little Indiana college which eventually became Indiana University.

Nevertheless, the Presbyterian Church in Indiana grew slowly but steadily, fueled by help from the eastern congregations. You will find Presbyterian records in the Genealogy Division of the Indiana State Library in Indianapolis, and some Presbyterian records might also be found in the individual churches in the state. Local church records vary in availability and content because no provision was made to preserve local records until fairly recently. The *Union Catalog of Presbyterian Manuscripts,* Presbyterian Library Association, 1964, lists Presbyterian and Reformed records. Major collections are at McCormick Theological Seminary, McGaw Library, 800 West Belden Avenue, Chicago, Illinois 60614, and the Presbyterian Historical Society, United Presbyterian Church in the U.S.A., 425 Lombard Street, Philadelphia, Pennsylvania 19147. The *Presbyterian Biographical Index,* a card index to periodicals, newspapers, and books for clergy and laymen is housed at the Princeton Theological Seminary, Speer Library, Mercer Street and Library Place, Princeton, New Jersey 08540.[41]

GERMAN BAPTIST BRETHREN

The German Baptists, also known as Brethren or Dunkers, were an offshoot of the Lutheran Church. Brethren believed in the Trine baptism, in which a person was baptized three times, face forward. From this type of "dunking," the names Dunker, Tunker, and Dunkard evolved.[42] Southern Indiana had German Baptist Brethren, or Dunker, congregations by 1809, all with ties to the South. The Brethren in southern Indiana had come from either North Carolina or Kentucky and, thus, had no real or spiritual ties to the eastern Brethren congregations.[43]

The first Indiana Dunker congregation was Olive Branch, which had been organized by 1803 in Owen Township, Clark County. Two of the earliest and largest Dunker churches were in Orange and Lawrence counties. The Lost River congregation in Orleans Township, Orange County, was organized in 1819. North of there in Indian Creek Township, Lawrence County, was the White River Church, which was organized in about 1821.[44] The Bethel Church was active in Morgan Township in Harrison County. There were Brethren settlements in Jackson, Washington, Monroe, and possibly Dubois counties before 1825.[45]

These southern Indiana groups formed their own independent association in about 1820 with possibly as many as fifteen hundred members. By 1827 they had merged with a group called the "New Lights" to form the Restoration movement, which soon became the Disciples of Christ.[46] North central Indiana, with its strong ties to the east, was a center of Brethren activity in the mid- to late nineteenth century. For information regarding the Church of the Brethren, contact the Brethren Historical Library and Archives, 1451 Dundee Avenue, Elgin, Illinois 60120.

THE DISCIPLES OF CHRIST (CHRISTIAN CHURCH)

The Christian Church was the melding of several frontier churches in Kentucky and Indiana. Some independent German Baptist (Dunkers) and Brethren congregations from southern Indiana merged with the "New Lights," or Campbellites, to form the Restoration movement, which became the Disciples of Christ. The original Restoration movement aimed to restore the simple, or "primitive," New Testament Christianity. The followers practiced baptism by immersion for believers only, weekly observation of communion, and the autonomy of local congregations.[47] The nucleus of the movement was organized by Alexander Campbell, a former Presbyterian minister turned Baptist reformer. The preacher Barton W. Stone, who had been at the Great Kentucky Revival of 1801 at Cane Ridge, joined with Campbell to form the nucleus of the group that would become the Christian Church.[48] When the first state convention of the Disciples was held in Indianapolis in 1839 the denomination was well-established.[49] Records of the Disciples of Christ Church are at Bethany College in St. Louis, Missouri, and at the Christian Theological Seminary, 1000 West 42nd Street, Indianapolis, Indiana 46208. The Disciples of Christ Historical Society Library Archives is at 1101 Nineteenth Avenue South, Nashville, Tennessee 37212.

LUTHERANS IN INDIANA

Members of the Lutheran church were mainly of German birth or German descent. Because Lutherans were linked to their religion by either birth or marriage, there were few converts to the Lutheran religion in Indiana. Lutheran records are generally complete, but the completeness can vary, depending on the competence of the minister or clerk who kept them. Lutheran records are similar in style and content to the records of the Reformed Church. The records, if found, include a register of the families of the congregation, a list of communicants who received communion every two or three months, confirmations, marriages, baptisms, and burials.[50] The Lutheran Church was one of the larger church groups in 1850 but was never a very strong denomination in the Hoosier state. Lutheran records for those people having German-American heritage can be found at the Lutheran Archives Center, 7301 Germantown Avenue, Philadelphia, Pennsylvania 19119, and also at the Abdel Ross Wentz Library, Lutheran Theological Seminary, Gettysburg, Pennsylvania 17325. Both repositories have important collections of congregational and pastoral records for Pennsylvania German Lutherans.[51]

INDIANA JEWISH RECORDS

Only a few Jewish synagogues were organized in Indiana, and these were established only in the larger cities in the later years. In 1849 a small group of Jewish people in Lafayette formed a burial society, Ahavas Achim, meaning "brotherly love," and soon after they established a synagogue and a school, and a temple in 1867; in 1919 the name was changed to Temple Israel.[52] The Ahavath Shalom Reform Temple was organized in 1867 at Ligonier, and its former temple now houses material on Ligonier Jews. The Ligonier Jewish Cemetery is on the south side of the city.[53] Temple Beth-El and Congregation Beth Israel are both on Hohman Avenue in Hammond.[54] In Bloomington, Beth Shalom Jewish Religious and Community Center and Hillel Foundation serve the Jewish community. Major collections of Jewish records are in the American Jewish Archives, 3101 Clifton Avenue, Cincinnati, Ohio 45220, and also in local Jewish historical societies.[55]

OTHER INDIANA DENOMINATIONS

There have been a large number of religious denominations in the Hoosier State since its organization. The Genealogy Division of the Indiana State Library has church records for the following groups: Baptist, Catholic, Church of God, Church of the Brethren, Congregational, Disciples of Christ, Evangelical, Evangelical United Brethren, Freewill Baptist, Society of Friends, Lutheran, Mennonite, Methodist, Methodist Episcopal, Methodist Protestant, Moravian, Church of the New Jerusalem, Presbyterian, Protestant Episcopal, and United Brethren in Christ.[56]

In 1850 Indiana churches ranked in descending order by size of membership thus: Methodist, Baptist, Presbyterian, Disciples of Christ, Friends, Catholic, and Lutheran.[57] Over the years, however, the principle church groups in Indiana have been the Baptist, Catholic, Methodist, Presbyterian, and Christian. Other groups who are now or have been active in the state are the Freewill Baptist, Church of God, Church of Jesus Christ of Latter-Day Saints (Mormons), Jehovah's Witnesses, and other smaller fundamentalist sects.

SOURCES OF INDIANA CHURCH RECORDS

Church records for the various religious denominations are often found at the national headquarters of each denomination. Some individual churches may also have a variety of church records in their custody. Contact the individual church in the town or area of search to inquire about the records it has, such as membership lists, christenings, baptisms, marriages, and other records. Then contact the local public library and the libraries of the historical and genealogical societies to learn whether they might also have church records for your ancestors. You may also be able to find copies of old denominational publications which contain the names of members and information about them. The Indiana State Library, the local library in the Indiana county of interest, or the local church may be able to help you locate old church publications. Many have been gathered together over the years and published, wholly or in part.

THE VALUE OF CHURCH RECORDS

Church records are valuable because they give names, dates, and events in the lives of the members, some of whom may be your ancestors. Church records can also give you a glimpse into the character of your ancestors and their daily lives. They can sometimes fill in missing information, add breadth to your family histories, and give clues which will suggest other places to search.

PROBLEMS WITH USING CHURCH RECORDS

The first problem when researching in church records may be determining to which church or denomination your ancestor belonged. This information can sometimes be learned from family traditions, from information found in a family Bible, from lists of church members printed in the county history, from baptismal and wedding certificates, from newspaper items and obituaries, death records and mortuary records, and from the county marriage records. If the name of the presiding minister is given in the marriage, baptismal, or funeral record, you can check in the county history and in the old newspapers of the area for the church or denomination served by this minister. If a couple was married by a justice of the peace, you may have to use the marriage records of their siblings to learn the church attended by the family. A wedding customarily took place in the bride's church; this is another clue to follow when determining religious affiliation. Another thing that can complicate your search is that either the bride or the groom may have joined the church of the new mate. Also, the couple may not have found their regular church when they moved to a new place and may have joined a similar church or an entirely different denomination.

The main problems with using church records is that they do not exist or are not available to the public. The individual church may no longer exist, and its records may have been lost or destroyed, and, unfortunately, some denominations do not let the public use their records. Check with the Indiana State Library, the county library, and the local historical and genealogical societies for the whereabouts of existing church records and cemetery lists. A society member could possibly know the family's denomination and the location of church records. That person might even be one of your ancestor's descendants, who can share family information.

CEMETERY RECORDS

Sometimes it isn't possible to find records for the church where your ancestors worshiped because those records were lost or destroyed long ago. The minister might have taken them when he left the church or the records may never have been made or kept. It is even possible that your ancestor did not belong to an established church or to any church at all; not everyone did. When no church records are available, you may be able to find the graveyard where your ancestors are buried and learn something about them from the tombstone inscriptions.

Finding the Proper Graveyard

You may already know the name of the graveyard, where it is located, and the location of the family graves. Many people have visited family burial places on "Decoration Day," as Memorial Day is sometimes called in Indiana. Other people are not so fortunate. They don't know the cemetery location or they've forgotten how to find it. If you are not sure where your family is buried, call on a helpful relative to go there with you or to draw a map showing the way. But what if you know only that your family is buried in a particular county and nothing more? How can you learn the name of the burial spot, and how can you find it?

The deceased's obituary, the mortuary record, and the death record generally give the name of the cemetery. Copies of old newspapers containing obituaries can often be found at the public library in the city or county where the person lived. Obituaries or death notices were published in the newspapers after about 1860–70. The newspapers or microfilmed copies of the papers are often stored at the newspaper office (if it still exists) or at the public library. If the funeral home is still in operation you can obtain mortuary records fairly easily. Mortuary records for defunct businesses are harder to find, but they, too, might be housed in the local public, historical, or genealogical society library. A society member might know the name of a descendant who has records from a defunct mortuary establishment. Death records are found at the county health department (for deaths occurring after 1882) and at the Indiana State Department of Health (for deaths after 1899).

Sometimes the "neighborhood news" columns in the newspapers mentioned the death of a resident, giving the date, time, and place of burial. Another way to locate a cemetery is to contact the library of the town, county, or one of the societies to see whether they have cemetery lists or indexes for the county cemeteries. Also, check the old county maps for the period when your ancestors lived there. It is possible that they attended a church in their neighborhood and you can determine the name of the church from the old map. If none of these methods reveals the burial place of your ancestor, place an advertisement in the local paper where he or she lived, asking for the name and location of the burial place. A local researcher or another descendant might tell you the name of the cemetery or help you to locate it. Many newspapers now carry genealogy columns which print free inquiries regarding area ancestors. A list of these newspaper genealogy columns is found in the frequently updated publication *Newspaper Genealogy Columns in Print,* compiled by Anita Cheek Minor.

Tombstone Inscriptions

Tombstone inscriptions are important to genealogical research because the information on the stone may be the only concrete proof that your ancestor ever lived at all. If you were unable to locate church records, an obituary, or a death notice, the tombstone can probably provide the important dates you seek. While not as accurate or dependable as the vital records, tombstone inscriptions will give the name and, usually, the birth and death dates for an individual. Some tombstones do not have dates on them, however, Military tombstones erected by the federal government for war veterans do not have dates inscribed on them. A government tombstone shows only the name of the veteran and the name and number of his Civil War (or other war) unit. This type of gravestone doesn't tell you whether he died during the war or many years after it.

During certain periods it was common for only the birth and death years to be placed on tombstones, omitting days and months. At other times, a tombstone might contain a mini-autobiography of the individual. For instance, in the Vernal

Baptist Cemetery in Monroe County we find this inscription: "Henry Sanders, born Oct. 1761, died 2-13-1831. Soldier in Rev. Volunteered in Fairfield County S.C. in 1776. Served under Gen. Green—captured at battle of Rock Mount but escaped. Services ended in battle of Yorktown in 1781. Was a Baptist preacher for 40 years."[58] This tombstone with its lengthy inscription was probably erected long after Henry's death, but it does tell a great deal more than most tombstones do about the deceased. The information given for Henry's wife includes her maiden name, their marriage date, and her birthplace.

Wrong Tombstone Data

Carving information in stone does not make it correct, and mistakes were sometimes made on tombstones. You may find surnames misspelled and erroneous dates on a gravestone, especially one that was erected many years after the death. By the time the stone was erected the person who ordered it may have forgotten exactly when the person died and made errors in other information about the person. Some tombstones bear the nickname, not the given name, and the wrong age of an individual because the informant didn't know the actual name or correct age. Sometimes even the spouse didn't know the deceased's real age, and thus the dates on the stone will be incorrect.

A mistake on a tombstone also could have happened when the stone carver misunderstood information he was given or just carved the wrong data on the stone. Either the deceased's family did not immediately notice the error or chose to accept the stone in order to save the expense of another stone. Generally, the error will not be a major one, and you may still be able to learn the correct information by using other contemporary records such as newspaper death notices, obituaries, old church publications, or even mortuary programs given out at the funeral.

You might also be able to pinpoint the year a person died by noting when he or she no longer appears on the county tax lists. But, because that person may merely have sold the property and not be deceased, don't jump to false conclusions until you have checked other sources. Check for the sale of land in the county and then look for a will, a death notice, or some other indication that the person indeed died. Despite the chance of error, you can still use tombstone inscriptions as clues that can lead you to other, more accurate sources. And, when no other information exists, you must use the information found on the gravestone. Any information is better than none at all. Now that you know that tombstone inscriptions can have mistakes but are still a valuable source, how do you find where they are?

Locating the Cemetery

You must first learn the location of the cemetery where your ancestors are buried before you can go there. Inquire at the local library for its whereabouts. If the cemetery is a city burial ground, it should be listed in the telephone directory and the city directory. If the cemetery is a country burying ground, you will probably need more than its name and the road it is on. Buy a good county map that shows where the various cemeteries are located. County maps are generally available in the office of the county recorder or at the local chamber of commerce office. Write well ahead of your visit to request a map from the county recorder in the county seat where you want to visit cemeteries. If the recorder doesn't have maps, then contact the chamber of commerce in the city nearest your ancestors' home. I once found county maps on sale at the county auto license branch. The Indiana Geological Survey has excellent maps showing the locations of existing cemeteries. Each survey map covers an area two and a half miles square and has excellent details. Of course, you need to know the exact map needed to find the correct cemetery. To order a survey map, write to the Indiana Geological Survey, 611 North Walnut Grove Avenue, Bloomington, Indiana 47405, noting the particular map you want.

The Large City Cemetery

After you have studied the map of the county, you can begin to make plans to visit the cemetery. If it is a fairly large cemetery, it may employ a sexton or caretaker who can help you locate the gravestones. The sexton's office usually has a list of persons buried there, as well as a map of the cemetery showing the location of their stones. Contact the sexton to learn when he or she will be available to help you find your ancestors' tombstones. Hunting for gravestones in a large cemetery can take many hours, and even then you may not be able to find the stones unassisted. It is important that you have someone available to help you find them. The sexton may also have information about the burial, the burial date, the next of kin, and other data that would be useful to you. Cemeteries which are owned by private corporations as businesses will usually have a paid custodian on duty during regular business days.[59] City-owned cemeteries are generally listed in the yellow pages of the phone book under the heading "Cemeteries." In some large city-owned cemeteries you must go through the city offices to telephone the cemetery custodian. Corporation-owned cemeteries are a relatively recent business venture in Indiana. Such a cemetery can be reached by telephoning the cemetery office, also listed in the yellow pages.

Church Cemeteries

When you visit a large church-owned cemetery, you will again need help in finding the gravestones. Contact the minister of the church or the sexton or caretaker to arrange a convenient time for your visit. Most ministers are very busy and won't have time to help you if you arrive unannounced. Advance notice and a polite and considerate approach might prompt the minister to look up information about your ancestors. The minister may have the old church records containing data about them, so a letter or phone call could help to pave your way. The pastor will certainly be more willing to help you if he or she knows exactly when you will arrive. A note of thanks later is also a nice gesture.

The Small Cemetery

The small cemetery might be a church cemetery, a private cemetery, or a family cemetery. If the cemetery is really tiny, you may be able to find the family graves without additional help. But "small" may begin to seem large once you begin to hunt for family stones. Even though it only involves looking for the right surnames and copying the information, this can be quite a chore to do unaided. You may still need the caretaker's help if you can't find your gravestones quickly. Perhaps another visitor or the caretaker will be there when you visit, but don't count on help being available. Don't count on finding cemetery records in the sexton's building, either. The sexton's building may actually be the caretaker's tool shed with no records found there. You may have to go to a nearby house or store to ask who owns the cemetery and how to reach the custodian. Then, you must contact the custodian, the sexton, or the minister to arrange a time for your visit.

Some church cemeteries are located right beside the church, but others may be some distance away. The church may have moved to a new location, or the original small cemetery may have been outgrown and a new one begun elsewhere. This may be the reason that there were once three separate Hogan Hill Baptist Church cemeteries in Dearborn County. To avoid the problem of a "removed" cemetery, write or telephone the pastor before you plan to visit. If you arrive unannounced and the minister or the caretaker is not available, you will have to return some other time. If you can't find the cemetery, your trip has been wasted.

Family Cemeteries

Many early Indiana burials were made in family cemeteries located right on the family farm. Because most family cemeteries are rather small, not all will be shown on the county maps. To locate a family cemetery, contact the public library or the local historical or genealogical society, which should know the location or can tell you who does know. Once you learn the location, refer to the county map to reach it. Some family cemeteries are still in active use and are well kept and easy to find. Others are neglected, run-down, and almost impossible to locate, let alone get to. For such an isolated cemetery, you will need not only a good map but also some definite directions to its site. Even if "your" family is buried there, you will need the permission of the present landowner to visit the cemetery. Again, show consideration for the owner. Politely ask to see the cemetery, but don't demand it. Your thoughtfulness might be the only reason the owner lets you onto the property to see the cemetery. The present owner may be another descendant of your ancestor who can tell you some family history. Or, if the owner doesn't know about your ancestor, he or she may know someone else who does. The owner may even be inclined to take you to the cemetery if you are considerate of the person's time and other obligations. After your visit, give the owner copious thanks and also send a letter of appreciation.

Paraphernalia for a Cemetery Visit

When you visit a large city cemetery, take a good camera and plenty of film to photograph the gravestones, a notebook, pens and pencils to record the inscriptions, and yellow or white chalk to highlight very old stones. By rubbing the side of the chalk across dim lettering you can increase the contrast and bring out an inscription for a better photograph. Try to have the sun at your back or to one side when photographing gravestones so that the lettering will show up better. Of course, you can't always wait until the sun is in perfect position, so try the chalk-rubbing technique to highlight worn or slim lettering when the sun doesn't cooperate. (Some conservationists insist that nothing touch a tombstone—not fingers, chalk, or even graphite and paper rubbing materials—unless the stone is wrapped completely and no tape or graphite touches the tombstone.)

Be sure to copy the complete inscription found on each tombstone even though you have photographed it. Should your camera malfunction, you will still have the backup information copied from the stone. Take time to draw a map showing the location of the various family stones in the cemetery and noting "landmarks" such as distinctive monuments or other permanent structures. Trees and shrubs can die or be moved, so use the roads, sexton's building, or other more permanent fixtures as landmarks. A photograph taken from a particular landmark can often serve the same purpose as a map, and can be used to later guide you back to the family graves. Some larger cemeteries, such as Rose Hill Cemetery in Bloomington, furnish a map on which the sexton will mark your family stones.

The Country Cemetery

When visiting a country cemetery that is clean and well kept, take the same items as when you visit a city cemetery—the camera, film, paper and writing implements, and chalk. If the graveyard is in a remote spot, you could take along a lunch to enjoy at midday. For a hot day add your sun hat and sunglasses, and if the day is rainy, a raincoat and boots. On a bitterly cold day take a tape recorder to record the inscriptions instead of hand-copying them. Always have at least two ways to record the data from tombstones. Photographs can be used to verify data copied from the stones, and vice versa.

Gear for the Isolated Cemetery

When you visit that out-of-the-way cemetery, the one reached by climbing several barbed-wire fences, fording a creek, and plunging through dense underbrush, your tools will be different from those used in the "easy" cemeteries. Wear heavy slacks, thick socks and sturdy shoes, a long-sleeved shirt, a protective hat, a sturdy jacket, and heavy gloves to thwart the thorns and weeds. This is just the basic gear needed to get to the cemetery. You will need all that and more at the cemetery. Take along a spade (folding, if possible) to uncover buried stones, clippers to trim away weeds and brush, a stiff (but not wire) brush to carefully remove mosses or lichens from the stones, and a trowel to lift clumps of sod from partially buried stones. You can wipe away mold and mosses with a spongeful of vinegar, so you may want to take that, too. It's wise to take someone with you when visiting an isolated cemetery in case of accident, wild animals, or mishap. That person can also carry half of your gear.

Take the usual equipment to the neglected cemetery—the camera, writing materials, a tape recorder if there is room, and maybe a backpack to hold everything. You might even need a hatchet for felling small trees and a can of wasp spray to discourage creeping and flying pests. Snakes and other varmints might live in that neglected graveyard, so the shovel and hatchet could also be useful for discouraging them. Just remember to use proper precautions when poking around in an overgrown cemetery. Finding information in a neglected graveyard can be a great deal more work than in a nice neat one, but it can also be a great challenge. Genealogists are diligent cemetery cleaners, and we can be thankful for this fact. Their efforts help to preserve the valuable hidden cemeteries. Remember to leave the cemetery in better condition than you found it.

Finding Relationships

Whether the cemetery you visit is large or small, city or country, community or church operated, corporation or private, look for evidence of relationships among the people buried near one another. If people are buried in the same cemetery lot or plot, you can be fairly sure that they are somehow related. Even though you don't see the relationship right away, copy the information from all of the stones in the family plot. The names of the other persons can serve as clues to further research. Look for birthplaces, dates when family members were in the county (and died there), church affiliations, land that was donated or willed to a church for a burial ground, bequests to maintain a cemetery in last wills, marriages involving the surnames of those buried in the family plot, and the proximity of those surnames in the township land descriptions. It's probable that the people buried in the family plot will eventually fit into your genealogy.[60] Because you can note those "others" buried in the same plot, a personal search is preferable to hiring an agent to search in the cemetery for you. A personal visit is also preferable to merely looking through a cemetery book or index because you can spot family relationships more readily at the cemetery. Use published cemetery lists or the index as guides before you visit the cemetery and as a supplement after it, but not as a substitute for a personal search.

Cemetery Lists

Cemetery lists are generally kept at the sexton's building in a public or private city cemetery, at the church in a church-connected cemetery, or with the minister in a small church cemetery. They may also be housed at the county library, in the libraries of the county historical or genealogical societies, at the Indiana State Library, or in the Library of the National Society, Daughters of the American Revolution (D.A.R.), in Washington, D.C. Use the cemetery lists to determine which cemetery your ancestors are buried in and to locate the cemetery in the township. Then, using the section number, the road or the street, you can locate the exact site of the cemetery. Most cemetery lists will include the name of the person, an abstract of the inscription, or sometimes the entire inscription. By using the cemetery lists, you may also be able to determine some of the other relatives who are buried there. But always try to make a personal visit to the cemetery so that you can be sure that the cemetery data agree with the actual gravestone inscription. Some cemeteries have been "copied" by persons who were not familiar with the surnames of the people buried there, and, thus, mistakes have been made in the cemetery books and indexes. Always look for any and every possible way your surname could have been spelled, or misspelled. You may find your ancestors listed under a name completely different from the one they always used, merely because the copier misread the inscription on the tombstone.

Dating Tombstones

Over the years and at different times in history, many different kinds of stone and styles of tombstones have been used in Indiana. The early tombstones were often crude wooden crosses which did not last long or large fieldstones which were scratched with the deceased's initials. It is not at all uncommon to learn that your early Indiana ancestors did not have tombstones. They were too busy clearing the land, building houses, and settling in to have time for such niceties. Family tradition may tell you that an ancestor is buried in a particular cemetery without a stone. This was particularly true during early settlement days when there were no resident stone carvers. Even at a later date, you may not find a tombstone for your ancestor, especially when poverty was a factor. If it was a matter of feeding the children or erecting a tombstone, there will be no stone. Vandalism of cemeteries has also reduced once large burial grounds to a few broken bits of stones, and there will be no record of your ancestor's burial there. It is sometimes difficult to prove that an ancestor actually died in a certain county at a particular time because there is no tombstone for him or her there.

The early Indiana tombstones were made of the softer native sandstone and limestone and were carved by itinerant carvers. The carvers traveled around the state, carved stones in one area, and then moved on to work in another place. It was not until fairly late in the nineteenth century that harder stone, such as granite and marble, were brought to Indiana for use as tombstones. The carving on native stone generally had deeper, wider downstrokes and thin, spidery cross-strokes. The thinner carving tended to weather badly and rather rapidly. Gravestones with such thin lettering are usually very hard to decipher and are easy prey for vandals. If you can't decipher the dates on a stone, the kind of stone and style of lettering might help you to determine the time period when it was carved. Thinner, slanted letters and heavy downstrokes were used during much of the nineteenth century, and heavier, plainer lettering was used after 1900.

During the early 1900s tombstones contained only inclusive dates (years only, not complete birth and death dates), such as "1818–1888." Before that, the complete date of death and age at death had been used, as in "Aged 45 years, 2 months, and 10 days." Later, the complete dates and other information were omitted in favor of shorter, and probably less expensive, inscriptions. The harder stone used at this time may also have encouraged the carver to shorten and simplify the inscriptions. Frequently, only the deceased's initials and surname were used, making verification of the name of a person difficult. To try to learn the given name, use Bible records, censuses, church records, school records, and other contemporary records.

Misleading Tombstone Inscriptions

Because of carving errors, incorrect information (due to faulty memory or misrepresentation), and unreadable inscriptions, the data on tombstones can be misleading. You can easily make mistakes when trying to read the thin, spidery carving on old tombstones. The fine cross-strokes on the letters and numbers are the first to wear away, leaving only the heavier downstrokes. For this reason, the numbers 1, 7, and 4 can all look alike without the cross-strokes. Likewise, 3, 8, and 9 also tend to look alike after years of weathering. And any of these rounded numbers can also look like zero. When you find such undecipherable carving, write down all of the possible interpretations of the inscription. Then try to check the data against contemporary records, such as the tax lists, censuses, and church records, to determine which of the interpretations is probably the correct one.[61]

Figuring Exact Birthdates

When you find a complete date of death and age in years, months, and days on a tombstone, you can figure an almost exact birthdate by using those data. By merely using subtraction you can replace "born about 1848" with an almost exact birthdate. If the tombstone inscription reads "John Jones died December

22, 1848, aged 35 years, 10 months, and two days," you have all of the ingredients for determining his birthdate. You must, of course, remember the number of days in each month and which years had a leap day. This childhood rhyme will remind you: "30 days hath September, April, June, and November. All the rest have 31 except February which hath 28, and in the leap year, 29." In order to figure John Jones's birthdate, first write out the date of his death numerically in this order: year, month, and day. (This is the reverse order of proper genealogical recording of dates.) John's death date would then be: "1848-12-22." Next, write his age numerically under the first set of numbers: "35-10-2" (years, months, days) and subtract the bottom numbers from the top ones, beginning with the set of numbers to the right and moving to the left. This particular example involves no "borrows" or "carrys" and results in the answer: "1813-02-20," or February 20, 1813, as John Jones's birthdate.[62]

Another man, George Smith, presents a more complex problem involving "borrowing." George died on January 5, 1880, aged 40 years, 10 months, and 8 days. Set up the subtraction problem just as in the example above. His death date becomes: "1880-01-05," from which you subtract his age at death: "40-10-08." You will quickly see that some borrowing is necessary. In order to subtract, you must borrow 31 days from January (the 01 in the top set of numbers) to add to the 5 days, giving a total of 36 days from which to subtract the 8 days, leaving 28 as the day of George's birth. Next, you must borrow 12 months from the year 1880 to replace your lost "1" in the months column, giving you 12. Subtract 10 months from 12, leaving 2, or February, as the month of birth. The year 1880 has become 1879 because of borrowing 12 months from it. From 1879 you subtract 40 (his age at death), leaving 1839. Thus, George Smith was born on February 28, 1839.[63]

Some dates are harder to determine because of leap years, leap days, and odd mathematical combinations requiring several more adjustments than those in the examples given above. It is also possible that the informant figured the age at death incorrectly or gave the wrong death date. In such a case, the date you determine may not be correct because the dates were given incorrectly. Nevertheless, this method is helpful in determining most birth dates. Practice doing some dates from your own genealogy to see how the process works. Exact dates aren't necessary, of course, but genealogists are happier when they find the closest dates possible.

If, however, the inscription reads "Aged 65 years," you may have some problems. Since a person rarely dies on his or her birthdate, you must assume that the inscription is an approximation and that the months and days have been omitted. It is impossible to tell whether the person was a few days younger or older than 65 or was a few months or days from 66. If the person had passed the 64th birthday, he or she was then in the 65th year; or if actually 65, in the 66th year. Until you can verify the person's actual age and birthdate, use a probable date of the two possible years when he or she might have been born, such as "1838/1839."[64]

The Value of Tombstones

Finding a tombstone is rewarding even when the data carved on it might be incorrect or misleading. This is because so many of our ancestors were buried without tombstones or the stones may no longer exist. It can be very important to find that stone because it may be the only tangible evidence that the person ever lived. But don't feel that all is lost should you learn there is no stone. This is when your ingenuity enters in. When there is no tombstone, you must use other contemporary sources to learn about your ancestor. The particular method used for one ancestor may not, and probably won't, work for another ancestor, so that you need to try all kinds of methods and sources. Sources which often prove fruitful are the land records, tax records, censuses, court records, newspaper items and obituaries, mortuary records, city directories, and the biographies in county histories. In fact, some very unusual and unlikely sources may finally answer your genealogical questions. So don't give up if the church and cemetery records aren't helpful in your search. There are many other avenues of search to try, and one of them will eventually help you to solve your genealogical problems. Your ancestors made many records during their lives and those records are waiting to be found.

Indiana County Records

CHAPTER

8

Although a few records exist from territorial days most county records in Indiana began when the individual county was formed. There are literally hundreds of different records that might be found on the county level. Some of the kinds of records found in the county include marriage records, probate and civil court records, land records, tax records, divorce records, naturalization records, and many other related records.

INDIANA LAND RECORDS

The desire for plentiful and inexpensive land was one of the chief reasons that people came to America, and Americans remained land-minded throughout the colonial period and well into the twentieth century. Land was of the utmost importance as long as most men were farmers and until most of the available land was taken. In fact, most men owned land at some time in their lives and records of that ownership will be found in the land records. Land records began with the onset of permanent settlement in Indiana and before other types of records began. The land records are often the only means of locating an individual in an area during the period of early settlement. The very early land records, especially those involving private land transactions, are valuable because of the relationships given and the genealogical information found in them.

Land was transferred in two ways, from the government to the individual, and from one individual to another. Records of private land claims in Indiana, which was originally part of the Northwest Territory, are in the National Archives in Washington, D.C. The original copies of patents for the public domain are in the Bureau of Land Management, Eastern States Office, 350 South Pickett Street, Alexandria, Virginia 22304. They are recorded in chronological order by state and then by land district but are not indexed. If you know, or suspect, that your ancestor was an original purchaser of land, check the Tract Books in the county and, after that, look in the patents for land in the public domain.

Two important provisions regarding land were included in the second Northwest Ordinance of 1787. The first provided that the widow of an intestate landowner should get one-third of the land in *fee simple. Fee* meant an inheritance in land, and fee simple meant the estate would last forever, descending to the heirs if one died intestate (without a will), or could be devised by a will, or could be sold, in part or entirely, by the owner. The rest of the land was to be divided equally among his children. The second provided that in order to be valid, wills and deeds had to be proved and recorded within one year of the death of the person making the will. Landowners, whether or not they lived on the land, were made subject to taxation; government land was exempted from taxation.

Before 1800, tracts of government land had been too big and too expensive for most people to be able to afford. The size of the tracts was reduced by the Harrison Land Act of 1800, which permitted land to be purchased on credit (five years') for as little as $2 per acre, allowing most people to buy land in the Old Northwest. Credit sales were in effect from 1800 until 1820, when the minimum size of a tract was reduced to eighty acres (or one-eighth section), and the minimum price reduced to $1.25 per acre. This made it possible for more people to buy government land.

DEED RECORDS

The first type of records kept by the Indiana counties were the *deeds* which recorded the sale of land. A deed is a legal document of transfer, bargain, or contract, or warranty where the seller guarantees (warrants) the title to the land being sold. At first the deeds for a county were kept in a single record book containing only the deeds, but many early deed books contained other miscellaneous records which the clerk deemed savable. By about 1848 a separate mortgage record book began to be kept by the County Recorder in each Indiana county. From the 1870s on, a separate Chattel Mortgage Record was kept, and at the present time, over seventy separate types of records are kept by the office of the County Recorder.[1]

Indiana was the first state in the public domain to be set up entirely under the new rectangular survey system. For the first time, using this system, land was transferred directly from the federal government to an individual citizen. The transfer began with the Land Ordinance of 1785 (also known as the Northwest Ordinance), which was set up by the federal government for this purpose. The first government land office opened at Vincennes in 1807 and was followed by five other land offices throughout the state. The last land office closed at Indianapolis in 1876. The records of the Government Land Office (G.L.O.) are in the Indiana State Archives in Indianapolis, and the early surveyor's field notes are housed in the adjacent Indiana State Library. The field notes can provide descriptions of the area where your ancestors first lived in Indiana.[2] The drawings of existing buildings found in the field notes might be useful to descendants of the original purchasers. Land entries for the Cincinnati land district, 1801–1840, and the Vincennes land district, 1807–1877, are indexed in *Indiana Land Entries,* by Margaret R. Water, and are available at the Indiana State Library.

The County Recorder in each Indiana county has custody of the land records. The first good source for legal descriptions of land are the *deed records.* The deed contains the names of the buyer and the seller, the residence (township, county, or state) of each, and sometimes the name of each person's wife. The seller's wife was required to sign a statement of her consent to the sale of the land, and her full name will be found on the deed. The Deed Books are arranged chronologically and are indexed under the name of the *Grantee* (the buyer) and the *Grantor* (the seller). These books are located in the office of the County Recorder and are open to the public. Some county deed records have been microfilmed, and copies of the films are found in the courthouses and the libraries.

Many types of title conveyances and contracts are also found in deed books: *deeds in fee simple* granting absolute ownership; *mortgages* transferring property rights as security for a debt; *dower releases* waiving a wife's rights; *quitclaim deeds* releasing title or right held, whether valid or not; *deeds of gift* transferring land without payment except "love and affection"; *powers of attorney* appointing legal agents; *marriage property settlements,* either before or after the marriage; and other bills of sale of property, usually not land. Although not usually recorded in the deed book, you might also find various contracts such as leases, partnerships, indentures, and other performance bonds.[3]

TRACT BOOKS

The names of the first purchasers of land in a county are recorded in a volume called the *Tract Book.* This book records the name of the original purchaser of land from the federal government; the section of land, township and range, and the date of purchase. Because the Tract Book lists only the initial purchaser, any later land transactions will be recorded in the Deed Book, not in the Tract Book. The Tract Book and a separate index are in the office of the County Recorder in each county, usually near the township plats. Try the Tract Books before you investigate the plat books, as the plat books are often hard to read because of constant use. The Tract Books can be used as a kind of index to these first land buyers in the townships of a county. They are also an excellent "finding tool" for locating the legal description of a piece of land. They can help to place a person in the county at a specific time. (See above, chapter 3, for an explanation of land descriptions.)

GRANTOR-GRANTEE INDEXES

Use the Grantor-Grantee Indexes to find the deed for your ancestor in the county where he purchased land. *Grantor Indexes* record the names of the sellers of land, and *Grantee Indexes* record the names of the purchasers. Because names were constantly being added to a page, the names are arranged in chronological, not alphabetical, order. These indexes generally group together on a page all of the names of buyers whose surnames begin with the same letter of the alphabet. Thus, all the "A's" will appear on one page and all the "B's" on the next page, and so on. In other words, the books were kept in running order just as the names and transactions were added to them. Deeds involving more than one buyer or seller are usually recorded under the name of the first person only, and unless your ancestor was the first person listed you won't find his name listed there. To find his name, you will have to go to the original document. Some deeds were recorded many years after they should have been. If you can't find a deed you think should have been recorded, look for it in the later Grantor-Grantee Books.[4]

PLAT BOOKS

Plat books are historical atlases which were produced periodically by the county. They contains maps on which were printed the names of the landowners in each township of the county. The county map was broken up into townships and then further divided into sections and the smaller half, quarter, and eighth sections therein. The name of each landowner and the amount of land he owned was printed on the section or partial section of land he owned. Plat books also show plats of subdivisions, towns, and cemeteries. The plat books are helpful in determining whether a man was a landowner in a township at a particular time, how much land he owned, and where the land was located. Plat books are kept in the courthouse. Some plat books have been photocopied or microfilmed and can be found in the particular county library or at the Indiana State Library.

TYPES OF LAND RECORDS

There are various kinds of land records which researchers can use in their search for information about their families. One of these is the *abstract of title,* which is the condensed history of the title to the piece of real estate that should contain a

This Indenture Witnesseth That N
Nicholas Burst and Mary Bur
his Wife of Monroe County and
State of Indiana Warrant and
Convey to Hiram Hanson of the
County and State aforesaid for
the Sum of Two Hundred and
Seventy five dollars. The followin
Real Estate Situate in the County
of Monroe and State of Indiana
and described towit
The North West quarter of Section
ten (10) Township Seven (7) Range
No. one (1) East Containing one
hundred and Sixty acres more
or less. The Said Grantee hereby
accepts the payment of a Mortgage
on said lands to Sarah Burham
for two Hundred & fifty Seven
dollars (257.00) due August the 1st
1881.
In Witness Whereof the Said Nichola
Burst and Mary Burst his Wife
have hereunto Set their hands
and Seals this March 24th 1879

Nicholas Burst (Seal)
Mary Burst (Seal)

An indenture from the loose papers of the Auditor, Monroe County, Indiana.

summary of every change of title to the land and the restrictions, easements, and liens against it. It may also contain maps, plats, and other descriptions. Private abstracting firms generally sell an abstract of the title to real estate in the county. The abstract serves as an index, although an expensive one, to the original records.[5]

The *acknowledgment,* or certificate, is a formal statement at the end of a deed where the official certified that the persons who executed the document declared to him that they signed the instrument of their own free will.

The deposition, is a written statement of facts, made voluntarily and affirmed by oath of the party making it. It is often used as evidence.

An *agreement* found in a deed implies that two or more parties have given mutual agreement to a matter that could change some of their rights and obligations. An agreement is similar to a contract but is broader in application.

An *antenuptial (premarriage) contract* (also called a *marriage settlement*) is made between a man and his wife-to-be outlining the property rights of one or both of them. Such a contract was usually made before a second marriage to secure properties for children of a former marriage; such contracts are not too common in early Indiana land records.[6]

The *deed,* by which title is transferred from one person to another, is the most important document in a land transfer. The most common type of deed is the *deed in fee,* which conveys a fee simple title; it is commonly referred to simply as a deed. The other kinds of deeds of interest to the genealogist are the warranty deed and the quitclaim deed. The *warranty deed* is the means by which the grantor warrants the title of the property he or she is selling. Should the title prove to be faulty the grantee can sue the grantor or the grantor's heirs. The *quitclaim deed* is the document by which individuals release all title, interest, or claim to certain real properties (without making warrants) and by which they convey all they have. The quitclaim deed is used to remove potential problems from real estate titles.[7]

A *gift deed* is one in which real property is transferred without payment of money. Such a land transfer is generally made by a parent to his or her child or children. If you see the phrase "for the natural love and affection which I bear toward" or "and for other valuable considerations," you will know that the transfer is a gift deed.

The *power of attorney* is a document which grants a person the right to act for another person who is unable to act for himself or herself, whether because of incapacity, distance, or other circumstances.[8]

The *petition* is a request made to the court for an action, such as the need for a sale of property to benefit a penniless widow and her children. Very good genealogical data is often found in these petitions.

A *release of dower* is the release by the wife of her right to her husband's real estate under common law. A woman always had the right to a life estate and could legally claim her right to property unless she had signed the deed or

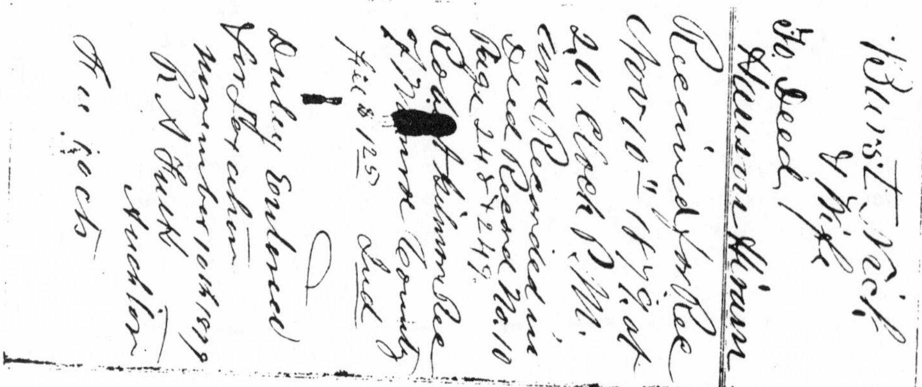

County of Monroe }
State of Indiana }

Before Me Isaac A Chandler a justice of the peace in and for the County and State aforesaid on this March 24th day 1879 Nichlas Burst and Mary Burst his Wife acknowledged the Execution of the forgoing Deed Given under My hand and seal March 24 1879

Isaac A Chandler (Seal)
Justice of peace

A justice of the peace record from the loose papers of the Auditor, Monroe County, Indiana.

executed a release of her dower rights when the sale took place. This is why you will always find the release of dower at the end of a deed. Although it may merely give the name of the grantor's wife, it can be valuable. This may be the only place where you will find her legal name recorded.

THE VALUE OF LAND RECORDS

Land records are valuable to the genealogist because they can provide the dates when persons bought land in the county and, perhaps, when they later sold it. Land records can sometimes show names of places where persons had formerly lived, although they usually gave their present residence, not the former one. The name of the former residence can be extremely valuable if you hadn't previously found this information. Relationships can also be given or inferred in the land records, such as when a group of heirs sell inherited land. Look for the names, which might be in-laws or other relatives, in other contemporary records to help you distinguish between two persons who have the same name. You can often determine which is your ancestor by studying the legal descriptions of the land and that of his or her close relatives, who often lived nearby.[9]

PROBLEMS WITH USING LAND RECORDS

Family researchers usually try to use the land records to locate the piece of land an ancestor once owned, to prove relationships between persons, and to find former places of residence in another county or state. Land records were intended to record the transfer of a piece of land from one person to another, not to contain genealogical information. Therefore, any genealogical information found in deeds is usually not stated but merely implied. Thus, a man may convey property to his son without mentioning that he is his son. He may say that he is a resident of the county he has just moved into instead of naming the state or county he recently lived in. The suggestion is there but you must find ways to prove the relationship.

Descendants also try to find the signatures of their ancestors by using the deed records. Not everyone realizes that after the original deeds were entered in the deed books, the books were recopied by the clerk. The deed book is actually a copy of the original document, and the signatures on the deed copy are usually not those of your ancestor and the other party involved. Although some jurisdictions required the signatures of the buyer and seller on the copy, most did not, and the names were generally written by the clerk. If the signatures are all in the same handwriting, they belong to the clerk; if not, they may be the actual signatures of the buyer and the seller.

INDIANA TAX RECORDS

The early Indiana tax records are an important genealogical source because they, too, can be used as a kind of census record for your ancestors, showing where they lived and their financial worth at different times. There are two kinds of tax records, those for payment of *real property taxes* and those for *personal property taxes.* Personal property tax was levied primarily for livestock. Real estate tax records usually show the amount of land, its location, the name of the person who originally entered the land, and the appraised value. The personal property taxes are valuable because they name people who lived in a place but who owned no land. You won't find the people who owned nothing taxable in these records.

Indiana county tax records began in 1817 and go up to the present time. The tax records are in the custody of the County Treasurer in the county of interest. Most noncurrent tax records are now in storage, either at the courthouse or in some other storage facility. Some counties use an old barn, an empty warehouse, or some other decrepit and out-of-the-way place to store older records. Luckily, most of the tax records have been microfilmed by the Mormon Church (LDS) and copies of the films are found in both the county courthouse and the Indiana State Library in Indianapolis. Because the microfilms kept at the courthouses are not always available to the public, try to determine whether they are accessible before you make a trip to use them. Often, the county public library or the library of the historical or genealogical society will have copies of the microfilmed tax records.

The records kept by the County Treasurer are the tax duplicates, from 1841 to the present. These are the records of taxes payable, the name of taxpayer, and the taxing unit; the value of real and personal property, the amount of taxes due, and the payment made. The tax duplicates are good sources for historical and genealogical research, as they often contain good genealogical data. They can also be useful in determining the economic and social development of your family.[10] The Mormons microfilmed Indiana tax duplicates in the 1980s and these are available at the Indiana State Library and the individual courthouses.

THE INDIANA COURT SYSTEM

There are forty-nine County Courts in Indiana, which meet in the county seats to hear contract and tort disputes, misdemeanors, traffic and local ordinance violations, and some criminal matters. A separate probate court for St. Joseph County sits at South Bend. Forty-seven counties have Superior Courts, which are courts of general jurisdiction that sit in the county seats of those counties. The Superior Courts deal with law, equity, domestic relations, felonies, misdemeanors, preliminary hearings, and some juvenile matters. The Courts of Marion and Vanderburgh counties also have probate divisions.[11] The Circuit Courts handle all civil and criminal matters except where exclusive jurisdiction is conferred on a lower court in the county. The Circuit Courts sit in each county seat, although two Indiana circuits contain two counties: one circuit includes Dearborn and Ohio counties, and the other, Jefferson and Switzerland counties. Although not county courts, two other higher courts sit at Indianapolis, where they are the "next steps" in the court system. The first of these is the Court of Appeals, which is divided into four districts and sits at Indianapolis. The second higher court is the State Supreme Court, which is the Indiana court of last resort.[12]

John J. Newman, Indiana State Archivist, reports in his paper "Research in Indiana Courthouses: Judicial and Other Records" that over four hundred different types of records have been created by the Hoosier courts. The courts classify their jurisdiction thus: civil; chancery/equity; criminal; naturalization; probate (estates, guardianships, and trusts); juvenile, and conciliation. These jurisdictions began with the establishment of a court in the county, with the exceptions of the juvenile, which began in 1867, and conciliation, which was handled by a separate court, the Court of Conciliation, between 1853–1865).[13]

Indiana Circuit Courts

As the name implies, the early Indiana Circuit Court consisted of one judge who "rode circuit" for all of the counties in the territory. This judge traveled to each county seat to conduct court on a regular, or nearly regular, basis. Two associate judges were elected locally. The records of the Clerk of the Circuit Court began with the establishment of Indiana Territory in 1790 and continue to the present. Current records are in the custody of the Clerk of the Circuit Court in his or her office, and the older records are usually in storage. The records of this court run from 1817 to 1852, when the second state constitution took over.

Local-Level Territorial Courts in Indiana

The court handling the business of the county, criminal and administrative, during territorial days was the General Quarter Sessions of the Peace. A General, or Criminal, Court, meeting at Vincennes and Brookville, handled criminal actions from 1788 to 1814. General Court did not "ride circuit." The Court of Common Pleas handled civil actions and first met in Knox County on June 20, 1790. The Probate Court first met there at the same time.[14]

The Clerk of the Circuit Court keeps the records of the Circuit Court in the county, files nonjudicial records, and has acted as the chief election officer since 1933. The clerk files the original papers, records the pleadings into the ledgers, and keeps the official record of court proceedings in the order books and ledgers. You must search in both the pleadings and the order books for data regarding your ancestors, because pleadings in a judicial action are seldom recorded in an order book. It is estimated that more than 600 different types of records have been generated in this particular office.[15] Archivist Newman suggests using the Tippecanoe County WPA Historical Records Inventory as a guide in order to learn functions, procedures, and types of records which might be available in this office.

PROBATE RECORDS

The probate records are a family-oriented source, the most valuable kind to the genealogist. Because property was so important to our ancestors, more people in frontier America left wills than you might imagine. This is especially true if your ancestor lived in a farming community, not in a large city, because most "city people" didn't own enough valuables to warrant making a will. Of course, until the late nineteenth century Indiana's population was largely rural and nearly everyone owned land, so that the proportion of persons leaving wills was larger than in the eastern industrial states.

Probate records are court records and they relate to court actions that take place after the death of a person. The probate process sees to it that taxes are paid, dependant family members are cared for, debts are paid, and property is transferred to the rightful heirs through an *executor* or *executrix,* when there is a will, and through an *administrator or administratrix,* when there is not. If there are heirs who are incompetent or ones younger than twenty-one, the court appoints a guardian for them.[16]

The two classes of probate records are the *testate records* and the *intestate records.* If a person died leaving a valid will, that person is said to have died testate. If one did not leave a valid will, one died intestate. Anyone could make a will if he or she was of sound mind, of legal age, and free from restraint (not in jail). It was legal, however, not to make a will, and many of our ancestors did not make them. But, because most people owned property, it was the court's duty upon their death to see that the estate went to the legal heirs, whether or not there was a will. A *will* devised real estate or land and the property attached to it, and a *testament* bequeathed personal property consisting of movables and receivables, hence the term "last will and testament." "Movables" could be money, jewelry, a house, furniture, livestock, tools, and such. "Receivables" might be debts, loans, or mortgages owed to the deceased, which would be collected by the court.[17]

Kinds of Probate Records

The number of documents which might be found in the probate court can sometimes be astounding, and the amount of information in many of them is often amazing. The following documents are ones which you might be lucky enough to find in the probates: *court records;* various kinds of *petitions; wills,* of various types—written, nuncupative (oral, not written), holographic (in the handwriting of the deceased), and codicils (additions) to wills; *bonds of various kinds*—administrator, appraiser, executor, guardian, and trustee; *inventories* of real estate, personal property, guardian's, and so forth; *publications,* such as advertisements, announcements, notices of sales, notice to heirs, and notice to creditors. There were also various *accounts,* such as the administrator's, executor's, guardian's, trustee's, and conservator's, and *miscellaneous documents,* which could include unrecorded wills, widows' allowances, orders to find heirs, sales documents, marriage settlements, waivers, changes of name, legitimatizings, memoranda, appeals, judgments, and records of estate taxes.[18]

Only wills were proved, and to be proved they had to be valid. To be valid a will had to be properly prepared, signed, and witnessed. The people who witnessed the will had to swear that they had seen the deceased sign the will, and that the deceased was of sound mind and had signed it of his or her own free will. If it was judged valid, the will was recorded in the will book. Wills not properly made or signed were *invalid,* and they were not proved nor were they recorded in the will book. The loose papers from such an invalid will can sometimes be found with the miscellaneous records of the court, but they will not be found in the probate index.[19] Unfortunately, most court officials will not be eager to hunt the miscellaneous records for you. Ask at the courthouse for their location, and if no one can tell you where they are kept, try the public library or the local historical and genealogical societies. Someone should know their whereabouts and how to gain access to them. It sometimes helps to hire a local genealogist to help you with these records, because he or she will be familiar with their location. At times, court records are kept in strange places, and their whereabouts are often unknown or nearly forgotten.

Bondsmen were usually relatives or friends of the deceased or of the deceased's spouse, and you can look for family relationships among them. Bondsmen can also be heirs to the estate. In recent years bonding companies have replaced personal surities. In all intestate estates and in most testate cases, three disinterested persons were appointed by the court to inventory and appraise the property in the estate of the deceased. They should not have had an interest in (expect to inherit or profit from) the estate. The estate *inventory* was to be returned to the court within ninety days, or by the beginning of the next court term. The inventory was intended to protect the executor or administrator from false or excessive claims against the estate and to protect the heirs from fraud or the theft of their inheritance.[20] An auction was generally held to sell farm tools or produce or to raise money for the widow and the children. There probably would have been no need for an auction if the widow was wealthy. The accounts of a sale record the kind of furniture and tools the deceased owned, the names of people who made purchases at the sale, and what each bought. Because people who attended the sale were generally friends, relatives, and neighbors of the deceased, you can look for relationships among these people. If you aren't sure where your ancestor lived, you can use the sale list to compare the buyers' names with the names on a county map of landowners.

When the inventory was completed and submitted to the court, a public notice of the probate was "to be published." In the early days these notices were nailed to trees, to the courthouse door, and to the doors of churches and other public buildings. Later on, the notices were published in area newspapers for three successive weeks, giving people plenty of time to file claims against the estate. Some jurisdictions kept copies of these notices, which you might find preserved in the probate or the inventory case packets. In recent years probate officials have stopped keeping the bound newspaper volumes because of space limitations, but you can often find the probate notices printed in the old newspapers that carried such notices. The case was closed when all heirs had been located, property was divided and distributed to them, and all debts were paid and collected.[21]

You might find old newspapers containing the published probate notices on microfilm or in bound volumes at the newspaper office, the public library, or the libraries of genealogical and historical societies in the town or area where the newspapers were published. Newspaper offices, however, seldom have space to store the bound copies of the older newspapers. The Main Library at Indiana University in Bloomington has some bound volumes of newspapers, although that facility has also been forced to dispose of many of them because of lack of space. The Indiana State Library in Indianapolis also has bound copies of many of the newspapers published in Indiana over the years, but the collection has not been indexed. The 1982 Indiana Historical Society publication *Indiana Newspaper Bibliography,* by James W. Miller, lists 8,000 newspapers which have made "at least a brief appearance" since the first one was published at Vincennes in 1804.

The Value of Probate Records

The probate records are a valuable source for the genealogist because they give relationships between persons. Because a will was meant to leave a person's worldly goods to those he loved, the people mentioned in the will are usually members of his family. You can learn where the nonresident heirs lived, whom daughters married (last names), and a lot about the family's financial worth. When there was no will, the intestate person's family members were also considered the heirs. In such a case, it was the court's duty to determine the rightful heirs and to see that the estate was divided fairly among them. Whether a person died testate or intestate, a great deal of material was generated during the estate proceedings. The *estate papers* are a wondrous collection of papers generated during the probate and the administration. They can show relationships, residences, names of neighbors, business associates, and the debts and assets of the deceased. For this reason you should always try to find and use the estate papers and, if possible, photocopy them.

The probate records are also valuable because they usually contain the names of a lot of other people besides the heirs. Every person mentioned in the probate records and the wills was recorded—the witnesses, executors or trustees, beneficiaries, and sometimes a neighbor or business associate who had sold property to the deceased. It has been estimated that half of the people in America have either left wills or have been mentioned in them. Thus, you have a good chance of finding your ancestor mentioned in at least one will. Witnesses to wills were usually near neighbors, fellow church members, or close relatives who would not have inherited from the estate.

Wills are valuable not only because they give names and relationships but also because they give glimpses into the daily lives of your ancestors. By studying the tools and possessions listed in the will or the estate papers, you can often learn your ancestor's occupation, his economic worth, who lived in his household, and how generous (or stingy) he was with his loved ones. Did he provide for his children before his death? Did he leave some of them out of his will or cut them off with a one dollar bequest? How did he provide for his widow or for incapacitated family members? Did his wife lose her inheritance if she remarried? If so, who got her part of the estate?[22]

You can also learn about the amount of education and the social standing of the family by the bequests made in the will, such as books, paintings, musical instruments, and carriages, or a bequest of one Bible, a cow, and a hand plow. In 1875 in Huntington County, Indiana, George W. Detamore left "my large family Bible" to his daughter, Sarah C. Carl, and his property in Jefferson Township to his wife (no name given).[23] How did your ancestor dispose of his money and land? Did he leave it to his church, to the school, or to his favorite political party? Did he provide for the education of his younger children? Was he well-educated? If he signed his will with an "X" you know that he probably was not educated, although he might have been able to read but not write. You can often discern your ancestor's character and personality by reading his will, especially if it is not written entirely in "legalese." Local expressions and words often creep into even the legally worded documents.

You can learn a great deal, too, about the family from the probate inventory. If it lists all of the household items of the deceased you sometimes find that there were fewer beds than family members, that they had only a few bowls and spoons, and that the only cooking utensils were a kettle and a spider (a three-legged skillet). You may have to dash to the dictionary to learn what some of the items were. What were froes, settles, and piggins?

Problems with Using the Probates

There are obviously some problems encountered when using the probates. First, as mentioned, not everyone made a will. If your ancestor did not make a will, you won't find one and must hunt in the estate papers to find information about him. Second, not all heirs are named in probate records, not even the spouses and children of the deceased. It is not uncommon for the deceased to have mentioned "my beloved wife" without giving her name. After all, he knew her name and so did most of the people in his neighborhood, so why mention it? He also would not have mentioned his deceased children, but he probably would have named the children of a deceased child if they were to inherit. He might, however, have mentioned "my deceased daughter Eleanor's children" and not have named them. A man might even have mentioned "all of my children" and never listed their names. He might have mentioned the children who would inherit by the will but not those previously provided for. Stepchildren are seldom identified as such, and the fact that a second wife is not related to some or all of the children is also seldom mentioned. Sometimes, too, people are mentioned as receiving considerable amounts of money or land without any relationship being given. In such a case, assume that a relationship could exist and hunt for proof of it.[24]

Death dates aren't recorded in a will. The only dates given will be the date the will was written and the date it was probated. You must assume that the death took place between those two dates, that is, after the date the will was written and somewhat before the date it was probated. If no other record exists to establish an exact date of death, the death date will have to remain an approximation based on the two dates given. The establishment of an approximate date of death by using the probate records is usually considered sufficient proof of a death date, because the probate would have been within about ninety days of the death.

Also, the places of residence of heirs are seldom given in the probate records, although you might find them in the estate papers or the newspaper advertisements when a search had to be made for an heir. Maiden names of spouses of next-of-kin are also seldom mentioned, although you might find the names of sons-in-law and brothers-in-law mentioned. Daughters' married surnames are usually given, however, and if they are, you can go to the marriage records to determine whom the daughters married.

If the deceased was very old when he died, it may be a problem to learn where he died and where to find the probate records. A very old person may have gone to live with a son or married daughter in another county, and his probate record would be found there instead of in the county where he lived most of his life. You might look for an obituary for the deceased in his usual place of residence and for the sale of his land there if he still owned property. Otherwise, try to learn where his children lived at the time of his death.

In Indiana the probate records are found in various places: the County Probate Court has exclusive jurisdiction in Marion, St. Joseph, and Vanderburgh counties; the Superior Court has exclusive jurisdiction in Allen, Madison, and Hendricks counties; and in all other counties the Circuit Court in the county has jurisdiction, although in Bartholomew, Elkhart, Grant, Lake, LaPorte, and Porter counties the Superior Court and the Circuit Court have concurrent jurisdiction.[25]

An index to the probate records is usually available in the courthouse in the county where the deceased filed his will. These indexes are generally only for the *testators* (the persons who made wills) but sometimes they cover everyone named in the wills, including the heirs, beneficiaries, witnesses, and executors.

Printed *abstracts of wills* containing the names of all the people mentioned in each will are often found in area libraries. Hunt for the will abstracts to determine whether your ancestor did, indeed, make a will and to learn the names of the people mentioned in it. You can then go to the appropriate will book to see the complete will and get a photocopy of it.

You may have noticed that the person who made a will has been referred to as "he," not "she." A woman, unless she was a widow, could seldom make a will without her husband's consent. Special premarital agreements might have been made, but they weren't common. However, a widow or an unmarried woman could make a will. Therefore, you will seldom find a will for a married woman who died before her husband. The widow's dower, usually one-third of the estate, was reserved for a widow, and the other two-thirds went to the children of the couple. Grown children sometimes took their legal shares, leaving their mother in poor circumstances. An illegitimate child could only inherit from the father if the father had made the child legitimate; otherwise the child could inherit only from the mother. Thus, you will not find illegitimate children mentioned in wills as such. If the deceased had no children or spouse, the estate passed to his or her parents and siblings.[26]

MARRIAGE RECORDS

By 1800 marriage licenses were required by law in Indiana Territory, and the licenses were issued by the office of the county clerk from the date the particular county was established. *Marriage records* are in the custody of either the County Clerk or the Clerk of the Court in the county where the ceremony was performed. The kinds of marriage records include *licenses,* which were issued before the marriage took place and *ministers' returns,* which were made by the officiating minister and "returned" to the clerk after the wedding ceremony. Hence the name "marriage returns." Written *affidavits* of consent were required when one or both of the people to be married were under legal age, but a parent could appear to give oral permission for the marriage. The name of the parent who gave permission for the marriage is usually recorded in the marriage record. The father of the minor generally gave consent, although it might have been given by the minor's uncle or brother. When the minor's mother gave consent, it generally meant that the father was deceased. If both parents were dead, the minor's legal guardian would have given consent to the marriage. And, if the guardian was a relative, the family connection might be given on the marriage document.[27]

Licenses were issued by the county clerk in the county where the bride, not the groom, lived. The earliest marriage records are the marriage returns, those one-line entries which include only the name of the groom, the name of the bride, the date of the marriage return, and the name of the person officiating.

The name of a parent or guardian appeared only when either the bride or the groom was under legal age to marry. In territorial days, the legal age for marriage in Indiana was seventeen for a male and fourteen for a female.

Problems with Using Marriage Records

Marriage applications or licenses were required in Indiana from the formation of the county. After the marriage ceremony was performed, the minister or justice of the peace returned the license to the county clerk, who, in turn, compiled the *marriage registers.* The registers, large books containing those "one-liners" previously mentioned, are often the only existing record of the marriage. The registers are far from complete because many ministers' records were lost or destroyed before they could be officially recorded. Some ministers and justices simply neglected to return the forms, and no record will exist other than the names of the couple, the application date, and the notation "License. No return." This entry does not mean that the marriage did not take place but merely that the license had been obtained but was not returned to the court. Often the couple took out the license in one county and then proceeded to be married in another county. Because a minister filed returns only in his own county, no return would be found in the county where the marriage actually took place. When no return is found in the probable county, look in nearby counties for it.[28]

The marriage registers are kept in chronological order by the year, although overlap is often found in registers that were updated frequently. If such updating caused duplication of the records, a couple's marriage might be recorded in two separate marriage books. Of course, it is possible that the couple actually did marry twice, so check the marriage dates carefully to make sure. Unfortunately, the information found in the marriage registers is often erroneous or subject to misinterpretation. The information was provided by the person who performed the marriage ceremony, and he could have recorded the wrong names or dates. Later, the information would have been copied into the marriage register by a clerk, where it was subject to further errors. Mistakes might have happened if the clerk was poorly educated, was deaf, couldn't see well, or was an "indifferent" speller. In the early days not all public officials were well educated, and it was not until about 1850 that spelling began to be standardized. Even then, many a man spelled his name a different way each time he wrote it. All of these problems might be met when searching in the public records, so be on the lookout for them.

Later Marriage Records

Indiana marriage records didn't contain much genealogical information until 1882, when statewide registration of vital statistics began. At that time, marriage data were obtained on the county level and then sent on to the state to be recorded. Many more questions were asked of the couple who intended to be married. Recorded were the given name and surname of the groom; the given name and maiden name of the bride; the age, birthplace, and birthdate of each; the sex of each; the names of each person's parents; and whether each person was white (W) or colored (C). Any previous marriages of the bride or groom were also noted. From 1905 until 1949 this information was kept in the Application Books of the Board of Health in the county.

When searching for a marriage record, always try to think of every conceivable way a surname might have been spelled and all of the possible variations of that surname. The names "Robinson," "Robertson," "Roberson," and "Roberts" were often used interchangeably in the court records. Instead of having the couple write their names, the clerk often asked for the names and entered them himself. If he did not hear the names correctly or spelled them strangely, or if his handwriting was illegible, the entries may be almost impossible to decipher. "Louchs" was recorded one time as "Schultz" and another time as "Loutz" in the marriage records of Huntington County. Because the bride was quite old, she may have mumbled due to some missing teeth. Faded ink, torn pages, water-stained books, and poorly filmed copies can also make the marriage records difficult to use. Be inventive in your approach to these records and look for the many ways your ancestors might have been identified.

Supplemental Marriage Records

A lot of additional information about a marriage can be found in the books called "Marriage Supplements," which are found in the county courthouse. The additional data from marriage records after 1882 can help to determine the names of the parents, other siblings, birthdates, and, sometimes, the birthplaces of the people who were married. By noticing all of the people with the same surname and parents with same given names, you can often determine which ones were siblings or were somehow related. The Marriage Supplement, alphabetical by surname, also serves as a kind of index to the marriages in a county, giving the book and page number where the complete marriage record can be found. A representative entry in a supplemental marriage record might read: "SMITH, Angie J; Leander [father], Lizzie Gobble [mother's maiden name]; F W [female, white]; [birthdate]; Book 7, page 275."[29] Similar information about the groom in this marriage would be listed under his surname. If you don't know his name, you will have to go to the marriage book listed for the bride to find his name, because there is no cross-index in the marriage supplements. In many counties members of the D.A.R. have compiled indexes to the marriage records, which make locating the complete marriage records much easier. Information usually contains the surname and given name of the groom, the complete name of the bride, the date of the marriage, the name of the officiating minister (D.M.V.) or justice of the peace (J.P.), and the page number of the particular marriage book where the complete record can be found. These records are indexed by the surname of the bridegroom and, frequently, by the maiden name of the bride.

Justices of the Peace Records

Justices of the peace were elected or appointed to take care of the lesser legal actions in a county, including the marriages. Justices, like ministers, were required to submit to the county government a record of any marriages they performed. Justices kept duplicate records of their official actions in personal account books, which sometimes contain further information about the marriage and perhaps genealogical data not found in the county records. The account books of the justices are sometimes found in the custody of the county clerk, in area libraries, with local historical and genealogical societies, or perhaps in the custody of the descendants of the justices.[30] Descendants who have such records should deposit the documents (or copies) in the appropriate county office or the State Library.

Finding Marriage Records

If you know the name of the county where a marriage took place, contact the County Clerk in that county to obtain a copy of the marriage record. Costs for copies vary from county to county in Indiana. The Division of Vital Records of the State Board of Health in Indianapolis has custody of the marriage records for the entire state of Indiana since 1882. At that time the county clerks were required to send copies of the marriage returns to the state, but not all clerks complied. The percentage of nonreturns is rather large for the early days, and you will not always find the information you seek about a marriage at the state level. Even as late as the 1920s marriage returns were heavily underreturned. Inquiries to the Division of Vital Records will be forwarded to the appropriate office to be answered. An index to Indiana marriages has been kept by the state only since 1958; to obtain earlier marriage records you need to know the name of the county where the marriage took place. Certified copies of marriage records are not available from the State Health Department, but must be obtained from the County Clerk in the county where the marriage was performed. The names of all ninety-two Indiana counties, along with the names of the corresponding county seats and the dates of formation, are found at the end of this chapter.

If you are researching in the area of the "gore" of Indiana (which was originally made up of Switzerland, Ohio, Dearborn, part of Franklin, most of Union, and slivers of Wayne, Randolph, and Jay counties), and you find no marriage record in the county where you think the couple should have married or in any nearby county, look for the local "Gretna Green." Cincinnati fit the bill as a "no-questions-asked" marriage spot for couples up and down the Ohio River and in a wide area of counties in Indiana, Kentucky, and Ohio. Check in Cincinnati for that elusive marriage if you don't find it elsewhere.[31]

INDIANA DIVORCE RECORDS

Until 1852, divorce actions in Indiana were handled by the Indiana General Assembly and not by the local courts. At times, the Assembly did not actually grant the divorce but gave permission for the divorce petition to be filed in a local Circuit Court. Since the General Assembly usually met from December of one year through the spring of the next year, divorce actions are filed under the spring year rather than that of the winter before. *Divorces Granted by the Indiana General Assembly Prior to 1852* is a complete listing of divorces granted before 1852.[32] A companion volume, *Name Changes Granted by the Indiana General Assembly Prior to 1852,* can often be useful in genealogical research when you know of, or suspect, an ancestor's name change. The book is an alphabetical cross-index to personal names, both the original and the newly assumed name. The kinds of information given might include the county of residence; relationships; the reason for the name change (restoration of maiden name following a divorce; an adoption; legitimization, or merely a desire for a different name); and the date the name change became effective. After 1852, name change petitions were filed in the local county circuit courts.[33]

Divorces were handled by the courts, and the resulting records are part of the court records. If your ancestor was divorced, the divorce records can be a valuable genealogical tool. Divorce records are found in the county where the divorce was granted, and although divorces weren't common in the early days, they did take place and the records do exist. Divorce records can be especially valuable if the couple had children, because the names and ages of the children will be recorded in the court records; they will not be on the certificate. Information usually given on the divorce certificate includes names of both parties; ages or dates of birth of both parties; state or country of birth; date and place where marriage took place; the date and the grounds for the divorce. Divorce records are found in the court which has control over other equity matters. In Indiana either the Circuit Court or the Superior Court in the county had authority to grant divorces, and the County Clerk or the Clerk of the Circuit Court has custody of the divorce records.[34] *The County Courthouse Book,* by Elizabeth Petty Bentley, has information regarding the jurisdictions in Indiana.

Divorce records are generally indexed and, as public records, are easy to see and use. To obtain a copy of a divorce record, write to the proper court, sending the names of both parties involved, or, at least, the name of the plaintiff, and the year the action took place. A fee is charged for the copy of the divorce record, with a certified copy costing slightly more. The fee varies considerably from one court to another. Some courts will not undertake a search but will advise you to use a professional genealogist to get the desired records. In such a case, the clerk will usually send the names of researchers who are willing (for a fee) to search the records. If a divorce was a part of the life of your ancestor, you will want to know about it and include it in your family records.

Finding Divorce Records

You can find divorce records recorded with the regular court cases or in separate volumes of divorce cases. The court dockets give the *plaintiff* and the *defendant* in the divorce case, the term of court, and the day. The court *minute books* give the court judgment and a description of the case. The *case files* contain affidavits, lists of children and their ages, and inventories of the property, and give the grounds for the divorce. Sometimes, you will find the names of relatives who got custody of minor children during or after the divorce.

GUARDIANSHIP RECORDS

A guardian was appointed to look after minor children and mentally or physically handicapped persons and their inherited property when a parent died. When the mother did not want to assume guardianship, a guardian was appointed by the court to serve in her place. She would have still cared for the children, however. You sometimes find a child referred to as "an orphan" even when one of the parents is still living. Technically, a minor whose father is deceased (or whose deceased mother, excluding the father, left separately held property to the child) is called an orphan. Thus, an "orphan" can actually have one living parent. This is valuable knowledge, especially when you feel sure that one parent should still have been alive. It is also common for a mother or a father to be appointed guardian of her or his own children (when the other parent died) without implying an adoption. A male relative was often appointed guardian in the place of the mother when the mother waived guardianship.[35]

A guardianship may be a separate court process handled by a separate court, or it can be a part of the probate process and be handled by the Probate Court. In Indiana guardianships have been handled by the Probate Court from 1790 to 1805; by the Orphans' Court from 1795 to 1805; by the Circuit Court from 1814 to 1829; by the Probate Court again from 1829 to 1852; and by the Court of Common Pleas from 1806 to 1813 and again from 1853 to 1873. Since 1873 the Circuit Court has handled guardianship matters. In order to handle the affairs of an orphan, the guardian had to post a bond equal to the value of the orphan's estate, and a record of this action should be found with the guardianship papers.

The Value of Guardianship Records

Guardianship records are valuable to the genealogist because they can show relationships, give names of children who were minors when the parent died, and give the dates when minor children reached legal age, when the minors married, and perhaps, when they, or the guardian, died. All of these incidents appear in the guardianship records, and guardianship reports were often published in the area newspapers.

NATURALIZATION RECORDS IN INDIANA

Naturalization was provided for and administered by Congress. The process is performed by "a court of record," that is, one having a seal and a clerk who maintains permanent records. Because of broad interpretation of this requirement, many courts naturalized which shouldn't have. Also, not all resident aliens were naturalized, and, in fact, many people were never naturalized. Early immigrants merely signed an oath of allegiance as they exited the boat, and later ones may not have felt it necessary to be naturalized. At first, only European immigrants had to be naturalized. People from the British Isles and English subjects in the American colonies did not have to be naturalized after the colonies became the United States. Some immigrants began the process of naturalization by filing "first papers" but never went any further in the naturalization process. It was common for a person to begin the process in one state, then to move on to another spot where he continued the process, and finally to be naturalized in still a third place. The records for each "step" in the process will be found in a different place and probably in a different kind of court. The naturalization process can be difficult to unravel because of overlapping jurisdictions and the way our ancestors went about being naturalized.

The first federal naturalization law required a two-year residency in the United States and one year in the state, good moral character, and an oath to support the Constitution. The application could be filed in any common law court of record. An act of 1795 required aliens to file declarations of intention three years before they could become citizens, five years' residency and one in the state where naturalized, an oath of allegiance, good moral character, renunciation of any titles of nobility, and foreswearing of allegiance to the sovereign of the former land.[36] The basic naturalization code was enacted in 1802, requiring that a declaration of intention be filed three years before admission as a citizen; residence of five years in the United States and one year in the state where naturalized; an oath of allegiance; good moral character; renunciation of any title of nobility; and renunciation of allegiance to the reigning sovereign of the former country. Copies of declarations of intention, the report of registry, and naturalization proceedings were to be sent to the Secretary of State of the U.S. These requirements, slightly modified, became the basis of all future naturalization proceedings.[37]

From 1856 to 1906 the Indiana State Supreme Court was the principal court of naturalization, but other courts may also have been created to exercise specific jurisdictions. Thus, by being "a court of record," the other courts also naturalized, and such naturalizations could have been recorded in any number of places: probate minute books, chancery order books, or civil order books. All of these books should be searched for nineteenth-century naturalizations, especially when jurisdictions overlapped. In 1868 the Fourteenth Amendment granted citizenship to all persons born or naturalized in the United States, with the exception of tribal Indians, people living in unincorporated territories, and the children of foreign ambassadors. Until 1906 the record of the court's order of naturalization was to be entered in the official record the court, whether it was called a *minute book* or an *order book*.[38]

During the Civil War, aliens who had served in and been honorably discharged from United States military forces could become citizens merely by petitioning to be naturalized. Previous declaration of intention and proof of residency were eliminated and the procedure applied to any war, including the Mexican, Indian, and Spanish-American wars.[39]

Content of Naturalization Records

Records before 1906 usually contain name, country of birth or allegiance, date of application, and signature, and some give date and port of arrival in the United States. Records after 1906 include name, age, occupation, personal description; date and place of birth; citizenship; present address and last foreign address; ship and port of embarkation; U.S. port and date of arrival; and date of application and signature.[40]

Finding Naturalization Records

In order to find naturalization records for an ancestor, you need to locate the person in a certain place at a specific time and then use the citizenship laws there to deduce when and where the person might have been naturalized. Determine which court would have had jurisdiction and what procedures would have been followed. Learn what forms were required, such as registration, declaration of intention, certificate of arrival, petition, oath, affidavits of witnesses, or certificates of naturalization. Would your ancestor have gotten special consideration because of military service, employment, or obtaining a passport?[41] If your ancestor's name appears on voting lists in an area, check to see what the state requirement for voting was at the time. Were a declaration of intention or first papers required? When checking the various courts, begin with local civil court records and then go on to the other courts whose jurisdiction might have overlapped. If you find no records, go to the courts which had statewide jurisdiction, such as the State Supreme Court or the federal court. Knowing about the laws in effect when your ancestors may have been naturalized can give you a better chance of finding their naturalization records.

Always remember that, as your ancestors migrated across the country, they might have filed first papers in an eastern state, taken the next step toward citizenship in a state farther west, and have been naturalized in yet another state. Knowing the migration route of your ancestors, the probable time when they would have been naturalized, and the laws in effect there at that time can help you to find their naturalization records. Then, you can check for naturalization records in the various places they lived during their migration.

Naturalization records created after September 26, 1906, by U.S. federal courts are housed in the National Archives and in its field branches. The list of holdings of the various field branches is on pages 63–68 of the *Guide to Genealogical Research in the National Archives.* These later records can be found in the courts and also at the Immigration and Naturalization Service. Former restrictions on providing information from, or copies of, naturalization records were removed in 1973.[42] The Genealogical Society of Utah has been microfilming the naturalization records found in the local courts throughout the United States, generally for the period before September 26, 1906. Recently, records through 1935 have also been microfilmed, and naturalization records created by federal courts are currently being microfilmed.[43]

For records before 1906, the extensive step-by-step research procedure is necessary. For records after 1906, contact the local court, or file form #G641 with the Immigration and Naturalization Service, 425 I Street N.W., Washington, D.C. 20536. A search fee is charged for this service. Some states are beginning to transfer naturalization records, especially the older ones, from state and local courts to regional depositories or state archives. It might be wise to check with these places before starting a search in the courts.[44] An excellent booklet, *American Naturalization Processes and Procedures, 1790–1985,* was prepared by Indiana State Archivist John J. Newman, in 1985. It is probably the best source for information about the naturalization process. The book is available from the Indiana Historical Society in Indianapolis. The Society has also published many naturalization lists in its various publications.

ADOPTION RECORDS

Adoption records are closed to the public in Indiana to protect the privacy of all persons involved in the action. The records are sealed by the court and can be opened by the court only for "good cause," which seldom happens in Indiana. In the case of health problems requiring medical information, the court may release medical history but not the identities of persons involved. In July 1988 an Indiana adoption history program was inaugurated to handle consent registrations regarding adoptees and birth parents. To open the adoption records requires the consent of an adult adoptee (over age 21), a birth parent, and the adoptive parents. This three-way consent is sometimes waived if one or both adoptive parents are dead, or if one adoptive parent has abandoned the mate or the adoptee and the other parent has consented. Once the three-way consent is given, the persons seeking information will receive names, addresses, original birth certificates, and a wealth of other information about each other. Request consent forms from the Indiana State Board of Health. The completed consent form is then filed and the person filing the form is notified if others involved in the adoption have also filed consent forms. Unless all three consent forms are filed, no information will be given to any one person.

A separate adoption medical history registry can, however, provide the adoptee access to certain medical records of the adoptee's birth parents and relatives. Adoptions finalized since January 1, 1986, require that a comprehensive medical history of the adoptee be completed and filed with the State Board of Health. Birth parents can file medical information with the State Board even if their child was given up for adoption before 1986. A free brochure is available from the State Registrar of Vital Records, Indiana Adoption History Registry, P.O. Box 1964, Indianapolis, Indiana 46206-1964.[45]

BIRTH AND DEATH RECORDS

Birth and death records, the so-called *vital records,* are considered primary sources of genealogical information. Vital records are the records kept by the government for the vital events in one's life. Unfortunately, vital records are available for only relatively modern times. It was not until 1882 that Indiana began to require that the county clerks in the respective counties record the births and deaths which took place there. Enforcement was haphazard and physicians often forgot to return certificates to the county clerks. Eventually, the state began to require that the clerks send copies of the birth and death records to the state. Compliance with the order to forward copies to the state was incomplete until 1916 for the birth records and until 1919 for death records. It has been estimated that records may still have been slightly incomplete into the 1920s. Even today, persons wishing to retire sometimes learn that they have no birth certificate and must provide proof of age in order to do so. The United States Census Bureau will provide proof of age upon request and use of the proper form. Records of births which took place before October 1, 1907, are in the office of the county health officer in the county seat where the child was born. After that date, birth records are in the office of the Indiana Division of Vital Records, State Board of Health, 1330 West Michigan Street, Indianapolis, Indiana 46206.

The Indiana birth certificate will contain the name of the child; birthplace; birthdate; sex; name of the hospital; time of birth; father's name, race, birthplace, age, and occupation; mother's name, race, birthplace, age, and occupation; parents' residence and how long lived there, marital status; number of other living children, number of deceased children, and any stillbirths. In order to get a birth certificate for someone other than yourself, you must have that person's permission or a valid reason for wanting to obtain it. This ruling is necessary to prevent fraudulent use of birth certificates. Write to the proper office, either in the county or the state, to request the needed birth certificate.

INDIANA DEATH CERTIFICATES

Death records before October 1899 are found in the office of the county health officer, and records after that date are in the office of the Division of Vital Records in Indianapolis. The death certificate generally contains the name of the deceased; age; sex; race; marital status; name of spouse; birthplace; occupation; name and birthplace of father and mother; name of informant; place of burial; funeral director; date of death; cause of death; duration of illness; signature of attending physician; physician's address; and date certificate was signed. Later death certificates will also contain the person's social security number; whether foreign-born; and whether a war veteran and, if so, of which war. For a death before October 1899, write to the health office in the proper county and request the death certificate. For a death after 1899, write to request a form, fill in all the known information, and send to the state office along with the proper fee. It is helpful to know the exact date of the death because the office will search only one year on either side of the year you designate.

Most county health offices have indexed both the birth and the death records, but not every county office will allow you personally to inspect the indexes or the actual records. You will get a record, but not necessarily the one you wanted. This is why it is helpful to know something about the deceased, such as the birth date, the spouse's name, or anything which might help the clerk locate the correct record for the person. If two or more persons with an identical name died during the same year, it might be necessary to have further information about the person to get the correct record. A copy of the actual death record can be quite valuable because of the wealth of information it may contain. Unfortunately, most counties do not provide photocopies of the actual records. Instead, the information is typed onto a standard form, which omits much of the valuable data found on the original copy. If possible, try to get a photocopy of the actual death record.

Problems with Using Vital Records

As with other records, there are problems encountered when using the birth and death records. The first concerns legibility of the records. If you cannot read the entries, you won't find them too helpful. The given name or surname might be incorrectly recorded on the certificate or on the index, or on both, making it difficult to recognize it as the name of "your" individual. Also, you may not find the record you seek because it was never made or, if made, was not forwarded to the proper office by the attending physician. Another problem might be that the

PERSONAL DEATH.

County of Grant

Township of Center

Town of ______ or

City of ______

No. ______ St.

______ Ward.

Indiana State Board of Health.

CERTIFICATE OF DEATH.

Record Number 01

(If death occurred in a Hospital or Institution, give its NAME instead of street and number.)

Full Name Michael Myers

PERSONAL AND STATISTICAL PARTICULARS.

Sex Male Color White

Single, Married, Widowed or Divorced, } Married

Name of Husband or Wife, Nellie Myers

Date of Birth Dec (Month) 30 (Day) 1841 (Year)

Age 64 years, 6 months, 7 days.

Occupation Retired Farmer

Birthplace Ohio (State or Country.)

Place of Death Marion 408 W. Sixth St.

Name of Father Benjamin Myers

Birthplace of Father Unknown (State or Country.)

Maiden Name of Mother " "

Birthplace of Mother " " (State or Country.)

The above stated personal particulars are true to the best of my knowledge and belief.

(INFORMANT) Nellie Myers

(Address) Marion Ind.

MEDICAL CERTIFICATE OF DEATH.

Date of Death July (Month) 7 (Day) 1906 (Year.)

I HEREBY CERTIFY, That I attended deceased from ______ 190__, to ______ 190__ that I last saw h__ alive on ______ 190__, and that death occurred on the date stated above, at 10 o'clock P. M.

To the best of my knowledge and belief the cause of death was as follows:

Chief Cause [illegible]

Immediate Cause Pyemia Duration Three [illegible]

(Signed) Edmonston [illegible] M. D.

July 10" 1906 (Address) Marion Ind.

SPECIAL INFORMATION ONLY FOR HOSPITALS, INSTITUTIONS, TRANSIENTS OR RECENT RESIDENTS.

Former or usual Residence ______

How long at Place of death ______ days

Where was disease contracted if not at place of death?

Place of Burial or Removal: IOOF Marion

Proposed date of Burial: July 9 1906

Undertaker: [illegible]

Address: Marion Ind.

Filed July 12" 1906

[illegible] Health Officer or Deputy.

(Address) Marion Ind.

(IF UNABLE TO ANSWER ANY OF THE ABOVE QUESTIONS, WRITE "UNKNOWN.")

Death certificate of Michael Myers, July 7, 1906, Marion, Grant County, Indiana.

informant did not know the answers to many of the questions on the form. If the word "unknown" appears many times on a birth or death record, it probably means that the informant simply didn't know the information asked. It is even possible that an informant could have invented a fictitious name for the father of the person to conceal his/her illegitimacy. Such a deception could cause the researcher to devote many hours of fruitless search for a nonexistent person.

MISCELLANEOUS RECORDS AT THE COURTHOUSE

You might also find other useful records at the courthouse, such as cemetery deed records, 1925 to the present, which record deeds to cemetery plots; plat books, showing plats of towns, subdivisions, cemeteries, and such; turnpike reports; leases; election returns for churches and organizations, and even Bible pages; soldiers' discharge records from 1865 to the present, which record the discharge of soldiers, sailors, and marines in the Civil War and later wars; registry of farm names, 1913 to the present, which records farm names registered by owners; nineteenth-century records of marks and brands, recording owners' animal brands and marks, which are useful if a person did not own land; and the newspapers of two political parties, 1865 to the present, which were kept by the recorder on orders of the commissioners. Only about forty-five Indiana counties originally kept the newspapers, and fewer than twenty-five counties currently have these files.[46]

THE VALUE OF COUNTY RECORDS

It is easy to see that the court and vital records found in the county are among the best sources of genealogical information available to the family researcher. Although subject to the kinds of errors found in other records, the county records are still extremely useful when researching one's family. If you remember that these records usually begin with the erection of the county, you will be able to determine when you might find certain kinds of information about your ancestors.

COUNTY RECORDS OF INDIANA MICROFILMING PROJECT (CRIMP)

The County Records of Indiana Microfilming Project (CRIMP) was a statewide program organized, funded, and operated entirely by the Indiana State Library, the Indiana Historical Society, and the Genealogical Society of Utah. The program preserved on microfilm the basic records of the people of Indiana and has made them available to the public. The records include the more important courthouse records, family, church, cemetery, funeral home, and other public records listing names, dates, and connections of Hoosiers. Courthouse records microfilmed were marriages, wills, probate orders (estate settlements), naturalizations, deeds, deed indexes, and some miscellaneous records.[47]

Courthouse records from the beginning of the county through 1917 were microfilmed, and by January 28, 1988, the records of courthouses in 42 Indiana counties had been filmed. A free set of film of all the noncourthouse records was given to each principal county library or libraries. With the approval of the County Clerk and Recorder, the principal county library can also purchase a set of the microfilm of the courthouse records. Two other libraries also have copies of the local noncourthouse microfilms: the Indiana State Library in Indianapolis and the Genealogical Library of Salt Lake City, Utah. CRIMP was discontinued in 1990.[48]

COURTHOUSE FIRES

In 1977 Willard Heiss, Indiana's premier researcher and genealogist, prepared a list of the known and reported courthouse fires which took place in the state. By 1976 twenty-seven Indiana courthouses had been destroyed partially or totally by fire. Many of the court records were lost unless they had been stored in other buildings away from the courthouse. Sometimes the records were kept among the personal papers of court officials or justices and have therefore survived. Surprisingly, some records have been saved from even the totally destroyed courthouses because townspeople dashed into the burning buildings to save them.[49]

The second courthouse in Boone County, at Lebanon, had been torn down in 1856 to make room for a third courthouse, and temporary offices of the Recorder, Auditor, and Treasurer were destroyed by fire on October 12, 1856, and practically all of the records were lost. The second courthouse in Nashville, in Brown County, was destroyed by fire, but some of the Clerk's records remain. The second Clay County courthouse, then located in Bowling Green, burned on November 30, 1851, but only the Recorder's records were lost. The third Daviess County courthouse at Washington was built in 1878 and burned just one year later; the marriage records, Index to the Probates, and deed records are extant. The first courthouse in Dearborn County was built in 1810 and was destroyed by fire in 1826; some early marriages and will records remain.[50]

In 1913 a fire in the Dekalb County courthouse at Auburn caused the loss of all of the probate records before 1860. The Dubois County courthouse, located in Jasper since 1830, was destroyed on August 17, 1839, with all of its contents, although ten file boxes of deeds, dating from 1812, seem to be complete. The third courthouse of Franklin County also burned in 1852, but no records were lost. In the Gibson County courthouse fire of 1935 only the belfry burned and no records were lost. Hancock County's courthouse at Greenfield burned in 1940 but the records were not damaged. The second courthouse of Henry County at New Castle was also destroyed in 1864, but records of the Clerk, Recorder, Auditor, and Treasurer were kept at offices elsewhere and were not harmed.[51]

There were no records lost in a reported fire at Brownstown, in Jackson County, which happened either in 1872 or 1881. Jasper County's third courthouse and its contents were destroyed in a fire in 1864, and the Clerk's records were lost; the Deeds and Deed Indexes were spared, however. The second Johnson County courthouse at Franklin, built in 1832, burned, and the third courthouse burned in 1874, but many records are extant: marriages from 1830, court records from 1823, Recorder's Entry Books from 1822, and the Deeds and Deeds Index from 1824.[52]

Knox County had an explosion and fire which destroyed the courthouse in Vincennes in 1814 and many records were lost. The records that are largely extant from then on are Deeds from 1814, Marriages and Marriage Certificates from 1807, Order Book from 1811, Wills from 1806, Minutes Book, 1816–1818, Orphan's Court Minutes, 1796–1805, Minutes of the Common Pleas Court, 1790–1810, General Indexes to Administrations, 1795–1886, and perhaps others, and the recently discovered Knox County tax lists for the years 1802, 1804, and 1805. Madison County's third courthouse at Anderson burned on December 10, 1880, destroying Marriage, Circuit Court, and Common Pleas Court records; extant records are Wills from 1879, Deeds from 1825, and General Index to Deeds from 1829. The Martin County courthouse at Shoals was built in 1871 and it burned in 1876, but records of interest to genealogists were saved. Morgan County's third courthouse burned in 1876; some records were destroyed and others have been restored.[53]

The first Noble County courthouse burned in 1843 and the county offices burned in 1859; extant are Marriages from 1859 and Deeds and Deed Index from 1836. Parke County's first courthouse burned in 1833 and records exist only from that date. Porter County lost its third courthouse in 1934 but, fortunately, lost none of its records. Marriages and Deeds were saved when the second Spencer County courthouse was destroyed by fire in 1833. The first Sullivan County courthouse burned in 1850 and only the Wills from 1841 and records after 1850 remain. Documents of general interest were saved when the first Tipton County courthouse burned in 1857. Union County lost its second courthouse in 1903 but, fortunately, the records suffered only water damage. The second courthouse also burned in Vermillion County in 1844 but all records were saved. Wabash County's first courthouse was destroyed in 1870 but the nearby offices of the Treasurer, Auditor, Recorder, and Clerk escaped harm.[54] It is amazing that all of the courthouses did not burn, what with the open fireplaces and woodburning stoves used to heat them.

ADDRESSES OF INDIANA COUNTY SEATS

County	*Year Formed*	*County Seat*
Adams	1835	Decatur 46733
Allen	1824	Fort Wayne 46802
Bartholomew	1821	Columbus 47201
Benton	1840	Fowler 47944
Blackford	1838	Hartford City 47348
Boone	1830	Lebanon 46052
Brown	1836	Nashville 47448
Carroll	1828	Delphi 46923
Cass	1829	Logansport 46947
Clark	1801	Jeffersonville 47130
Clay	1825	Brazil 47834
Clinton	1830	Frankfort 46041
Crawford	1818	English 47118

County	*Year Formed*	*County Seat*
Daviess	1817	Washington 47501
Dearborn	1803	Lawrenceburg 47025
Decatur	1822	Greensburg 47240
Dekalb	1835	Auburn 46076
Delaware	1827	Muncie 47305
Dubois	1818	Jasper 47546
Elkhart	1830	Goshen 46526
Fayette	1819	Connersville 47331
Floyd	1819	New Albany 47150
Fountain	1826	Covington 47932
Franklin	1811	Brookville 47012
Fulton	1835	Rochester 46975
Gibson	1813	Princeton 47570
Grant	1831	Marion 41952
Greene	1821	Bloomfield 47424
Hamilton	1823	Noblesville 46060
Hancock	1828	Greenfield 46140
Harrison	1808	Corydon 47112
Hendricks	1824	Danville 46122
Henry	1822	New Castle 47362
Howard	1844	Kokomo 46901
Huntington	1832	Huntington 46750
Jackson	1816	Brownstown 47220
Jasper	1835	Rensselaer 47978
Jay	1835	Portland 47371
Jefferson	1811	Madison 47250
Jennings	1817	Vernon 47282
Johnson	1823	Franklin 46131
Knox	1790	Vincennes 47591
Kosciusko	1835	Warsaw 46580
Lagrange	1832	Lagrange 46761
Lake	1836	Crown Point 46307
LaPorte	1832	LaPorte 46350
Lawrence	1818	Bedford 47421
Madison	1823	Anderson 46011
Marion	1822	Indianapolis 46206
Marshall	1835	Plymouth 46563
Martin	1820	Shoals 47581
Miami	1832	Peru 46970
Monroe	1818	Bloomington 47401
Montgomery	1823	Crawfordsville 47933

County	*Year Formed*	*County Seat*
Morgan	1822	Martinsville 46151
Newton	1859	Kentland 47951
Noble	1835	Albion 46701
Ohio	1844	Rising Sun 47040
Orange	1816	Paoli 47454
Owen	1819	Spencer 47460
Parke	1821	Rockville 47872
Perry	1814	Cannelton 47520
Pike	1817	Petersburg 47567
Porter	1835	Valparaiso 46383
Posey	1814	Mount Vernon 47620
Pulaski	1835	Winamac 46996
Putnam	1822	Greencastle 46135
Randolph	1818	Winchester 47394
Ripley	1816	Versailles 47042
Rush	1822	Rushville 46173
St. Joseph	1830	South Bend 46601
Scott	1820	Scottsburg 47170
Shelby	1822	Shelbyville 46176
Spencer	1818	Rockport 47635
Starke	1835	Knox 46534
Steuben	1835	Angola 46703
Sullivan	1817	Sullivan 47882
Switzerland	1814	Vevay 47043
Tippecanoe	1826	Lafayette 47901
Tipton	1844	Tipton 46072
Union	1821	Liberty 47353
Vanderburgh	1818	Evansville 47618
Vermillion	1824	Newport 47966
Vigo	1818	Terre Haute 47801
Wabash	1832	Wabash 46992
Warren	1827	Williamsport 47993
Warrick	1813	Boonville 47601
Washington	1814	Salem 47167
Wayne	1811	Richmond 47374
Wells	1835	Bluffton 46714
White	1834	Monticello 47960
Whitley	1835	Columbia City 46725

Census Records

CHAPTER

9

After the thirteen colonies became the United States of America, a provision of the Constitution was that the inhabitants of the new country should be enumerated (counted) within three years after the first meeting of Congress and every ten years thereafter.[1] The purpose of the census was to apportion representatives and direct taxes according to the number of inhabitants in each state. The United States instituted a federal census before any other country except Sweden, whose census preceded it by only a few years. Censuses actually have been taken since Roman times for the purpose of taxation or simply to "count heads" in an area. The word "census" comes from the Latin word "censere," meaning an official count of population and recording of age and sex.

THE 1790 CENSUS

The first census, taken in 1790, did a count and not much more. It counted the population, but only within limited age categories and by sex. It is useful, however, for locating an individual in a certain state at that time, because it did list the names of the heads of families. This type of census format remained unchanged through the next five censuses taken from 1800 through 1840. Age groupings grew more precise, but only male or female heads of households were actually listed by name. Other members of the household were given only numerical listings by sex but not by name. The first federal census, ordered to be taken in 1790, was to list the name of each male inhabitant over the age of twenty-one, the number of free white males sixteen years of age and upward, the number of free white males under sixteen, the number of free white females, the number of all other free persons, and the number of slaves, giving the name of the county, and sometimes the town, or district of an individual's residence.[2]

While the census schedules for 1790 don't seem to have much information for the family researcher, they do show where a man was living at a particular time in history. Even though there may have been several men living in an area who had the same given and last name, this first census is still a valuable finding tool. It is particularly useful for locating your ancestor after the Revolutionary War at a time when a great deal of migration was taking place. The 1790 census schedules are available for the following states: Connecticut, Maine, Maryland (except for Allegheny, Somerset, and Calvert counties), Massachusetts, New Hampshire, New York, North Carolina (except for Caswell, Granville, and Orange counties), Pennsylvania, Rhode Island, South Carolina, and Vermont.[3]

Several of these "censuses" are really reconstructed listings of inhabitants that have been compiled from the existing tax lists for the same time period. States having reconstructed censuses in place of the missing 1790 census schedules are Delaware, Georgia, Kentucky, New Jersey (1793 military list), and Virginia. West Virginia, which separated from Virginia at the time of the Civil War, is enumerated as part of Virginia until the 1870 census, although separate census indexes for the area which became West Virginia have been compiled and printed for the years before 1870. While there is no 1790 federal census for Indiana, which was then a part of the Northwest Territory, it is conceivable that men who were later living in the state might be found in the reconstructed 1790 census for Kentucky or some other "feeder state."[4]

THE EARLY CENSUSES

The early censuses, 1790 through 1840, not only place an individual in a specific place at a given time but they also give clues to the makeup of his family. Although persons living in the household may not have been related to the head of the family, those of the correct age to have been his children can be assumed part of his family until proved otherwise. Families often took in orphaned children, whether related to them or not, and sometimes considered them part of the family. Older children, and even younger ones, were sometimes hired hands or mothers' helpers and not actually part of the family. It was fairly common for siblings and relatives of the couple to live with them before going out on their own. One or more parents of the couple might also have been living with them and would have been counted as part of the household.

The 1800 Census

Indiana became a part of the Northwest Territory in 1787 and was organized as the Indiana Territory in 1800. It was not enumerated as a territory in the 1800 census, and no 1800 census exists for Indiana. If your ancestor was then living in nearby Ohio or Kentucky, however, you might find him listed in the census or tax lists there. The 1800 census was still principally a listing of the heads of households, with no names of other members of the household given. The age categories of the 1800 census schedules were made more exact, with separate columns which list number of free white males and females aged 1–10, 10–16, 16–26, 26–45, and 45 and upward; number of other free persons except Indians not taxed; number of slaves; town (or district), and county of residence.[5] The 1800 census is more exact than the 1790 census and can be used to provide clues to ages and sexes of the various members of a household at that time. Later censuses and other types of records can then be used to verify or disprove any conclusions you may have made. Marriage, church, cemetery, and the various county records found where your ancestors lived in Indiana can be used to substantiate the conclusions you have made from the scanty information found in the earlier census records.

The 1807 Territorial Census

The people of Indiana Territory were eager to advance from territorial status to statehood. They kept badgering the federal government to take a census of the territory in hopes that Indiana could become a state. In 1807 the county sheriffs in Indiana Territory were instructed to take a census of free white male inhabitants twenty-one years of age and upward by June 1, 1807. Indiana Territory then was made up of Knox, Clark, and Dearborn counties in Indiana, and Randolph County in Illinois.[6]Sometimes the sheriff would list only the head of a household, omitting other males over the age of twenty-one, but generally he enumerated all of the males of the proper age, as instructed. Because the names are listed one after another, it is not always possible to tell whether a man was then the head of his own household or if he was still living in his father's household or with some other relative. Look for the number of other persons living in the household for a clue as to his marital status. If your ancestor was living in Indiana Territory, which then included Illinois, he should be listed on the 1807 Indiana Territorial census. The schedules for Clark County could not be found, so the original 1807 voters list was used in its place. The Kaskaskia poll list for Randolph County is also added to the 1807 census.[7]

Because each sheriff was paid the grand sum of three cents per name, which was really not bad pay for those days, he was careful to list each and every male adult living in his district. He not only contacted every family but he also kept careful records of the money owed to him. Knox County sheriff Parmenas Beckes was paid $32.40 for his services as Knox County census enumerator.[8] Because the purpose of the 1807 census was to determine whether there were enough male inhabitants to advance Indiana to statehood, and Indiana did not become a state until 1816, it is evident that there were not then enough inhabitants. The 1807 Indiana Territorial census is available in a book, *Census of Indiana Territory for 1807,* compiled by Rebah Fraustein and published in 1980 by the Indiana Historical Society. The book contains photocopied pages of this early Indiana census. There is no 1810 census enumeration for Indiana except for Randolph County, which was later in Illinois. A few years ago, the 1810 census schedules for Exeter and Harriston townships of Harrison County were found at Corydon and were reproduced in the June 1976 issue of *The Hoosier Genealogist,* an Indiana Historical Society publication.

The 1820 Census

Indiana, as the nineteenth state admitted to the Union (in 1816), was enumerated in the 1820 federal census. The format of the 1820 census was more or less the same as the two previous "head counts," which had named only the male or female head of household and had enumerated the broad categories of age groups. The male groupings were enlarged to include categories for men aged 16 to 18 and 18 to 26, which were the prime ages for military service. This was just a few years after the close of the War of 1812, and with Britain still considered a threat to America the enumeration of available manpower was deemed necessary. Number of all other free persons, including colored, and number of slaves, by age groups, were continued from the 1810 schedules. Added were foreigners not naturalized and the occupations of agriculture, commerce, and manufacturing. The 1820 census schedules for Indiana are complete except for Daviess and Dearborn counties, which are missing.[9] Because marriages were routinely being recorded at the courthouses of the existing Indiana counties by 1820, and other official records were also being kept, the censuses after 1820 are especially useful for locating persons and determining the makeup of families. The 1820 Indiana census schedules are available in a book, *1820 Federal Census for Indiana,* compiled by Willard Heiss and published by the Indiana Historical Society in 1966; it was reprinted in 1975 by the Society. Note that the Daviess county schedules are missing, and Delaware and Wabash were still the "New Purchase" counties.

The 1830 Census

It was not until 1830 that a uniform printed census form was used by all census takers to record census information. These forms, unlike earlier ones, were printed and provided by the federal government. They replaced the hodgepodge of different-sized paper and homemade forms previously used. The schedules were sometimes written in ledgers, account books, and journals and often had bindings made from old newspapers, wrapping paper, or wallpaper.[10] Even with the uniform census forms provided for them, each census taker still used his own method of filling out those forms. Some enumerators carefully recorded the name of the county and district on each page, while others wrote the name of the county only on the first and last pages. An occasional enumerator would use the initials of the person instead of the full name, and each enumerator could decide whether the surname led or followed the given name.

The schedules of the 1830 census follow the same general format as the earlier schedules, with the age groupings being made even more exact by 1830. Many more categories are found in the 1830 census schedules, but they still list only the name of the head of each household. Given are male and female age groupings: under 5 years of age; 5–10; 10–15; 15–20; 20–30; 30–40; 40–50; 50–60; 60–70; 70–80; 80–90; and 100 and over. Other categories included slaves; free colored persons; foreigners not naturalized. New categories were number of deaf and dumb, with white and colored persons given separate columns, and with whites separated into the age groups under 14, 14–24, and 25 and over; blacks were not separated by age groups; number of blind, separated by white and colored persons; and total number of persons in the household. The column for the number of insane or idiotic people in a household, given on the 1820 schedules, was removed from the 1830 forms. The enumerator did not always fill out the columns for those who were deaf, "dumb" (mute), or blind, even though such afflicted people might have been living in the household. Finding such a category for an ancestor's family can often be quite revealing. The *Index 1830 Federal Population Census for Indiana,* compiled under the supervision of Leona (Tobey) Alig of the Genealogy Division of the Indiana State Library, was published by the Family History Section of the Indiana Historical Society in 1981.

The 1840 Census

The 1840 census format was essentially the same as that for 1830, with the addition of the following listings: number of persons engaged in agriculture, commerce, manufacturing, mining and the trades, navigation of the ocean, and learned professions or engineering; names and ages of pensioners for Revolutionary War or other military service; and number of white males over twenty-one years of age "who cannot read or write." This last listing possibly indicates that the country was becoming more interested in cultivating the literacy of its inhabitants. At least, it was interested in counting those who could and could not read and write. The total number of persons living in a household was again taken in this 1840 census. Divided and listed separately are the insane and the idiotic. A notation of whether these persons were in private or public charge was also made. The index, *1840 Federal Population Census for Indiana,* was published by the Indiana Historical Society. The book is now out of print, but it is available on microfiche from that organization.

A book containing a list of 25,000 living Revolutionary War pensioners, with their ages and the names of heads of households with whom they were living in 1840 (unless heading own households) was compiled from the returns by marshals of the several judicial districts. *A Census of Pensioners for Revolutionary or Military Services, 1840, with Their Names, Ages, and Places of Residence . . . Under the Act for Taking the Sixth Census* was first published in 1841, reprinted in 1965 with the index as a companion volume, and reprinted in 1989 with the index included as part of the book. In Switzerland County, Indiana, Pleasant Township, we find Stephen Rogers, age 80, living with Henry Rogers, and Charles Seward, age 82, living with Charles Seward, presumably himself but possibly his son or another relative.[11]

THE 1850 CENSUS

The name of Lemuel Shattuck of Massachusetts should be forever immortalized, because he is the person who designed the format of the 1850 census schedules. These forms were greatly improved because they listed the name of each and every person in a household. Also given were the age, sex, color, occupation, and the value of real and personal property owned by the person; place of birth of each person (state, territory, or country); place of birth of each person's father and mother (state, territory, country). Also given was whether a person was married within the year previous to June 1; whether any person attended school prior to that date; whether a person over age twenty-one could not read and write; whether any person was "deaf and dumb, blind, insane, or idiotic"; and whether a person was a pauper or a convict. The words "deaf," "insane," and such were written out in the blank provided for this information.[12] The index to the 1850 census for Indiana has been published by Accelerated Indexing Systems.

THE 1860 CENSUS

Census forms used to enumerate the 1860 federal census were identical to those used in 1850 with the exception that both males and females over fifteen years of age were enumerated in the "profession, occupation or trade" category. This might indicate that the government was becoming more interested in younger workers. Industrial development was becoming much more important by 1860, and many factory and mill workers were aged fifteen and sometimes considerably younger. A droll entry was made by an enumerator in 1860 when he listed one male occupant of the Morgan County jail in this manner: "Residence: Jail; Occupation: Criminal." The 1860 federal census is notoriously difficult, if not impossible, to read. It is generally blurry and faded and leads one to think that the federal government supplied an inferior grade of ink to the enumerators. Only scattered counties have made copies of the 1860 census, and those are generally available from the particular county historical or genealogical society. Two separate indexes, one for the northern Indiana counties and one for the southern counties, was published in 1987 by Accelerated Indexing Systems.

The staff of the Indiana State Library also indexed the 1860 census for blacks, Indians, and Chinese. In 1981 Ruth M. Slevin compiled the *Report of Blacks and Mulattos as Enumerated in the 1860 Federal Population Census of Indiana.* Slevin also compiled seven pages of names for the *Index to Indians in 1860 Federal Population Census of Indiana.* These books are available in the Genealogy Division of the Indiana State Library in Indianapolis.

THE 1870 CENSUS

Fortunately for the genealogist, the people who designed the census forms added more and more categories over the years. The questions added to the 1870 census forms were these: whether a baby was born within the year prior to June 1, 1870, and, if so, its birth month; whether the person's mother or father was foreign-born; and whether a person was a male citizen of the United States over age twenty-one or "whose right to vote was denied or abridged on grounds other than rebellion (Civil War retribution) or other crime." Inability to read and to write were recorded in separate columns, perhaps because some individuals could read English but could not write it. Occupations were recorded for all persons regardless of age. The industrial revolution was in full swing by this time, and many young children were employed in the mills, factories, and mines. This may account for the recording of workers of all age brackets. As yet, the 1870 census for Indiana has not been indexed statewide, but several counties have indexed their own 1870 census schedules.

THE 1880 CENSUS

The enumeration schedules for 1880 continued all of the previous additions and categories and added many more. In addition, each of the categories for "deaf and dumb, blind, insane, and idiotic" was given a separate column on the forms. Added were relationship of each person to the head of the household, such as "wife," "son," "brother-in-law," or "boarder"; whether married, single, widowed, or divorced; the number of months each person was unemployed within the year prior to June 1, 1880. Also given were any sickness or disability; temporary disability when enumerator visited; and whether a person was maimed, crippled, or otherwise disabled.[13] One aged woman was listed as having "a broken arm" as her disability. The 1880 federal census is particularly valuable because of the many added categories and also because no 1890 census schedules are available for Indiana. The Soundex index for the Indiana 1880 census is described later in this chapter. Ruth M. Slevin compiled a partial index in *Index to Blacks, Indians, Chinese, Mulattoes in Indiana 1880 Census,* a 676-page typescript which is found in the Indiana State Library.

THE 1890 CENSUS

The 1890 census was taken by the government, but in 1921 a disastrous fire in the Commerce Department in Washington, D.C., destroyed most of the schedules. Only fragments of schedules for a few states remain from this valuable census, and none of the Indiana census schedules remain. This loss leaves an unfortunate gap of twenty years between the 1880 census and the extant 1900 census. Thus, no census information is available for the Indiana researcher for a period of twenty years. Where researchers had been using the censuses to verify names, ages, occupations, and other such information for their families, they must use other records in the place of the missing 1890 schedules. Births and deaths which occurred during this twenty-year period may not be accounted for. And, even though death records should have been kept in Indiana from 1882 onward, many of them were never recorded. Births were not recorded until after the turn of the century, in 1907, and those were also badly underrecorded.

The 1890 census would have been particularly valuable because it was the first one to use a separate schedule for each family enumerated. A family having ten members would fit on one schedule, and another complete schedule was used for additional children in larger families. Other valuable information was recorded on the Civil War Union Army Veterans' schedules, which were taken in conjunction with the 1890 census. These schedules from "A" through "Kansas" and part of "Kentucky" were lost in the same fire which destroyed the census schedules. Some of the Civil War veterans' schedules are still available, but none exist for Indiana. These veterans' schedules gave a great deal of information about the veteran or his widow which could be of genealogical value. If "your" Indiana veteran was then living in another state whose schedules survive, you may still be able to find information about him.[14]

THE 1900 CENSUS

The 1900 census was even more complete than the previous censuses. This census identified the name of the street, gave the house number, the dwelling number, and the family number for each family enumerated. Identification was made by a block of numbers found in the upper right-hand corner of the census page. These numbers are the Supervisory District Number, the Enumeration District Number, the sheet number, and the page number. When using this census, each of these numbers should be copied from the census page just as it is recorded. These numbers are used as an index number and are needed to find a family in this very large census. The name of the county and the page number are enough information to find a family in previous censuses but not in the 1900 census.

Information given on this census includes name of individual; relationship to head of family; color; sex; month of birth; year of birth; age; whether single, married, widowed, or divorced; number of years married; mother of how many children (if female); number of those children still living in 1900; place of birth; place of birth of person's father; place of birth of person's mother; year of immigration to the United States; naturalization information; occupation; number of months not employed during the year previous to June 1, 1900; whether attended school and how many months; whether can read; whether can write; whether can speak English; whether home is owned or rented; whether home is owned free or mortgaged; and whether home is a farm or a house.[15]

A great many facts and numerous clues can be gathered from the 1900 census, starting with the family's address and proceeding through the various categories. It is a veritable gold mine from which you can learn the month and year of birth of each person in the household. Sometimes the actual date can be found by searching through old newspapers from the time and place where the person reported being born. You can also learn the various occupations that an ancestor had worked at. You may be surprised to learn that Uncle Joe was a bartender and bouncer in 1900, when later he became a clergyman. And your grandad sold tombstones and insurance? Very interesting, when family legend said he was a school teacher all of his life. Did great-aunt Clemmie really become the first "typewriter" (typist) in the county? And her sister, Belle, was the only telephone operator? You may learn that your ancestors came from Russia in the 1870s even though their English-sounding name doesn't suggest Russian origins. The birthplaces of the children may also show that the family moved around a great deal. You may also learn that several of the children born to the couple had died by 1900. The 1900 census, although relatively recent by genealogical standards, is nonetheless a very valuable source for family research. It can often disprove family legends and can add greatly to your knowledge of the family. Don't pass up the 1900 census as being "too recent."

THE 1910 CENSUS

The 1910 census follows the same basic format as the 1900 census. Added are columns for Confederate or Union veterans and whether blind in both eyes or "deaf and dumb." Identification is made using a format similar (Superintendent's District, Enumeration District, sheet number, and page number) to that used in the 1900 census. A great deal of information recorded on this particular census can be helpful to the family researcher. Although you may believe that you know a lot about your family, there may still be some surprises. Aunt Grace may have been several years older than she admitted to being, and she may have been married more than the twice she claimed. Tillie may have had a child long after her husband died, too. And, once again, the occupations may be surprising to you.

Because so much information is recorded on the 1910 census schedules, try to find a microfilm printer to make copies of the census pages regarding your family. Not only will you save a great deal of time, but a photocopy will ensure that you have not miscopied an entry or an entire line of the census schedule. You can then photocopy the copy of the entire page for anyone who wants it. All of the data found on the 1910 census page may ultimately prove helpful in piecing together a history of your family.

THE 1920 CENSUS

The 1920 census is the most recent census to be released by the federal government. Any census less than seventy-five years old is considered confidential and is therefore closed to public scrutiny. This rule can be waived only for the purpose of proving one's age (for retirement or pension benefits, et cetera) or to prove one's parentage (not involving adoption). Every ten years a "new" census is released to the public, and for the next nine years the genealogical world waits.

The public no longer is allowed to see or handle the fragile original census schedules. The original census records have been microfilmed, however, and copies are made available for sale to libraries and individuals. Because a complete set costs many thousands of dollars, many city and county libraries can afford to buy only the films for their own county. Complete sets are found at the larger genealogical facilities in Indiana. The Genealogy Division of the Indiana State Library at Indianapolis and the Fort Wayne and Allen County Public Library at Fort Wayne have complete sets of all United States censuses.

THE VALUE OF THE LATER CENSUSES

The 1900 and 1910 censuses are valuable to the researcher because they give birth month and year of each person, suggest possible marriage and death dates for absent individuals, identify relationships of persons in the household, give ethnic origins, occupations, degree of education, economic standing, and possibly verify family traditions.

THE CENSUS INDEXES

Each of the Indiana censuses for the years 1807 through 1860 has been printed (1807 and 1820) or indexed (1830, 1840, 1850, and 1860). An index to a census is arranged alphabetically by surname and gives the name of the county, township or district, and the page number where an individual can be found on the actual census schedules. Census indexes are particularly useful because, even in the early censuses, finding a person can be difficult. Using a census index can save you a great deal of time and frustration. Most larger genealogical libraries have copies of the census indexes as well as microfilmed copies of the actual census schedules. Because indexes make searching in census microfilms faster and easier, always check to see whether one is available for the state or county you are researching. Many county groups have prepared indexes for their own censuses, and some have produced printed books of the complete census reports. These complete printed censuses with accompanying indexes can be very helpful, but they should always be compared with the microfilm of the actual census to verify information and to be sure no copying mistakes were made in the typescript copy. Photocopied pages of the census film are preferable to hand-copied and other transcribed copies of the censuses because you can read the census for yourself, watch for family surnames, and avoid making mistakes.

When using a census index always look for every conceivable way that a surname might have been spelled. Look, too, for the inconceivable ways. So often the enumerator wrote the name phonetically, and he may have been half-deaf or semiliterate, or an inventive speller. Spelling was not standardized until well after 1850, so that names, places, and occupations were often spelled purely at the whim of the census taker. In 1850 the same enumerator spelled the occupation "wagon-maker" six different ways in his Morgan County schedules. Imagine what he did to the more complicated occupations and to such names as Umbarger and Lincithicomb! In the 1820 Monroe County, Indiana, census the ancestors of Hoagy Carmichael are listed as "Comical" and "Kommickle," which was probably the way they pronounced it then. Some indexes, particularly the computer-generated ones, have formed some completely unbelievable surnames that never were and never could be—Mraton for Martin, Psaoc for Isaac, and so on. The computer programmers and data-entry people were obviously not familiar with the surnames prevalent in the county or they were careless typists. It generally takes someone familiar with the surnames common in a county to do a good job indexing a census record. The person should also be familiar with old-time handwriting and spelling and should watch for the many possible variations of a surname.

The Soundex Indexes

In 1930 the Federal Works Project began a plan to index the longer and more complex censuses, such as the 1880, the 1900, and the 1910 census schedules. These resulting indexes are known as the "Soundex Indexes," although they are more familiarly called the "WPA Indexes." In the Soundex system the indexing was given phonetic or "shorthand" coding to make it easier to use. This coding system groups all names which sound alike or which use the same letters (consonants, not vowels) in sequence in the surname. Each letter of the alphabet is given a number:

1 = b, p, f, v
2 = c, s, k, g, j, q, x, z
3 = d, t
4 = l
5 = m, n
6 = r

No code is assigned to the letters a, e, i, o, u, y, w, and h. Each surname thus coded is filed under the initial letter of the alphabet with which it starts, as in "D" for "Dean." In the name "Dean" the vowels "e" and "a" are not coded, and the "n" is given the number "5" from the code and is followed by two zeros (because there are no more consonants), thus forming the code number "D500" for the surname "Dean." The Soundex code for the name "Grant" is "G" plus the number 6 for "r," 5 for "n," and 3 for "t." Thus, the Soundex code for "Grant" is "G653." When requesting a Soundex film, first ask for the state by name and then give the Soundex code (first initial of surname and the three-number code) for the surname you want to find. Because many surnames have the same code as Grant's G653, you will have to wade through many other surnames with identical codes.[16]

Soundex information was first written onto index cards and then microfilmed, so the information you seek will appear on the screen as an index card. These G653 cards might be for Garnett, Gerrand, Grende, Grund, and so on.[17] The surnames are also not arranged in alphabetical order, but all of the various coded surnames which have the same given name are grouped together. Thus, all the Alberts will be given first, then all the Alphonses, and so on through the alphabetical listing of given names. By watching for the correct given name you may find your individual on the first pass through the microfilmed Soundex. If not, when you reach the end of the code number, go back through it again to make sure you did not miss it on the first time through. You can easily be fooled into thinking the name is not there or that it should be in a more logical place than where you finally find it. It may also be that the person you seek was not then living in Indiana or was missed by the enumerator or by the person who made the index.

The 1880 Soundex is not a complete index because it covers only those families or households having children ten years of age or younger. If a child in the household was not the son or daughter of the head of the family, that child was given another separate card in addition to the card for the family, even when the surnames were identical. While not as exact and as detailed as the complete microfilmed census records, the Soundex cards will contain names, ages, relationships, birth month and year, birthplace, and citizenship. Be sure to follow the Soundex search with a thorough search of the actual census page because even more complete information about all of the individuals in a household will be found there. Each library having Soundex microfilms also has a sheet of detailed instructions on how to use the system. If you are unsure about any step, ask a librarian for help. Some cards for the letter "O" were omitted from the 1880 Soundex. A book entitled *The 1880 Illinois Census Index: Soundex Code O-200 to O-240, the Code That Was Not Filmed,* has been published by Nancy Gubb Franklin.

Names and pertinent information about the people counted in the 1900, the 1920, and part of the 1910 census schedules were also copied onto index cards by the Works Progress Administration in the 1930s. The Soundex coding is identical. It is almost mandatory to use the Soundex when searching in even a very small town in the later censuses. The small amount of time spent in finding the correct Soundex card on microfilm will actually save you countless hours of searching in the census. Once you find the correct Soundex card for your family, be sure to copy everything that is written on the card. Note, especially, the four descriptive numbers given in the upper right-hand corner of the card, because these are vital to finding your family quickly in the actual census records.

The Miracode Index

The 1910 census index is called a Miracode index. This index uses the Soundex codes but lists the visitation number instead of the page and line number used for the 1900 and 1920 indexes. The Miracode uses a separate index card for each family or household and gives the volume number and enumeration district number. Another index card follows for each person who is not a member of the immediate family with whom he or she resided or whose surname is different from that of the head of the family. Both the Miracode and the Soundex systems give the surname, given name, state and county of residence, city, race, age, and place of birth. Only twenty-one states are covered by the Miracode index: Alabama, Arkansas, California, Florida, Georgia, Illinois, Kansas, Kentucky, Louisiana, Michigan, Mississippi, Missouri, North Carolina, Ohio, Oklahoma, Pennsylvania, South Carolina, Tennessee, Texas, Virginia, and West Virginia.[18]

Problems with Using the Indexes

The census indexes are an excellent finding tool, generally saving lots of research time. They also have a number of pitfalls. In addition to problems previously mentioned in this chapter there are others you need to know about. One such problem concerns page numbering. In order to find your ancestors you need the right page number, but there are sometimes two or even three separate sets of numbers on a census page. There are the printed page number made by the book manufacturer and one or two sets of handwritten numbers made by the enumerator. It is hard to determine which of the page numbers the indexer used when compiling the census index. Is it the printed number or one of the handwritten ones? Try the printed number first, and if your ancestor isn't on that page, go to the first written number. If neither of these numbers locates your ancestor, go to the second written number.

You may search for hours for the "right" number on the census page. Must you divide the number in half to find the correct page, as you do when using one index for the Dearborn County, Indiana, 1850 census? Should you suspect that the indexer transposed the first number with the second one? Or with the one above or below it? Sometimes none of these numbers proves to be the one which will lead you to your ancestor. Actually, the name, page number, county, and township listed so confidently in the census index may not even exist. The indexer may have copied the information incorrectly or the typist or the computer programmer may have transposed the names and numbers during compilation. Names are often misread, misinterpreted, or miscopied, especially the surnames. When a surname seems to have a strange combination of letters, it is probably a typographical error, not a new surname.[19]

Computerized indexes are also wonderful. They, too, can save the researcher much time and energy, but they can also present problems. The indexes compiled "by computer" (implying no humans involved?) have been known to "lose" whole districts because of a power blip or operator error. An entire county was lost from the 1800 Pennsylvania census index. This index was withdrawn from publication and corrected, but similar, smaller errors in other census indexes may not have been found and corrected. Names listed in computerized indexes may be wildly incorrect because the copier or programmer was not familiar with the surnames common in the area or because he or she was not a proficient programmer. The earlier computerized indexes, such as the Pennsylvania 1850 census index, are full of errors and omissions. Those made more recently, however, seem to be more complete and correct.

Sometimes you won't find your ancestors listed in a census or in the index at all, even though you are fairly sure they were there when it was taken. It is always possible that the family was away on a visit and was missed by the enumerator, but some people deliberately refused to answer the door. New immigrants, in particular, tended to be fearful of census takers and pretended to be out when they called. In the "old country" the census takers seemed to bring about higher taxes, conscription for military service, or some other undesirable result. Even if the immigrants came to the door, their broken English might have been hard for the enumerators to understand. The immigrant's surname, recorded phonetically, often bears little resemblance to the person's actual surname. Thus, Martin Carl, American-born but with a heavy Pennsylvania German accent, was listed as "Caarroll" on the 1880 census of Huntington County,

Indiana. Many German names were incorrectly recorded—Tetrow as Deterow, Streich as Strike, and so on. Given names can be recorded in a manner so different from the real name that they completely mystify the researcher.

THE MORTALITY SCHEDULES

Mortality schedules were taken in conjunction with the population schedules in the censuses of 1850, 1860, 1870, and 1880. The mortality schedules recorded deaths that had occurred during the twelve months prior to the taking of the census, for instance, between June 1, 1849, and up to and including May 31, 1850. The census enumerators began to take each census on June 1 of the particular census year and were to end it on May 31, although some enumerators stopped on May 30. A mortality schedule was also taken prior to the 1885 state censuses. Because the mortality listings were made before the recording of vital statistics in most states, they can be very helpful. They are a valuable source even though the deaths recorded on the schedules are for only one year out of the ten years between censuses. Assuming that they were not so underreported as is sometimes suspected (about 13 percent), the mortality schedules can be especially useful if an ancestor died during the short period covered by the report.

Information found on the mortality schedules includes the name of the deceased, sex, age, color (white, black, mulatto; Chinese and Indian, on the 1870 only); whether free or slave; whether married or widowed; place of birth (state, territory or country); month in which death occurred; profession, occupation, or trade; disease or cause of death; and number of days ill. The birthplace of parents was added to the 1870 schedules. In 1880 the place where the fatal disease was contracted and how long the person was a citizen or resident of the area, including fraction of months less than one year, were included.[20]

Although the original mortality schedules were offered to the states some time ago, not all states accepted them. Thus, the schedules are scattered among some state archives and the National Archives, and many are in the library of the National Society, Daughters of the American Revolution (D.A.R.) in Washington, D.C. However, Indiana accepted its mortality schedules, and these are housed in the Genealogy Department of the Indiana State Library in Indianapolis. Originals and typescript copies for Jefferson County, Indiana, are also found at the D.A.R. Library in the nation's capital. The 1850 Indiana mortality schedules were transcribed and indexed in 1971 by Lowell M. Volkel in a three-volume set, *The 1850 Indiana Mortality Schedules,* which can be used at the Indiana State Library. A complete surname index to all mortality schedules was made by the Indiana State Library staff. *The Index to Indiana Mortality Schedules for Indiana, 1850, 1860, 1870, 1880* consists of eight volumes, and the microfilm copy of the schedules and the index are available for use in the Genealogy Division of the State Library.[21]

The Value of Mortality Schedules

If your Indiana ancestor died in the year preceding the taking of the census, the mortality schedules can be used to learn date, place, and cause of death (valuable when doing a genetic profile), to document ethnic background for those having Indian, Chinese, or black ancestry, and to obtain other useful genealogical information. Tracing genetic diseases and documenting ethnic ancestry are possible when using information found in the mortality schedules. The schedules may also suggest other avenues of research to use in order to learn more about your ancestor. These might be obituaries, mortuary records, gravestones or cemetery records, and the probate records—wills, administrations, and possibly guardianships—if young children were orphaned by the death. You may also be able to note migration dates and places by using data from the mortality schedules. You can then turn to the censuses themselves to verify information found in the mortality schedules.

VETERANS' INFORMATION IN THE CENSUSES

You may never think to look at or record the data found on the *second* page of the 1840 population schedules, but, if you had an ancestor who was a pensioned Revolutionary War veteran and who was still living in 1840, you should. Revolutionary War pensioners were recorded on the second, or right-hand, page of this census, as were slaves. Check this second page on the same line where the number of persons in a household and the number of persons engaged in various occupations were recorded. You may not find your pensioner listed under his own name on this census because he was probably very old by 1840. Some pensioners were living alone, but others lived with a married daughter or son and were recorded under the name of the daughter's husband or the name of a son.[22]

The 1890 census also surveyed veterans of the previous wars, and the information found in that census can be valuable. The veterans' schedules can be used to verify military service, to locate burial places unknown to you, and to document the surnames of married daughters or grandchildren with whom the veteran was then living. In the 1890 veterans' schedules, the specific unit in which the veteran served is given. Like the 1890 census schedules, the veterans' schedules were also destroyed in the disastrous Commerce Department fire. Only a part of the 1890 veterans' schedules remain, and for only some states. Missing are the schedules for states beginning with the letter "A" through "Kentucky," which means none exist for Indiana. Thus, only those researchers having Revolutionary War veterans who lived in Indiana in 1840 will be able to benefit from the veterans' schedules in the 1840 census.

OTHER SCHEDULES

The population and mortality schedules were not the only enumerations taken by the federal government. Other schedules which can be useful are the agriculture schedules, 1840–1910, and the manufacturing schedules for the same dates. None exist for the years 1890 through 1910 because of the Commerce Department fire, and, unfortunately for Indiana researchers, neither of these schedules exists for Indiana.[23]

INDIAN CENSUS RECORDS

Another census taken by the federal government and the Bureau of Indian Affairs was for Indians who were living in Indiana in 1854. This census was taken of only the members of the Miami tribe who were then living on the Miami Indian Reservation in northern Indiana. The Miami Indian census is in the custody of the Bureau of Indian Affairs, Record Group 75, in the National Archives. It is also printed in the government publication "Preliminary Inventory, #163, Records of the Bureau of Indian Affairs," which is available from the United States Government Printing Office.

The federal censuses of 1860 and 1870 noted Indians only if they were living in non-Indian households. Members of tribes who were living in unsettled territories were not enumerated. In 1880 a special enumeration was taken of Indians who were living near military reservations in California and in Dakota and Washington territories. The four-volume *1880 Census of Indians, Not-Taxed* is in NARS Record Group 29, in the National Archives. If you have Indian ancestors who left Indiana before this period, you may be able to find them in this special census or in the 1885 enumeration taken for Colorado, Dakota Territory, Florida, Nebraska, and New Mexico Territory.

PROBLEMS WITH USING THE CENSUSES

The federal censuses are only as good, only as accurate, and only as reliable as the person who recorded the information and the person who gave the information. Censuses are valuable only if the information is correct and if it is legible. If the information was wrong or was recorded incorrectly, or if you can't read it, the census is not so valuable and may possibly be worthless. Another problem, involving the peculiarities of the enumerators' systems of recording information, was the way they entered names. Some census takers recorded only the initials instead of the entire given name and middle initial, causing untold problems for genealogists who need to know those missing names. Nicknames were often recorded instead of the given names, and those nicknames often bear no resemblance to the actual names which are now unknown to descendants. Was Aunt Lyda really named Eliza? Was Uncle Will named William or Wilhelm or Willard? Some people never ever went by their given names, and it may take some additional research to determine whether these people are who you think they are.

Some census takers also omitted the "touchy" categories, such as lack of education and being insane or idiotic, blind, or deaf and mute. Other enumerators omitted the place of birth, the value of real estate, occupations, and other nonsensitive categories merely to save time or ink. If the family was not at home when he called, the enumerator might have "guessed" at the names and ages of family members instead of returning to get the right answers. This laxity might account for the garbled names and ages sometimes found on a census record. Also, the enumerator might have asked a small child or forgetful elderly person for information about the family. When the ages of family members are so far removed from reality as to be unbelievable, you might suspect that the neighbors gave the information.

The enumerator might even have skipped the family or the entire neighborhood if he missed the road as he enumerated, which sometimes happened. "Padding" of census figures and inhabitants also occurred at times, and it is possible to find "your" family listed twice in some censuses, although not necessarily in Indiana. Repetition of the same names further on in the enumeration (with different ages, birth states, and other information) might have been an effort to increase the number of inhabitants for tax purposes or for some other reason. This "padding" does not seem evident in the Indiana territorial census of 1807, but it is possible that it might have happened at other times and for a variety of reasons. Where tax increases were feared, the population might have been underreported to keep per capita tax lower. Is this what happened when people on one road were omitted from one county's schedules in 1860? Or was the enumerator just lazy that day?

Some age discrepancies can't be blamed entirely on the census taker, however. When you notice that an entire family aged by the normal ten years on each census but that the mother, or some other family member, grew progressively younger each time, don't blame the enumerator. If, after several such censuses, the mother appeared to be not much older than her eldest child, you must blame vanity, not the enumerator. Of course, this also happened among the male population, especially when a man had married a much younger woman or wanted to seem younger than he really was. Many wives actually did not know how old their husbands were and merely guessed when they reported their ages to the census taker. An unmarried daughter might also have been reported younger to increase her marriage chances, especially if the enumerator was single or had marriageable sons.

The later censuses, which give the birthplaces of individuals, are extremely valuable for pinpointing the place of origin of an individual and his or her parents. It is wise to use this information as a clue instead of the absolute truth, because birthplaces given for parents can vary from one census to the next. Frequently, each child would give a different birthplace for his or her parents, and sometimes this birthplace changed on each succeeding census. Sometimes even the individual did not know his or her own birthplace or the birthplaces of his or her parents. And, since it was generally the wife who answered the census taker's questions, the information she gave about her husband might have been pure speculation. If she had heard that the family once lived in a certain place she might have concluded that they were born there and given that place. "Unknown" given for a person's birthplace doesn't always mean that the person didn't know where he or she was born. This could have been the case, but generally it meant that the person giving the information (the informant) simply didn't know the answer to the question. The informant might have been a neighbor, a friend of the family, a visiting relative, or even a small child playing in the yard. This may also explain why the birthplaces, ages, and other information about an individual may vary radically from one census to the next.

Until the 1930s the actual census volumes were available to the public at the National Archives in Washington, D.C. But frequent handling and age caused the pages to begin to deteriorate, and it became necessary to try to preserve them in some way. It was decided that the census pages should be microfilmed and the microfilmed reels be made available to the public instead of the originals. This made the censuses accessible to many more people and in other parts of the nation besides Washington. Unfortunately, the quality of the microfilm varies—from excellent to awful—depending on the ability of the photographer and the condition of the actual census pages.

Some schedules cannot be read because the microfilm is too blurry or because the original pages are badly deteriorated. Some suffer because the photographer's thumb was photographed over some vital piece of information. An entire page was occasionally missed during the microfilming, and it might have been "your" family whose page was missed. For example, nine pages of the 1820 Virginia census schedules were missed when it was originally microfilmed. Fortunately, those missing pages have since been restored to later microfilm copies. Legibility is another big problem. The ink supplied to the enumerators by the federal government must have been really inferior because so many censuses, especially the 1860, are next to impossible to read. It often looks as if a blunt pencil were used instead of pen and ink. Having to guess at the contents of a census record isn't a good practice, and guessing provides highly questionable results. Try to find another copy of the microfilm to see whether it is clearer and the writing more legible.

THE VALUE OF THE CENSUS RECORDS

The census records are one of the most important genealogical sources, second in importance only to the vital records. The censuses are especially valuable because they generally precede the vital records in most places. You can use the early censuses to place a person in a specific place at a particular time, to learn the approximate makeup of his household and the approximate ages of his wife and children, and to follow the family's migrations across the land. Use the censuses after 1850 to learn the names, ages, birthplaces, occupations, education (or lack of it), economic worth, and other specifics about the family. Remembering the pitfalls and possibilities for errors in the census records, use them to find facts and clues, and to direct you to other possible sources to research. The censuses are one of your best sources for genealogical information. If you get "hooked" on one particular type of resource it will probably be the censuses. They are more fun and more informative than most other records, and if your eyes can stand the microfilm very long you may use them more than any other record.

STATE CENSUSES

The first Indiana State Constitution in 1816 ordered that a state census be taken of all white male inhabitants over the age of 21 beginning in 1820 and every five years thereafter for the purpose of apportionment. Surviving records, compiled as *Enumeration of Persons Over 21 Years for the Year 1820,* are for the Indiana counties of Crawford, Gibson, Jackson, Jennings, Knox, Monroe, Orange, Perry, Posey, Ripley, Vanderburgh, Washington, and Wayne. The records are in the Indiana State Archives in Indianapolis.[24]

In 1850 the interval between state censuses was extended to every six years and the township assessors were made responsible for the enumerations. Each assessor was to submit a copy to the Auditor of the State, who was to abstract and publish the lists in two Indianapolis newspapers. The Auditor's records have never been located and are presumed missing or destroyed. An Act in 1865 ordered the township assessors to obtain the specific age for every male over 21, and in 1877 an act added blacks to the list. Reports were to be filed with the county auditor in each Indiana county, and if any of these schedules exist, they will be found with the county auditors. Very few of these schedules are housed in the State Archives.[25]

Indiana County Histories and Other Sources

CHAPTER

10

There are many resources in the county which can be extremely helpful in your genealogical research. Among these are the county histories, county atlases, county and city directories, county and city telephone directories, Geological Survey maps and other older county maps, older newspapers which contain obituaries, notices of births, marriages, and deaths, newspaper query columns, and holdings of the various county libraries.

COUNTY HISTORIES

You can often find good genealogical and historical information in the old Indiana county histories. County histories began to be very popular in Indiana during the 1876 celebration of the Centennial of the United States. Representatives of publishing companies toured the state drumming up interest in writing and publishing county histories. The company agent would first approach the man considered the most educated in each county and would encourage him to write or to supervise the writing of the county history. Generally, that man wrote the body of the book but he sometimes may have "farmed out" parts of it to others. It probably took several years to write and compile the entire county history. Because of the big push for county histories after the Centennial, most Indiana histories date from the 1880s.

Each county history generally contains a brief history of the state and of the county, a description of the county's topography, and histories of the several townships in the county. The first buyers of land in each township are nearly always listed, along with the section or sections of land they purchased. Many county histories also contain accounts of the various military engagements and the military groups in which county men had served. The histories often have lists of county officials, officers of fair boards, members of churches, school boards, early tax lists, and those often-sought biographies of the county's leading citizens.

The lists of military men range from a few members of the earliest militia companies to the many men who served in the various Indiana units during the Civil War. Lists of the men (and their ranks) who enlisted and served in the various companies are often included in the county history, and sometimes lists of the men who died in battle, where they died, and from what causes. Some county histories also contain lists of Civil War pensioners or their widows and the amount of compensation they received for wounds incurred in the "War of the Rebellion." These lists can help you to learn the name of the unit and the rank attained by your ancestor who served in the Civil War, where he died if he died during the war, the approximate date of death, and possibly the wounds he suffered.

Biographies of the leading citizens were solicited by the county history chairman or his committee. Because the inclusion of a biography in the county history cost the individual somewhere between twenty-five and fifty dollars, the biographies will be chiefly for the affluent people of the county. The biographer (or autobiographer) usually received a "free" copy of the volume, for which he had paid to have his biography printed, and if he submitted several biographies (for sons, for instance), he might have received several "free" copies. Even though your ancestors may not have been wealthy and not included in the biographical section, you may still find mention of them elsewhere in the history. An ancestor who was less rich and influential might still be listed as the spouse, parent, business partner, or relative in another person's biographical sketch. The biographies may or may not contain factual accounts of the individual's life. Many a self-made man invented or embellished his "illustrious parentage" and ancestry, gave himself a grand education, and exaggerated his personal accomplishments and current wealth in the biographical sketch. Hence the name "mug book," which is given to the county history, implying that the biographies contain puffed-up, self-aggrandizing biographies of people who could afford to buy space in the history. The biographies can be very helpful, however, so use them whenever you find them, always checking the information against other contemporary sources to verify it.

The lists of public officials, members of churches and organizations, and taxpayers found in the county histories are valuable because they help to locate individuals in the county at a certain time. The history can also suggest other sources and resources to search in for information about your ancestors. If your ancestor was a first purchaser of land in the county you can learn when and where he first settled there. You may find him listed first in one township, and then later in another one at a later date. This tells you in which township to search and the approximate years in which to search tax records, federal censuses, and other pertinent records. If the man was a large landowner, you can sometimes learn how much tax he paid from lists of taxpayers. You can then search in the county tax records, the deeds, wills, and other such records for further data regarding him.

The original county histories were indexed only by broad subjects, and only the names of people who had submitted biographical sketches were printed in the surname index. The names of persons who appeared on the various lists or in the body of the history were not given in the index. In recent years the old county histories have been indexed, and the indexes list the names of everyone mentioned in the histories. These every-name indexes are extremely helpful for locating every place where an individual's name appears. Using the index will save you a great deal of research time, so always check to see if the original volume has a separate index. Or, if the book is a reprinted copy of the original, check to see if the index is included in the body of the reprinted volume. Oddly, the index can be found in the front, the center, or the back of the volume. There might also be two indexes, the original one and a new, every-name index. Some larger counties printed two-volume histories and each may have a separate index, or the combined index may be in the second volume. Search for an index before you start a page-by-page scan of the book because the index may be hidden in an unexpected place.

Some Indiana counties have never compiled a county history, and others have published several over the years. Monroe County, Indiana, has had three county histories—the original 1884 volume, an "up date" history in 1914, and the "new" 1987 county history. Each subsequent history is slightly different from the one before and contains more information, and the names are generally those of different people. The public library in each Indiana county should have copies of the histories of their own particular county, and many libraries have a complete, or nearly complete, collection of the existing Indiana county histories. Two books which list all of the county histories that have been published for every county in the United States can be found in most larger genealogical libraries. One is *A Bibliography of American County Histories,* compiled by P. William Filby and published in 1985 by the Genealogical Publishing Company. It is a state-by-state listing of all county histories, with title, author, place and date of publication, details of editions, reprints, and indexes for 5,000 county histories published to date. The other book is *Consolidated Bibliography of County Histories in Fifty States,* compiled by Clarence S. Peterson, published in 1961 and reprinted in 1980, which lists about 4,000 county histories, with author, title, and place and date of publication.

Many county histories have a contemporary map of the county as it was arranged when the history was published. Such maps can be very helpful to the genealogist and family researcher because they show the existing roads, churches, schools, villages, and towns of the period. By studying the old map, you can often determine where other relatives lived in relation to your ancestor.

You may even see how your ancestors might have met and courted their future spouses long ago, if their fathers' farms were on adjoining land. You may be able to see how they entered the county from their former homes and how they might have left to move elsewhere. If they lived in a village which no longer exists, you can often locate it on the old map and then find it on a modern map.

The older county histories contain few, if any, photographs. Instead, line drawings or etchings of houses, farms, churches, and other buildings were used. However, in the newer histories you will find a few photographs of the distinguished citizens of the county along with their biographies. These photos are often stiff and unnatural-looking, but the likenesses may be the only ones you will be able to find of these people. If you find a photo of your ancestor or one of his or her relatives, you will certainly want to get a photographic or xerographic copy of it for your records. Unfortunately, some libraries do not allow xerox copies to be made of the old and fragile county histories. If you meet this obstacle, look for a reprint copy of the same history to xerox. This is a wise move anyway because the reprint copy will generally be sharper and cleaner-looking than the older copy of the history.

The Value of Using County Histories

County histories are valuable chiefly because of the many persons mentioned in them. You can learn occupations, ethnic, regional, and genealogical backgrounds, military information, church affiliations, and all sorts of miscellaneous information from a county history printed when and where your ancestor once lived.

Problems with Using County Histories

Some counties never wrote histories, and others put forth minimal effort to produce only slim booklets. Only the wealthy and influential citizens will be found in the biographical sections, and the information found there may not be entirely factual in every case. The county histories are indexed only by broad classifications, and only those persons who have biographies will appear in the surname index. Thus, it can be time consuming to locate an individual in an unindexed volume.

COUNTY ATLASES

If you don't find your ancestors mentioned in the county history, you may still be able to locate their farms or homes in a county atlas. Atlases were put out periodically by an atlas publishing company for interested counties. Contents vary even in atlases which were published by the same company in the same year, but most county atlases contain a map of the entire county; maps of the various townships, marked with the names of the owners of particular pieces of land; locations of churches, schools, and settlements; and topographical features. Some county atlases contain alphabetical lists of the landowners in each township and the businesses found there. The name of the owner of a piece of land may be printed on that particular piece of land shown on the township map. Owners of very small parcels of land do not appear, nor do owners of town lots, which were even smaller. If your research is in a town or city, look for a city atlas for that place. Generally, only the larger cities had city atlases.

In 1968 the Indiana Historical Society reprinted *Maps of Indiana Counties in 1876.* This state atlas contains a map for each of the 92 Indiana counties, many of which have the names of the larger landowners printed on the parcels of land they owned as shown on the map. This atlas is available from the Society and is a useful addition to the library of anyone who needs to research in several Indiana counties.

Atlases of the towns or cities are similar to the county and state atlases, with owners of plats of land identified. Unfortunately, town atlases are not common in Indiana. It is often possible to locate the place where your ancestor lived in an Indiana city or town by consulting the directories of the time.

DIRECTORIES

City Directories

Only the larger Indiana cities and towns had city directories in the mid- to late nineteenth century, and it was not until about 1900 that the medium-sized towns had directories of their inhabitants. At that time, a section in the back of the volume sometimes listed residents of the county. It gave only the address, the amount of land owned by the individual, and, often, the tax evaluation.

The city directory contained an alphabetical listing of the names of heads of households in the city, the address of each person's residence, and each person's occupation and place of employment. If the resident was a married man, the name of his wife was printed in parentheses after his name. A letter notation suggested whether the person lived in a residence (r), was a boarder (b), was a domestic servant (dom), was a student (stu), and so forth. Advertisements completely circled the double pages and also crossed the centers in a one-inch horizontal band. No space was wasted because those advertisements helped to pay for publication costs, and the businesses who used the ads expected to gain increased business from them. Even though the ads helped to pay for the cost of the directory, the purchase of a city directory was then, as it is today, a fairly hefty investment. A list of all of the advertisers and the pages on which particular ads appeared was often the first section of the directory. Thus, if you want to know when an ancestor's business was operating in the town or when it was located at a certain address, you can check the city directories to learn the time period.

City officers, councilmen, committees, and members of the fire and police departments were often listed in the next section, along with members of the board of education and the school supervisors. Next followed the name and location of each school in the city. Also found in the directory were the names of the county officers, county commissioners, jury commissioners, and the county council; township trustees; county board of education; the judge, clerk, prosecuting attorney, and sheriff of the courts; the justices of the peace for the various townships; and the township constables. If your ancestor was serving on one of the boards or was an official at the time the directory was published, you will find his name listed there. Even if you don't know whether he served on a city or county board, look for him. He may have been quite active in some capacity and will be listed.

Each church of the town was listed under the appropriate religious denomination. Given for each church was the name, address, and location (northeast corner, east side of the street, and so forth), name of the pastor, hours of services, hours of Sunday school services, and the day and time of prayer meetings. Missions were also listed in this same section, with the address of the mission, the name of the mission pastor, and the times of Sunday services given. Christian associations (YMCA, YWCA), their addresses, and the names of the secretaries were listed. If the town had a hospital, the address and location was given, as well as the name of the director or superintendent and, often, that of "the nurse." Orphan asylums and the county poor farm were similarly identified. You might be able to find mention of your ancestor who was a minister of the gospel, the director of a hospital or asylum, or some other official, by checking the appropriate listing in an old city directory. You may be surprised at how active your ancestor was in city affairs when you search in these listings. Many of our ancestors were "joiners" as well as "movers and shakers."

Then, generally, would follow a list of all of the city's lodges, such as the Benevolent and Protective Order of Elks (B.P.O.E.), Eastern Star, I.O.O.F. (Odd Fellows), Daughters of Rebecca, G.U.O. of O.F., colored (or the black Odd Fellows), Knights of Pythias, Pythian Sisters, Grand Army of the Republic (G.A.R.), Red Men, Degree of Pocahontas, Haymakers, Fraternal Order of Eagles, American Legion (after 1920), Modern Woodmen of America, Woodmen of the World, Tribe of Ben-Hur, Knights of Columbus, and a great many other similar organizations of a patriotic, military, political, occupational, or philanthropic nature. Unfortunately, members of the organizations are not listed, but area newspapers should have published frequent items about the various lodges and their members. Such newspaper items, as well as listings in the contemporary county histories, can be used to augment information contained in the city directories.

Also listed in this informative section of the city directory are the town's cemeteries, with addresses and the names of their superintendents; its libraries, with addresses and name of "the librarian" of each; the city's banks, with addresses, capital, surplus, and names of bank officers, cashiers, assistant cashiers, and bank directors; local building and loan associations, along with similar information about officers. Next were printed the names and addresses of the principal clubs of the town, with the name of the director or the names of club officers, when applicable. Labor unions were listed in alphabetical order, with meeting nights and meeting place given for each union. Musical organizations, mostly city bands, were listed with the place where each group met and the names of the directors.

Places of amusement (theaters, parks, and baseball parks) and public halls and buildings were similarly listed along with their addresses, and if the town boasted a college or university, the names and addresses of the fraternities and sororities were given. Some club meeting places were listed twice, once with the name of the club and again with the name of the building, so that a sort of cross-index exists to help you locate a family-owned building. You can also determine when your ancestor's college fraternity or sorority was on a particular campus or when it may have moved from one address to another.

The Value of Using City Directories

The possibilities for using the city directories are almost limitless. Directories serve as a wonderful finding tool for people, places, businesses, and occupations. Directories can be used as an index to the later, larger federal censuses, because you can find the exact address, and sometimes even the ward, where your ancestor once lived. You then know exactly where to search for him or her in the actual census. The exact address can also be useful when obtaining an ancestor's military records, for locating a property deed record, and for determining approximate dates for marriages, deaths, divorces, and other events before you search in the vital records. If city directories exist for your place of interest, try to find and use them.

Sometimes the directory for a larger city contained a map of the city, which can facilitate locating your ancestor's home and place of business. But, even without a map, you can still locate the spot where your ancestor lived. The directory generally contained a section, arranged by streets, alleyways, and house numbers, with the names of householders or businesses, and the location of the particular house or business on a certain city block. All you need do is locate the ancestor's address in the directory proper and then find the location in this street and cross-street section. This is a wonderful finding tool, because it gives the intersections of streets (Adams North, Kirkwood Av. intersects), shows who lived next to or near whom, what businesses were in a particular block, which houses or businesses were then vacant, gives the side of the street (East Side Only, or South Side), and so on. You can proceed from one end of the town to the other, crossing various streets and noting landmarks and other signposts which can tell you the nature of the neighborhood, the exclusiveness of the area, when your ancestors moved, and when businesses changed addresses.

Following the residential section was a commercial directory which contained a classified list of all the professions, manufacturers, trades, and pursuits in the city. Each classification was alphabetically arranged, giving the name, address, and the location of the business' advertisement in the body of the directory. This is the section to search in when you want to learn when your ancestor owned a certain business in the town and to see who his competitors were at the time.

The final section of the city directory was a listing of the rural residents (titled R.F.D. or Rural Free Delivery) of the county. Here were listed the names, alphabetically arranged, the rural route numbers or name of the township, valuation of the person's property, and the number of acres he or she owned. This section can be helpful for finding your ancestor who lived in the county, not in the town. The name of the householder's wife, if any, is given in parentheses and can be a help in determining whether or not the person is your ancestor. You can travel through the city directories, year by year, and may be able to determine approximately when your ancestors married, were widowed or divorced, remarried, moved their residences or businesses, sold the farm, or died. If the name of a man's wife changes from one directory to the next, his first wife may have died (check the death notices, obituaries, and cemetery lists) and he remarried (check the marriage records for the years between directories). When an ancestor's name disappears from the directory, check for the sale of land (deed records), for notice of death (in the county death indexes and the cemetery lists), or scan the newspaper for an item noting the person's removal from the city or county, (he or she had gone to live with a son or daughter).

Except in the larger Indiana cities, city directories were usually not printed every year. Directories were generally printed only every two or three years, so that the listings of residents, officials, businesses, et cetera, may be correct for only a part of the period covered. Thus, they are not a good indication of exactly when a person lived at a certain address, when he acquired a wife, when he took a certain job, or even when he died and his widow was living alone in the household. However, the directory can give many excellent clues and many concrete facts that can be extremely useful in researching your family history.

County Directories

County directories, similar to city directories, show the names of landowners, their addresses, sometimes names of other members of a family, amount of land owned, property value, and other such data. In a largely rural county, there may be only county directories instead of city directories until well into the twentieth century. Currently published county directories might lead you to other descendants of your ancestors who are still living in the area, perhaps even on the old family farm.

Telephone Directories

After Alexander Graham Bell invented the telephone in 1876 there were for a time only three telephones in existence. Telephones were a rarity in most Indiana towns and cities until well into the twentieth century. In 1900 there were only 1,356 telephones anywhere, and in 1920 there were only 13,329, a total which breaks down to 23 telephones per 1,000 people.

Telephone directories did not exist for most Indiana cities until about 1920 or even later. Generally, the telephone operator, called "Central," knew everyone who had a telephone and knew each person's telephone number and "ring" (two longs and one short, for instance). Because the few people who had telephones also knew almost everyone else's phone number in the early days, at first, no directory of telephone users was needed. As more and more people got telephones, telephone directories became a convenience and then a necessity.

Just as the designs of the early automobiles were based on horsedrawn buggies, the first telephone directories were patterned after the existing city and county directories. Telephone directories were alphabetical in arrangement and gave the name of the individual and the telephone number. A few early directories contained addresses, but addresses were usually included only in the directories of larger cities. Some telephone directories might have contained maps of the city or cities covered by the particular directory, but this was not too common until more recently.

The Value of Telephone Directories

The old telephone directories are chiefly useful for locating individuals in a town or city in a particular year. Because only the more affluent people had telephones in the early days, you can often distinguish between two or more persons of the same name by noting which one had a telephone. Telephone directories are not nearly so useful as city directories in genealogical research, but use them when no other finding source exists.

Problems with Using Telephone Directories

Finding copies of the old telephone books is not always easy. Even the current telephone company may not have copies of the old directories because the original company no longer exists, and the current company may not even have copies of its fairly recent telephone books. Phone books, like catalogs—"wish books"—aren't kept very long. Because their use is temporary, directories are often discarded after the new one arrives. Look for telephone directories at the county library, in the historical and genealogical society libraries, or in the Genealogy Division of the Indiana State Library in Indianapolis.

Other Types of Directories

Other kinds of directories might help you find information about your ancestors, especially for the years before about 1920. These are the professional directories, which contain the names of doctors, lawyers, engineers, civil and military personnel, and other members of professions. These directories are arranged by state, are sometimes alphabetical, and are generally found on the local or state level. If you have an ancestor who was active in a profession you may be able to learn about him through one of these directories. Directories you might inspect are *The American Medical Directory, Medical and Surgical Register, Law Lists, Dental Register of the United States, Architects and Builders Directory of the United States, Marine Directory of the Great Lakes, Banker's Almanac and Year Book, Banker's Blue Book,* and *The American Blue Book of Funeral Directors.* For a listing of other directories see the *Directory of Directories.*[1]

MAPS

U.S. Geological Survey Maps

Topographical maps produced by the United States Geological Survey are great finding tools. They can be used to locate cemeteries, roads, landmarks, and topographical features in your area of interest. Each map shows a section of approximately two and one-half square miles in excellent detail. Such survey maps of sections of Indiana counties are available from the United States Geological Survey, Geology Building Survey Side, S-117, Indiana University, Bloomington, Indiana 47405. The Geological Survey maps are generally current and may not show inactive or destroyed cemeteries, old school houses, or the old roadways. The older maps are better for finding older buildings, roads, and such.

County Maps

A good current map of the county where you are conducting research is a necessity when hunting ancestors who lived there. County road maps are found in many different places, varying from county to county. They are usually available from one of the following: the county or state highway department, the county courthouse, the chamber of commerce, and, sometimes, the county license bureau. Usually the county library can suggest where maps are available. Most county maps will show existing cemeteries, schools, parks, and other features, but some recent county maps do not show all of these places. Always try to find the most complete map available for use in historical and genealogical research. The public library in the Indiana county where your ancestors lived should also have a collection of local maps showing where the cemeteries and other places are, or were, located. Generally, the librarian can photocopy a map for you for a small fee.

Always be on the lookout for old county maps or current reproductions of these maps. A map printed when your ancestors lived in the county will be extremely helpful in your research. Some county historical or genealogical societies have reprinted old county maps and have them for sale. Other groups have reproduced maps from old county atlases, which can be very useful to the genealogist because they show the schools, churches, roads, streams, railroad lines, and other features which may no longer exist.

MORTUARY RECORDS

Mortuary records were mentioned briefly in the chapter on church and cemetery records, but they deserve a bit more coverage as a useful source in the county. Mortuary records are a source which is seldom used. Sometimes it is possible to find information about your ancestor by contacting the mortuary which handled the deceased person's funeral arrangements. The information reported to the funeral director may be just what you need to learn more about an ancestor. Some mortuary records go back to the mid-nineteenth century, are very complete, and can be extremely helpful.

There are several ways you may be able to learn the name of the mortuary that handled the funeral arrangements for your ancestor. Obituaries printed in the local newspaper, especially the later ones, generally give the name of the funeral director or the mortuary which handled the burial. Obituaries giving the mortuary name were also printed in church periodicals of the various denominations. Death records, when available, usually show the name of the mortuary which handled funeral arrangements. If you are unable to find the name of the cemetery where the person was buried, you might be able to learn it also from the mortuary records. Mortuary records should state the name of the informant and his or her relationship to the deceased, the complete name of the individual, his or her age, the cause of death, the address of the deceased, the name of the person responsible for payment for the casket and the funeral, and details about the funeral arrangements and costs. Later data might include names of survivors, names of parents, the occupation of the deceased, and other useful information.

During early settlement, caskets were simple pine boxes made by a member of the family, and burial was on the family farm or in the church graveyard. In the early days the "funeral director" was probably the owner of the local furniture store that carried a line of caskets along with the customary beds, tables, and chairs. There are several ways to find the name of the funeral director. A section in the county histories listed the businessmen of the county during the various periods in the county's history, including the operators of mortuaries. Funeral home advertisements were also common in the newspapers of the late nineteenth century. Look in the old newspapers for advertisements for furniture stores to see whether caskets are also mentioned, because the man who sold the caskets might have been the funeral director. Mortuaries were also listed in the city and county directories in the commercial section.

Mortuaries came and went just as other businesses and it is often difficult to locate the records of the defunct ones. Unless such a business was purchased by another mortuary, the records are probably (if they still exist) in the possession of a descendant of the former owner. Not all people who have custody of mortuary records will allow someone else to inspect the records, feeling the information is private and should not be open to anyone. Perhaps you can persuade the holder the release the exact information you need, such as the name of the cemetery, whether the deceased was a widow or widower at time of death, or some other specific information. Descendants who have custody of such old records should be encouraged to deposit them in an archive or a library where they will be preserved. It is also possible that the local historical or genealogical society or area library might have a funeral director's records. Unfortunately, it is also possible that the records have been destroyed.

Because you might locate information about your ancestors in the mortuary records, don't overlook them. Check the county library's card catalog or computerized listing to see whether mortuary records are among its holdings. Although not many mortuary records have been published, records for two establishments in Bluffton, Wells County, Indiana, are available in printed form at the Indiana State Library. These are for the Jahn Funeral Home, 1922–1956, and the McBride Funeral Home (coffin purchase records), 1865–1975. Mortuary records from other towns may possibly have been published or made available to the public.

NEWSPAPERS

Some Indiana newspapers began publication very early and were long-lived but most lasted only a few months. These defunct papers left no trace of their existence except the fact that they had been published at one time. Most early Indiana newspapers were extremely short-lived and carried little local material. Editors relied on weeks-old material from the east, and the newspapers mentioned very few local people or printed little local news unless it was earthshaking or scandalous. Most of the news concerned persons and events from the east and had been copied verbatim from eastern newspapers. It is rare to find mention of local people in early Indiana newspapers, not even an obituary, unless the person was extremely important. Individuals might have been mentioned in the legal notices, in the lists of letters waiting to be picked up at the local post office, or in an account of a particularly scandalous event. Marriages and death notices, the items genealogists most often seek, were seldom printed in the earliest newspapers. The death of a national figure might have been written about at great length, but the demise of the local mayor or sheriff probably wouldn't have been mentioned. After all, everyone in the county knew about his death and the particulars surrounding it.

When unable to learn much about an ancestor, a descendant will sometimes try to find information in the obituary of the deceased person. Obituaries often contain pertinent facts about an ancestor. Generally, the researcher will contact the current newspaper office for the obituary for an ancestor who once lived in the town where the paper is published. Occasionally, the desired obituary is found and a copy is sent to the researcher. At other times, nothing is found because no obituary was printed, or the newspaper no longer exists, or the publisher no longer has the older papers.

The older Indiana newspapers are valuable to the family researcher because they record events which took place during the period before vital records were kept. Obituaries and death notices are particularly sought by genealogists when no tombstone exists or when none has been found for the deceased person. Only the most influential and wealthy people rated obituaries in the earlier newspapers, and unless your ancestor died in a bizarre accident, his death probably won't be recorded. However, by about 1870, newspapers had begun to cover more local events and persons, and more local news and obituaries were printed. Editors had evidentally learned that people would buy more newspapers if they could read about themselves and their neighbors.

Obituaries

You need to know the approximate date of death to find an obituary in the newspaper, and you also need to know where the person was living at the time of death. Not everyone who died had an obituary. Many newspaper editors charged a fee to publish an obituary, while others printed free obituaries only for their subscribers. The newspaper might also have published obituaries only for members of the political party supported by the newspaper. If several newspapers were published in the town at the time your ancestor died, be sure to check for the obituary in all of them. Your ancestor may have taken the "Democrat" paper and would not have had an obituary printed in the opposition's "Republican" paper. The obituary of a county resident might be found in the county paper but not in the one from the town or city. Thus, not everyone had an obituary printed when he or she died.

As a rule, obituaries were not printed in one particular spot in the newspaper but were found scattered throughout the paper. In the earlier papers the front page was dedicated solely to world and national news, and local events had to be earth-shattering to appear on page one. When editors finally began to use local news, the world events were moved to page two. The death of an important person might have rated front-page coverage in the newspaper, but the obituaries of less well known persons would have been printed in almost any available space. After searching through a few issues of a newspaper, you begin to learn where to look for different kinds of news, such as the obituaries and death notices.

Finding the Obituary

If you know the date of the individual's death, search all of the papers from that date onward for several weeks. Even though the death notice may not give the exact death date, you will often find "died on Tuesday last" or some other hint of the actual death date. By using a perpetual calendar (in the information pages of your desk calendar), you can work back from the day and date of the newspaper issue to determine the probable date of death. Unfortunately, some newspapers published death notices only once a month or even less often, and delayed death notices are difficult to locate. They can sometimes be found in gathered collections of newspaper clippings of area events which often include deaths. Fortunately, many local historical and genealogical societies have begun to compile collections of newspaper items from the past. Such collections, if they exist, should be available from the particular county society or library. Mary K. Meyer has produced *Meyer's Directory of Genealogical Societies in the U.S.A. and Canada,* seventh edition, which she published in 1988 at Mt. Airy, Maryland; it might help you find a society in your Indiana county. Also helpful might be *Genealogical Societies and Historical Societies in the United States,* compiled by J. Konrad and released by Summit Publications.

Even when printed in the newspaper, obituaries do not always contain all of the information you want to know about the deceased. Often he or she was extolled for "many Christian virtues," but the vital dates and places of his or her life are not mentioned. A man may have "left many devoted friends, a grieving widow [no name given], and several fatherless children" (again, no names), but nothing concrete was written about his life. This is true not only in the early days but even into the twentieth century, although it is possible to find wonderfully complete obituaries. Some of the better ones take the family ancestry back several generations, often stretching back to the "old country," and giving names, dates, and places galore. Obituaries, like tombstones, can tell you a lot about the deceased, or next to nothing. Fortunately, the obituaries in the later newspapers usually give more biographical data than the earlier ones did.

Death Notices

If you aren't able to find an obituary for your ancestor, look in the newspaper for a death notice. A death notice was usually just a line or two telling of an individual's death. Sometimes the deceased's place of residence (township, neighborhood, or town) was given, as well as approximate age at death. When a death notice was printed among the want ads, such placement generally meant that it was a paid death advertisement. The more precise the data are, the more likely that it was a paid notice. A sketchy death notice was probably free and was used to fill space, but it may also have been paid for. A death notice might also have been printed in the society column, in with the local news, or, occasionally, with several other death notices. Generally, death notices were put in any convenient empty spot on any page in the newspaper. If your ancestor lived in a smaller neighborhood served by the city paper, look for mention of his or her death in the "neighborhood news" column. Those neighborhood news columns often told much more about the individual, the family, the death, the funeral, and the burial than an obituary would have supplied. Sometimes week-by-week accounts of the person's illness or accident and subsequent death were given in blow-by-blow detail in the neighborhood news.

Neighborhood Columns

By the 1870s the newspapers in the smaller towns had regular "neighborhood news" columns which mentioned many of the residents of the area. Such columns were usually headed with the name of the neighborhood and often contained names, relationships, news of births, deaths, and occupations, and accounts of the events which took place in the neighborhood. These columns often recorded when residents moved away to another place, their return visits from their new homes, and their relatives' visits to them. When you know the name of the neighborhood where your ancestor lived in the county, the neighborhood columns can be valuable in family research. If the person lived in a city or town, he or she may be mentioned in the local news, the "society" columns, or in the legal notices.

Legal Notices

The legal notices should not be overlooked when researching your family. These notices often contain important information about members of your family in the announcements of land sales, foreclosure sales, sales of existing businesses, repossessions, administrations of probates, settlements of estates, searches for heirs, proving of wills, pending divorces and divorce actions (often in lurid detail), commitment of the insane, and other legal actions. Any one of these items might be helpful in locating and learning more about your ancestors. The legal announcement will contain the date of the event or court action and can lead you to the related county record for more details.[2] Some of the old newspapers have been indexed and can help you to find mention of your ancestors, but most of them have not. As a rule, a page-by-page search of the newspapers is the only way to find items about your ancestors. This is a painstaking and time-consuming task, which requires ample time to do properly.

If you suspect that your ancestor was involved in a trial or some legal action and you know the approximate date of the event, search in the area newspapers for any mention of it. Then you can search in the court records for an account of the trial. When you know or suspect that a divorce occurred in your family history but haven't been able to find record of the divorce action, you may find it prominently printed on the front page of the local newspaper. The gritty details, published right on page one, can shock and astonish you, because the papers "told all." Newspapers were not bothered by libel suits in the old days and, consequently, printed just about anything and everything about an event, and not all of it factual, unfortunately. Lists of divorce actions are found in the old newspapers, often with the complete details of the cases and the decisions of the court, including how much money and property women received, the names of the couples' children, their ages and their residences if they lived elsewhere.

Newspapers printed in the later years of the nineteenth century often published notices of marriage licenses obtained during the previous week or month. Such a notice might give the names and ages of the prospective bride and groom and where each lived. If you find the marriage license notice but no later marriage, the marriage may not have taken place. Look in later issues of the newspaper for a thinly, or not so thinly, veiled remark about "fickle females who change their minds" or about intended grooms who "vanish in the night." Newspaper editors cared more about the sale of a few extra newspapers than about wounded feelings. It is also possible to find that one of the parties was married to someone other than the original "intended" shortly after the first announcement. Then, you will have the task of finding why this "change of heart" happened, unless the editor also reveals the reason in a later edition of the paper.

Birth Notices

Birthdates are often the hardest dates to find for persons born before the state registration of vital records began. Birth announcements printed in the newspaper can, therefore, be very helpful because there may be no other way to learn the date of birth. Many birth notices were printed some time after the birth occurred, but usually they followed the birth fairly closely. The later newspapers often published birth notices but printed only the barest details: "A fine boy born to Able Suggs" or "A new little miss has come to live with the John Browns." Notice that the names of the child and the mother are not given, but the birth weight may be mentioned prominently. Sometimes the item reported only that a baby (no sex mentioned) had arrived on a certain day to the family (surname given) at a certain address and gave no other information. You may have to do some detective work to determine which son's or daughter's birth was being announced. If a child born at this time appears later in the next federal census schedule, you will probably be able to determine the name of the child and its place in the family. You may also be able to determine that a child has died before the next census when no child of the right age is listed on that census.

Until well into the twentieth century a woman was merely an adjunct to her husband, seeming to have had no given name and no identity of her own. Obituaries seldom gave the given name or maiden name of a woman. She was "Mrs. Jones" or "the wife of James Jones." She was seldom identified more fully or in any other way in the newspaper unless she was unmarried, and was then "Miss" So-and-So. Even then, she might have been referred to as the "spinster" daughter of John Jones or as a "maiden lady." You have to search in several places to learn the given name of a married woman; even her death record and the tombstone may list her merely as "Mrs. Jones." Hunt for the marriage record made when she married "Mr. Jones" or try to find her in the census records made when she was a child, unless that was before 1850, when only her father's name would have been recorded.

Social Events

In the 1880s and 1890s birthdays and wedding anniversaries were "big news," especially in the newspapers of the smaller communities. Long and extremely detailed accounts of the festivities reported who attended, what they wore, who gave what gifts, what foods were served, and how the home was decorated. The more prominent the individual and the guests, the more elaborate the write-up and the more likely it was to appear on the newspaper's front page. The collective gift of a rocking chair was popular at parties for "older folks" of sixty-five and over, and the honoree always obligingly "tried out" the chair on the spot! A husband honored at an anniversary party often showed off by wearing his wedding suit, which still fit perfectly. The gift list was printed, the winners of the games were mentioned, and the refreshments were described. Other social events, such as hayrides, riverboat trips, dances, and musicales were often deemed worthy of newspaper coverage, and all of the participants were named in the story. Needless to say, these people were more often from the more prominent families of the town, but you may also find items about the less prominent people, too.

The Value of Using Old Newspapers

You may be able to find a great deal about your ancestors by reading the newspapers printed when they lived. It is possible to find their names in almost any place in the newspaper, and one item may answer many questions you have about your ancestors. If the news item you find is sensational or even scandalous, use it to gain insight into the life and times of your ancestor. It's not often you can find concrete evidence of an ancestor's character on the front page of the newspaper! The newspapers of the late nineteenth century were particularly unkind to blacks, the poor, drunkards, and criminals. Blacks were often used as comic relief, and drunkards and poor people were treated condescendingly. Some people who were accused of crimes were prejudged as criminals before the trial, whereas locally prominent persons were excused of any wrongdoing without ever going to trial. Newspaper editors probably reflected similar attitudes among their readers. You merely need to locate the old papers printed when your family lived in a place to learn about the attitudes and prejudices of the time and of that place.

How to Find Old Newspapers

Most of today's newspapers are bound into books by the year, but the bound volumes are retained for only a few years before they are discarded. Sometimes the contents are microfilmed and the original books are destroyed. Huge volumes of older newspapers take up too much space, and today space is too valuable to store "obsolete material." Even libraries are following this microfilm-and-destroy procedure because of space restrictions. Local libraries and historical and genealogical societies generally try to preserve copies of the older newspapers or, at least, have newspaper-clipping files for their patrons to use, but these facilities have space limitations, too. The state of Indiana has undertaken a newspaper microfilming program and has microfilmed most or all of the existing old newspapers. Microfilmed copies of these papers are available at the Indiana State Library in Indianapolis and at many of the local public libraries throughout the state. Unfortunately, many newspapers no longer exist.

The *Indiana Newspaper Bibliography,* published by the Indiana Historical Society, lists 8,000 newspapers which have made at least a brief appearance since the first newspaper was published in Vincennes in 1804. By consulting this volume you can determine which newspapers were printed in your locality of interest, the dates the papers were published, and the current location of existing copies. Many of the repositories listed in the book have since disposed of many of their newspaper collections in favor of microfilmed copies. Check with the public library in your county of interest to learn whether microfilmed newspapers are available there.

Any newspaper still being published will be listed in *Ayers Directory,* along with the location and correct name of the paper. The earlier issues of this directory, published since 1869, list the various papers printed since that date. Each newspaper is listed under the name of the town where it is or was published. *Ayers Directory* is found in most larger libraries. *Union lists* can also be used to locate files of newspapers and are also available in the larger libraries. Also useful in a newspaper search are the following books: *History and Biography of American Newspapers, 1690–1820,* by Clarence Brigham; *Gregory's American Newspapers, 1821–1916,* and the Library of Congress's *Newspapers on Microfilm.* Most larger libraries should have these volumes.

The United States Newspaper Project was begun in 1973 to update the *Gregory's* newspaper list. Within a few years, historians and genealogists should be able to locate every existing newspaper file in the country. Almost every state in the United States has tried to update *Gregory's,* and each state currently has some form of newspaper program. Many have published lists of specific holdings or the whereabouts of other holdings in their state. The pilot project in Iowa was completed in 1979, and the Indiana Project, in 1982. Eventually, about 35,000 newspaper titles from all fifty states, as well as all extant copies of the 300,000 newspapers published in the United States since 1690, will be available on microfilm through Interlibrary Loan.[3]

If you do not find a newspaper listed in the town where you are researching, you may find that a newspaper from a nearby town carried news for the town. Consult maps of the area to determine which nearby town might have printed news of the area. Then contact the local public library to learn whether the older newspapers are available, either in book form, on microfilm, or as abstracts of obituaries and news items. Some libraries will photocopy material from the old newspapers for a small charge, but others are not sufficiently staffed to undertake such services. In such a case, the librarian may be able to send you the names of researchers who will do the research for you for a fee. Always ask for photocopies of any items found in the newspapers.

Newspaper Query Columns

While on the subject of newspapers, let's not forget the genealogical query columns carried by many of today's newspapers. A genealogical query column currently being printed in the place where your ancestors lived can often help you find information about them. A query you send to the columnist might put you in touch with people who have data about your ancestors, and you may even hear from their other descendants who live in the area.

Indiana has about eighteen query columns, possibly because so many people have lived in or passed through the state since territorial days. Only Texas has more newspaper genealogical query columns than Indiana does. To learn about columns currently printed in Indiana, check in the *Newspaper Genealogical Column Directory,* compiled by Anita Cheek Milner. This frequently updated book lists the columns published in each state and gives the following information about each one: name of columnist (byline) and address; research area covered by the column; papers in which column appears; frequency of publication of column; date column was first published; requirements for a query; charge for a query (if any); and availability of back issues and indexes.[4]

Should you wish to place a query in a query column printed in your Indiana county, you must first decide exactly what you want to know. Follow the "rules" for the column, which might include geographic area covered by column, length of query permitted, and style of query. Because most columnists have space limitations, keep your query short and to the point. Print or type the query, using complete names, surnames capitalized, at least one date and place, and say exactly what you want to know. If you want to know the death date for John JONES, say so. Offer to pay respondents for copying and postage costs for data sent to you; it may make a difference in replies. Send a stamped, self-addressed, legal-size envelope (S.A.S.E.) if you want a reply from the columnist. Don't expect your query to be printed "next week," because most query columnists have large query backlogs. If you don't get a reply from your first batch of queries, try again in a year or so. The person who can help you may not have seen your first queries but might see the next ones.[5]

If no query column exists in or near your research area, then you have several other ways to publish your inquiry there. One way is to write a letter to the editor, asking what you want to learn about your ancestor. Again, make it short and concise. The editor may or may not print your letter but will probably try to get it to someone who can help you. Another method is to place an advertisement in the want-ad section of the town or area newspaper. Making the ad short and sweet is easier when paying by the word, so be economical. Include your telephone number and suggest that the respondent reverse the charges when calling you. A third method, and one which often gets good results, is to send your query to the county historical or genealogical society for publication in its newsletter. Members of these groups are actively interested in families and the past and will be more apt to answer your call for help. Many societies offer free queries to members but charge a small fee to others. By using one or more of these methods you should be able to contact people in the area where your ancestors once lived and, it is hoped, gain information about them.

INDIANA LIBRARIES

There are three major Indiana libraries which have large collections of materials useful to genealogists and historians. These are the Public Library of Fort Wayne and Allen County in Fort Wayne, the Indiana State Library, and the Indiana Historical Society Library, the last two located in the Indiana State Library building in Indianapolis. Another library with extensive Indiana holdings is the Newberry Library in Chicago, Illinois. Each of these facilities will answer brief, concise inquiries by mail, but you need to send the name of a specific book or record and the page numbers to get copies regarding your ancestors. In other words, none of these libraries will undertake extensive research for you.

The Genealogy Division of the Indiana State Library is a major genealogical and historical repository for material on Indiana and the midwest. The facility has two important genealogical collections: the Indiana Division and the Genealogy Division, both excellent sources for the Indiana researcher. The collections of the Indiana Division include county and town histories, church records, directories, and newspapers; the collections in the Genealogy Division include more than 35,000 volumes and pamphlets and a large microfilm collection. The Genealogy Division has the complete federal censuses, 1790–1910, the index to the Revolutionary War military service records and pension and bounty land warrant application files; the index to the War of 1812 pension application files; the

Indiana Veterans' Grave Registration for Adams through Washington Counties, helpful although incomplete; Indian tribal census records; the federal mortality schedules, including the 1850, 1860, 1870, and 1880 Indiana mortality schedules in printed form; and numerous genealogies and family histories. State and county records for Indiana usually include indexes to various county court records, such as deeds, probates, marriages, wills, and tax records up to about 1900; various local special historical and genealogical collections; 42 reels of tax assessment lists for eleven collection districts of Indiana in 1862 in the *Internal Revenue Assessment Lists, 1862–1866.* Similar holdings are also available for other states. The collection is vast and constantly growing. The Indiana State Library, Genealogy Division, is located at 140 North Senate Avenue, Indianapolis, Indiana 46204. Parking is available one block south of the facility and in several nearby parking garages.[6]

The Indiana Historical Society is also located in the Indiana State Library building, although the address is not the same. The collections of the Indiana Historical Society include rare books, manuscripts, early Indiana and midwestern maps, more than 100,000 paintings, drawings, and photographs of people and scenes, and material pertaining to the history of the Old Northwest and Native Americans. Membership in the Indiana Historical Society is beneficial to anyone who is researching Indiana ancestry because of its excellent publications, which include *The Hoosier Genealogist,* a quarterly magazine which contains a wealth of early Indiana records, genealogical and historical book reviews, genealogical queries, lists of acquisitions; the quarterly magazine *Traces of Indiana and Midwestern History,* which covers Indiana people and places of the past; the *Indiana Magazine of History,* a scholarly collection of historical essays and brief reviews of current historical works; the bimonthly *Indiana Historical Society Newsletter;* and other special books, phonograph records, and publications. In addition, Society members receive a new hardbound book each year as another benefit of membership. The Indiana Historical Society is located at 315 West Ohio Street, Indianapolis, Indiana 46202.[7]

The Fred J. Reynolds Historical Genealogy Collection in the Genealogy Department of the Fort Wayne and Allen County Public Library is the largest genealogy collection east of the Mississippi housed under one roof. The Fort Wayne Library has one of the foremost genealogical collections and some of the top genealogical reference librarians in the country. Its holdings include 128,000 volumes and 132,000 microtext items. Included are the complete microfilmed United States federal census schedules from 1790 to 1910, Canadian census records from 1825 to 1891, ships' passenger lists, military pension records, city directories, indexes, bibliographies, maps, plat books, printed vital records, publications of patriotic and hereditary societies, county histories, cemetery records, and numerous other resources useful to the genealogist. The holdings for Indiana are particularly strong, although the library also has extensive material for the midwest, for the "feeder" states which populated Indiana, and for some foreign countries, particularly England, Ireland, Scotland, and Canada. The facility is large, well arranged, and has a helpful staff. A large section of books on the states sits on open stacks. The Public Library of Fort Wayne and Allen County is located in downtown Fort Wayne at 900 West Webster Street. The Genealogy Department is on the second floor in the new wing of the library building. There are convenient pay parking lots nearby. The mailing address for the library is P.O. Box 2270, Fort Wayne, Indiana 46801.[8]

Although not located in Indiana, the Newberry Library in Chicago is another rich source for Indiana genealogical research. The Newberry's Indiana material is considered to be among its strongest state collections. Its excellent holdings include voluminous amounts of genealogical source material and indexes and transcripts of vital records, probates, deeds, cemetery records, naturalizations, church records, and extensive land records. In the late 1970s an exchange program between the Newberry and the Fort Wayne libraries greatly increased the holdings of both facilities. Materials which were then in the Newberry Library are now also available in the Fort Wayne Library.[9]

Many other libraries in the state have extensive local, regional, and statewide genealogical collections. At the risk of leaving out some of the best, a few of these fine facilities are located in South Bend, Huntington, Vincennes, Lafayette, Evansville, Salem, Marion, Terre Haute, Bloomington, Richmond, Martinsville, and Jeffersonville. In fact, most Indiana counties have at least one outstanding genealogical library or collection to draw on when conducting family research. The public library may house the foremost collection, but there may be others that are equally fine.

FINDING GENEALOGICAL COLLECTIONS

Because genealogical collections can be found in any number of different locations, there is no one place which can be said to house the particular collection you want. The outstanding collection for your county of interest may be housed in the public library in the town, in the county seat, or in a nearby town. It may be housed in the local historical or genealogical society library or kept in an officer's home. Sometimes the material is owned by a private individual whom you must contact to arrange to see it. To locate genealogical collections in a particular county, contact the public library in the town of your interest to ask of their whereabouts. Write to the person or facility well ahead of your anticipated visit to arrange a time to see the collection. You will need to know the days and hours a library is open and when a visit to an individual would be convenient. If you know the whereabouts of materials and the times you can use them, you save much precious time for actual research when you arrive. If you are not able to learn about collections through a local source, check in the *Directory of American Libraries with Genealogy or Local History Collections,* compiled by P. William

Filby and published in 1988 by Scholarly Resources, Inc., Wilmington, Delaware.

Addresses of Indiana Libraries and Societies

The following list of Indiana county libraries, historical societies, genealogical societies, and other kinds of libraries is included to help steer you toward the possible location of material about your Indiana ancestors. The information has been gleaned from several sources, including *The Genealogical Helper* magazine and *The Handy Book for Genealogists,* both published by The Everton Publishers, Inc., P.O. Box 368, Logan, Utah 84321, and *The County Courthouse Book,* compiled by Elizabeth Petty Bentley and published by the Genealogical Publishing Company, Inc., 1001 North Calvert Street, Baltimore, Maryland 21202.

Adams County Historical Society, c/o Dick Heller, 141 South 2nd Street, Decatur, IN 46733.

Allen County Genealogical Society of Indiana; P.O. Box 12003, Fort Wayne, IN 46862.

Allen County Public Library, P.O. Box 2270, Fort Wayne, IN 46801.

American Legion National Headquarters Library, 700 North Pennsylvania Street, Indianapolis, IN 46204.

Anderson Public Library, 111 East 12th Street, Anderson, IN 46016.

Bartholomew County Historical Society, c/o Sue Wilgus, 524 3rd Street, Columbus, IN 47201.

Benton County Historical Society, 602 East 7th Street, Fowler, IN 47944.

Blackford County Historical Society, c/o Cecil Beeson, P.O. Box 1, Hartford City, IN 47348.

Bloomfield Carnegie Public Library, South Franklin Street, Bloomfield, IN 47424.

Bloomington Indiana (LDS) Stake Library, 2411 East 2nd Street, Bloomington, IN 47401.

Brown County Genealogical Society, P.O. Box 1202, Nashville, IN 47448.

Brown County Historical Society, Inc., P.O. Box 668, Nashville, IN 47448.

Carroll County Historical Society, P.O. Box 277, Delphi, IN 46923.

Cass County Genealogical Society, P.O. Box 373, Logansport, IN 46947.

Clark County Historical Society, P.O. Box 606, Jeffersonville, IN 47130.

Clay County Genealogical Society of Indiana, P.O. Box 56, Center Point, IN 47840.

Clinton County Historical Society, 609 North Columbia Street, Frankfort, IN 47130.

Danville Public Library, 101 South Indiana Street, Danville, IN 46122.

Daviess County Genealogical Society, c/o Eleanor Purdue, 703 Front Street, Washington, IN 47501.

Decatur County Historical Society, P.O. Box 163, Greensburg, IN 47240.

Dekalb County Historical Society, P.O. Box 66, Auburn, IN 46706.

Delaware County Genealogical Society, c/o Juanita Lewis, Y.W.C.A., 310 East Charles Street, Muncie, IN 47305.

Elkhart County Genealogical Society, 1812 Jeanwood Drive, Elkhart, IN 46514.

Elkhart Public Library, 603 South Jackson Street, Elkhart, IN 46514.

Emline Fairbanks Memorial Library, 222 North 7th Street, Terre Haute, IN 47807.

Fort Wayne and Allen County Public Library, 900 Webster Street, Fort Wayne, IN 46802.

Fort Wayne Indiana (LDS) Stake Library, Box 5250, Hazelwood Station, Fort Wayne, IN 46895.

Fountain County Historical Society, c/o Davey Lee Puckett, Box 148, Kingman, IN 47952.

Frankfort Community Public Library, 208 West Clinton Street, Frankfort, IN 46401.

Franklin County Historical Society, Route 4, Box 52, Brookville, IN 47012.

Fulton County Historical Society, c/o Shirley Willard, 7th and Pontiac, Rochester, IN 46975.

Genealogy Division, Indiana State Library, 140 North Senate Avenue, Indianapolis, IN 46204.

Genealogy Section, Kosciusko County Historical Society, P.O. Box 1071, Warsaw, IN 46580.

Gibson County Historical Society, P.O. Box 516, Princeton, IN 47670.

Goshen College Historical Library, Goshen, IN 46526.

Grant County Genealogical Society, 24 Herbal Drive, Marion, IN 46952.

Greene County Historical and Genealogical Society, c/o Gene Combs, 105 Mechanic Street, Bloomfield, IN 47424.

Greene County Historical Society, P.O. Box 29, Lyons, IN 47443.

Guilford Township Collection, Plainfield Public Library, 1120 Stafford Road, Plainfield, IN 46163.

Hamilton County Historical Society, P.O. Box 397, Noblesville, IN 46060.

Hancock County Historical Society, Inc., P.O. Box 375, Greenfield, IN 46140-0375.

Harrison County Historical Society, 117 West Beaver Street, Corydon, IN 47112.

Hendricks County Genealogical Society, 101 South Indiana Street, Danville, IN 46122.

Hendricks County Historical Society, P.O. Box 128, Danville, IN 46122.

Henry County Historical Society, 606 South 14th Street, New Castle, IN 47362.

Howard County Genealogical Society, c/o Kokomo Public Library, 220 North Union, Kokomo, IN 46901.

Huntington Public Library, 44 East Park Drive, Huntington, IN 46750.
Illiana Genealogical and Historical Society, P.O. Box 207, Danville, IL 61832.
Illiana Jewish Genealogical Society, c/o Sharon G. Blitstein, 3033 Bob-O-Link Road, Flossmoor, IL 60422.
Indiana African American Historical and Genealogical Society, c/o Coy D. Robbins, 502 Clover Terrace, Bloomington, IN 47404.
Indiana Genealogical Society, P.O. Box 66, Tunnelton, IN 47467.
Indiana Historical Society, 315 West Ohio Street, Indianapolis, IN 46202. (Genealogy Division at same address.)
Indiana Historical Society Library, 140 North Senate Avenue, Indianapolis, IN 46204.
Indiana Jewish Historical Society, Inc., 203 West Wayne Street, Suite 310, Fort Wayne, IN 46802.
Indiana Society, Sons of the American Revolution, William C. Roggie, Pres., 5401 Central Avenue, Indianapolis, IN 46220.
Indiana State Library, 140 North Senate Avenue, Indianapolis, IN 46204.
Indianapolis Indiana (LDS) Stake Library, 720 Woodale Terrace No. 18, Greenwood, IN 46142.
Jackson County Genealogical Society, 2nd & Walnut Streets, Seymour, IN 47274.
Jasper County Historical Society, c/o B. Arnatt, Augusta Street, Rensselaer, IN 47971.
Jay County Historical Society, Box 1282, Portland, IN 47371.
Johnson County Historical Society, 150 West Madison Street, Franklin, IN 46131.
Kosciusko County Historical Society, P.O. Box 1071, Warsaw, IN 46580.
Lagrange County Historical Society, Inc., R.R. 1, Lagrange, IN 46761.
LaPorte County Genealogical Society, 904 Indiana Avenue, LaPorte, IN 46350.
LaPorte County Historical Society, LaPorte County Complex, LaPorte, IN 46350.
Lawrence County Genealogical and Historical Society, Courthouse Museum, Bedford, IN 47421.
Lewis Historical Collections Library, Vincennes University, Vincennes, IN 47591.
Logansport Public Library, 616 East Broadway, Logansport, IN 46947.
Madison County Historical Society, Inc., P.O. Box 523, Anderson, IN 46015.
Madison-Jefferson County Public Library, 420 West Main Street, Madison, IN 47250.
Marion-Adams Genealogical Society, 308 Main Street, Sheridan, IN 46069.
Marion County Historical Society, 140 North Senate Avenue, Indianapolis, IN 46204.
Marion Public Library, 600 South Washington Street, Marion, IN 46952.

Marshall County Genealogical Society, 317 West Monroe, Plymouth, IN 46563.

Marshall County Historical Center, 317 West Monroe, Plymouth, IN 46563.

Martin County Historical Society, Inc., P.O. Box 84, Shoals, IN 46504.

Miami County Genealogical Society, P.O. Box 542, Peru, IN 46970.

Michigan City Public Library, 100 East 4th Street, Michigan City, IN 46360.

Middletown Public Library, Box 36, 554 Locust Street, Middletown, IN 47356.

Monroe County Genealogical Society, Old Library, 202 East 6th Street, Bloomington, IN 47408.

Monroe County Historical Society, P.O. Box 414, Bloomington, IN 47402.

Monroe County Public Library, Indiana Room, 303 East Kirkwood Avenue, Bloomington, IN 47408.

Montgomery County Historical Society, Genealogical Section, 212 South Water Street, Crawfordsville, IN 47933.

Morgan County Historical and Genealogical Club, c/o Becky Hardin, 133 Carter Street, Mooresville, IN 46158.

New Albany Public Library, New Albany, IN 47150.

Newton County Historical Society, Box 103, Kentland, IN 47951.

Noble County Genealogical Society, 109 North York Street, Albion, IN 46701.

Noblesville Public Library, 16 South 10th Street, Noblesville, IN 46060.

North Central Indiana Genealogical Society, 2300 Canterbury Drive, Kokomo, IN 46901.

Northern Indiana Historical Society, 112 South Lafayette Boulevard, South Bend, IN 44601.

Northwest Indiana Genealogical Society, 154 Granite Street, Valparaiso, IN 46383.

Northwest Territory Genealogical Society, Lewis Historical Library, Vincennes University, Vincennes, IN 47591.

Ohio County Historical Society, 218 South Walnut Street, Rising Sun, IN 47040.

Orange County Genealogical Society, P.O. Box 344, Paoli, IN 47454.

Owen County Historical Society, P.O. Box 222, Spencer, IN 47460.

Palatines to America, 716 Wallbridge, Indianapolis, IN 46241.

Paoli Public Library, N.E. Court, Paoli, IN 47454.

Perry County Historical Society, c/o Mrs. James Groves, Rome, IN 47574.

Pike County Historical Society, c/o Mrs. Marjorie Malotte, R.R. 2, Petersburg, IN 47567.

Plymouth Public Library, 201 North Center Street, Plymouth, IN 46563.

Porter County Historical Society, c/o Museum, 153 Franklin Street, Valparaiso, IN 46383.

Posey County Historical Society, P.O. Box 171, Mt. Vernon, IN 47620.

Public Library of Fort Wayne and Allen County, 900 Webster Street, Fort Wayne, IN 46802.

Pulaski County Genealogical Society, c/o Carolyn Case, R.R. 4, Box 121, Winamac, IN 46996.

Pulaski County Public Library, 121 South Riverside Drive, Winamac, IN 46996.

Putnam County Genealogical Club, Route 1, Box 28, Bainbridge, IN 46105.

Randolph County Genealogical Society, c/o Monisa Wisener, R.R. 3, Winchester, IN 47394.

Randolph County Historical Society, Route 3, Box 60A, Winchester, IN 47394.

Ripley County Historical Society, Inc., P.O. Box 224, Versailles, IN 47042.

Rockville Public Library, 106 North Market Street, Rockville, IN 47872.

Rush County Historical Society, c/o James Scott, 614 North Jackson Street, Rushville, IN 46173.

Scott County Historical Society, P.O. Box 245, Scottsburg, IN 47170.

Shelby County Historical Society, Box 74, Shelbyville, IN 46176.

Society of Indiana Pioneers, c/o Caroline Dunn, Secretary, 315 West Ohio Street, Indianapolis, IN 46202.

South Bend Area Genealogical Society, P.O. Box 1222, South Bend, IN 46624.

South Bend Public Library, 122 West Wayne Street, South Bend, IN 46601.

Southern Indiana Genealogical Society, P.O. Box 665, New Albany, IN 47150.

Spencer County Historical Society, Walnut Street, Rockport, IN 47635.

Sullivan County Historical Society, P.O. Box 326, Sullivan, IN 47882.

Tippecanoe County Area Genealogical Society, 909 South Street, Lafayette, IN 47901.

Tri-State Genealogical Society, c/o Willard Library, 21 1st Avenue, Evansville, IN 47710.

Union County Historical Society, 6 East Seminary Street, Liberty, IN 47353.

Valparaiso Public Library, 103 Jefferson Street, Valparaiso, IN 46383.

Vigo County Historical Society, 1411 South 6th Street, Terre Haute, IN 47802.

Vigo County Public Library, One Library Square, Terre Haute, IN 47807.

Wabash County Historical Society, Wabash County Museum, 89 West Hill Street, Wabash, IN 46992.

Wabash Valley Genealogical Society, P.O. Box 85, Terre Haute, IN 47808.

Warren County Historical Society, P.O. Box 176, Williamsport, IN 47993.

Warsaw Public Library, 315 East Center Street, Warsaw, IN 46580.

Washington County Historical Society, 307 East Market Street, Salem, IN 47904.

Wayne County Historical Society, 1150 North A Street, Richmond, IN 47374.

Wells County Historical Society, P.O. Box 143, Bluffton, IN 46714.

White County Genealogy Society, 609 South Maple Street, Monticello, IN 47960.

Whitley County Historical Museum, 108 West Jefferson Street, Columbia City, IN 46725.

Who's Your Ancestor Genealogy Society, District Public Library, 222 South Washington Street, Crawfordsville, IN 47933.

Willard Library of Evansville, 21 1st Avenue, Evansville, IN 47710.

Worthington Public Library, Worthington, IN 47471.

Other Libraries

Other major libraries which have extensive material concerning Indiana are the following:

National Archives and Records Service, General Services Administration, Washington, DC 20408.

Federal Archives and Records Center, 7358 South Pulaski Road, Chicago, IL 60629. (Serves Illinois, Indiana, Michigan, Minnesota, Ohio, and Wisconsin and collects records of field offices of U.S. Government agencies in the area.)

The National Genealogical Society, 4527 17th Street North, Arlington, VA 22207.

National Society, Daughters of the American Revolution (D.A.R.), 1776 D Street, N.W., Washington, DC 20006. (A superior library with original source materials, family and cemetery records gathered by local chapters; open to the general public.)

The Genealogical Society of Utah, 50 East North Temple Street, Salt Lake City, UT 84150.

Family History Library of the Church of Jesus Christ of Latter-Day Saints (Mormon), 35 North West Temple, Salt Lake City, UT 84150.

Basic Genealogical Principles

CHAPTER 11

RESEARCH BEGINS WITH YOU

When beginning to trace your family's genealogy, you, the genealogist (the one conducting genealogy), must always start with what you know and go back in time, step by step, to what is not known. Begin first with data about you. Record the basic information about yourself (birthdate and birthplace, marriage date and place, name of spouse, and so forth) on a standard family group sheet. Family group sheets are available from a number of genealogical supply houses, whose names and addresses can be obtained from your local genealogical society or from *The Genealogical Helper* magazine. The first family group sheet is headed by your name if you are a married man or by your father's name (as the head of the family) if you are unmarried, whether male or female. The family group sheet also contains the name of your mother and your siblings, with data (dates, places, events) about each of them and their spouses. A married woman appears as a child on the chart of her father and as a wife on her husband's chart. An unmarried woman never heads a family group sheet.

After you have completed the data about yourself, go back and record information about your parents on separate family group sheets. Your father will be recorded as a child on his father's family group sheet, and your mother as a child on her father's sheet. They are also recorded as parents on the initial sheet, where you and your siblings appear as children. Record all the known information for your mother and father in the blanks provided on each of their father's family group sheets. There may be blank spaces which you can't fill immediately, but don't be concerned about these at present. Blank spaces show you what research is needed to complete this part of your genealogy. It is not unusual to have quite a few blanks in a genealogy, even for people you knew quite well, such as your grandparents. As you go further back in your lineage even more blanks will show up, and some of them may stay blank for quite awhile.

Once you have found all of the information available for your parents and have recorded the data on family group charts, go back to your four grandparents and record similar information about them on their family group sheet and on their parents' sheets. Eventually, you will go back to your eight great-grandparents, and then back to your sixteen great-great-grandparents (or second great-grandparents), and so on, back to the very first ancestor who came to America. It is common to have about ten or eleven generations in a family whose first ancestor came to America in the 1600s. A generation can span anywhere from twenty to thirty-five years, with from three to four generations commonly found in a century.

Genealogy, as you can see, is a step-by-step adventure which cannot be begun with that first ancestor. In order for it to be a proper genealogy of your particular family, the lineage has to be proved, person by person, from you back to the original ancestor. Because you generally do not know who your original ancestor was when you begin family research, you must start with yourself and go back in time to that first ancestor. This is the only way to know positively that a person is your ancestor. Most people actually know very little about their great-grandparents, let alone their earliest ancestors. For this reason, you cannot simply choose a person with the same surname as yours and claim him or her as your ancestor. Even if you and he or she share a most unusual name, the chances of your being his or her descendant are slim. Instead, you must follow your own individual line back, generation by generation, until you can genuinely prove a connection with your first ancestor.

DEFINE YOUR GOALS

As you begin searching for your origins, you should decide what you really want to learn and how far you wish to proceed. Are you interested in only the line involving your surname, or do you want to research each and every family line you encounter? You may first decide to work only on your surname, and then become enchanted with your mother's line, and her mother's line, and so on, until you find yourself researching forty-odd lines instead of one. This is acceptable, so don't be upset if your goals change as you proceed to trace your lineage. It is advisable also to set a limit as to how far you want to research. These limits might be called (1) "to the shore," (2) "across the water," and (3) "to the traceable first." If you will be content to research a line only back to the first ancestor in this country, you will research "to the shore" where he or she landed. Perhaps you will learn his or her nationality in the process, but if you want to know the country that he or she came from, you will want to search "across the water." To learn the particular village, town, and province in a specific country, you will want to search "to the traceable first" in Europe, Africa, Asia, or wherever. Searching back "to the traceable first" ancestor is just what it says, and this step is limited by your energies, financial resources, and the availability or lack of existing records. So, as you begin tracing your family history, decide on your goals, but be aware that your priorities may change and that you may want to search further as you become infected by the "genealogy bug."

HOME SOURCES

Some of the best, least expensive, and most convenient sources available to a genealogist are the sources in the home. These are the papers, photographs, and mementos which can be found in your own home and in those of your relatives. Family documents suggested by Allan J. Lichtman, in his book *Your Family History,* published in 1978 by Vintage Books, might be family Bibles, letters, telegrams, postcards, diaries, journals, appointment calendars, ledgers, account books, bills, canceled checks, bankbooks, bank statements, credit cards, employment records, tax records, Social Security cards, identification cards, driver's licenses, fishing and hunting licenses, wills, deeds, bills of sale, insurance policies, stocks and bonds, school records and assignments, military records, medical records, church records, citizenship papers, passports, birth and baptismal certificates, marriage certificates, death certificates, confirmation certificates, yearbooks, scrapbooks, clippings, calling cards, greeting cards, invitations, baby books, memoirs, and family histories and genealogies.[1] Old family histories may have to be proved again, but they can give you a good starting point for your research.

Material objects Lichtman suggests as helpful home sources are souvenirs, trophies, medals, posters, jewelry, hobbies and collections, dated samplers and quilts, instruments, tools, clothing, dishes, paintings, photographs, albums, home movies, and other items which show the interests, tastes, and life-style of your ancestors.[2] The boxes, barrels, and trunks found in family attics and basements can hold treasure troves of "things" which were your ancestors' and which can tell you a great deal about the people and their lives. Search through every box, barrel, or trunk before you even think of discarding the contents.

When sorting through these papers and objects, look for names, dates, places, relationships, occupations, hobbies, interests, special talents, health problems, organizations belonged to, physical descriptions, photographs, and any other clues which suggest further research opportunities outside the home. You can generally learn a great deal by rummaging through the personal possessions and memorabilia of your relatives and ancestors. Your parents may even have old papers and mementos which belonged to their parents and grandparents. Make photocopies of papers you don't want to save and file the copies "for future reference." A union card made out to your relative in a distant city (where you didn't know he had lived) may show you where to look for data about him for the period when the card was issued. A military award sends you to the government records for the ancestor's military service. The value of birth, marriage, and death records should be evident. Analyze everything you find and make notes about the conclusions you draw about various objects and papers. Anything kept by your parents, relatives, or ancestors must be considered important to them. Even if you don't keep these things you will have observed them and learned much about the individuals who owned these keepsakes. You may even find a family legend or two among the memorabilia or hear family stories from your parents as you search through the trunk together.

FAMILY LEGENDS

Nearly every family has a tradition or a legend which tells something about the family's origins or about an illustrious family member. Some family legends prove to be true accounts, but others are just that—legends. If a family legend contains lots of fanciful details it may still be basically true but was overembellished as it was told and retold. Because some legends which are partially true can direct you to records about the events that inspired the legends, don't discard a family story just because it's a "legend." It could be one based on verifiable fact, or it could be a complete fabrication having, nonetheless, a few truths scattered among the elaborations. A family legend can thus offer some clues that suggest other research possibilities. You may be able to learn a great deal about your ancestors by keeping a family legend "on the back burner." Just don't accept it as fact until you find concrete and incontrovertible evidence that it is true. In order to prove that any information is true you have to use good records and resources and good basic genealogical principles. To be valid, genealogical proof must be reliable in nature and must be thoroughly documented.

DOCUMENTED PROOF

"Proof" and "documentation" are the two most important words to remember in genealogical research. "Guesswork" has no place in genealogy. You defeat your purpose when you guess that someone is your ancestor or that some piece of information is fact. You must prove a statement, a relationship, a date, a place, and an event. You must even prove the link between you and your parents, between them and their parents, and so on, back to your original ancestor. Following hunches or making assumptions are not allowed in genealogy. Without valid proof, your genealogy would be considered invalid by another genealogist, and all the time you spent on research, wasted. To be sure that you prove every bit of your genealogical material, you need to know what constitutes valid proof in genealogy.

Two Kinds of Records

For genealogical proof to be considered valid it must be obtained from a source that is considered reliable. Genealogists have to consult various kinds of records in order to obtain genealogical information about themselves, their parents, their grandparents, and their other ancestors. There are two basic kinds of records which genealogists use. Some kinds of records are considered more reliable than others. In genealogy, records are classified as either *primary* or *secondary* in nature. Primary records are records that exist as original documents which have never been copied. It is this very quality of *originality* which makes primary records the most valuable kind of record for the family researcher. Copying errors, possibly made during the transcription of original records, are eliminated in primary sources. For this reason the original records are considered much more reliable than records that have been copied. Primary records are *never* copies. Primary records include the original documents found in the various governmental offices of the county, the state, and the United States and records made by churches, cemeteries, businesses, organizations, and individuals. Always try to use the original, primary records whenever possible when conducting genealogical research.

Primary Sources Containing Errors

Although primary sources are considered the most valuable kind of record, they are not infallible. Admittedly, the information recorded in some original documents can be erroneous. Incorrect entries might have been made for a number of reasons: The recorder may have heard the information incorrectly or spelled it wrong, been an indifferent handwriter or partially deaf, or have received the wrong information from the informant, either intentionally or unintentionally. You may find the death certificate for an ancestor recorded and filed under someone else's name. You may find the surname of an ancestor spelled wrong or hideously garbled. You might even find the wrong birthdate recorded on your own birth certificate! When a name or some other information is recorded wrong, you might search forever, trying to locate records for your ancestor. In such a case, you might have to make a thorough search through all the records to determine whether a mistake was made or whether a record actually exists. When you do find such an error, whether in a primary or in a secondary source, please do not write the correction on the page. Get permission from the custodian to affix a small slip of paper to the original record correcting the error and giving your name and address. Do not write the correction on the page yourself because undocumented corrections are discouraged. Such a "correction" might be considered vandalism and you could be held responsible for defacing the volume.

Copied Original Records

Many original records are actually secondary records because, at some time and for some reason, they were copied. The recorder often copied deed records into the deed books in alphabetical order instead of in the chronological order that they were originally entered. The mere act of copying a record made it liable to errors, especially if another person originally wrote it. Sometime in the 1920s or 1930s, the original Gibson County estate papers were copied by a typist, and the originals possibly were destroyed. At any rate, the typescript is blurry with age and a photocopy of it is not so valuable as if it were the original document. Always try to get a photocopy of the original document. A typescript copy or an abstract is a poor substitute for an original document. The original document often has signatures of the people involved and is, thus, more valuable in your search. The indexes to the various court records and to the marriages, births, and deaths were also copied from the originals, and errors in names, dates, and other data often resulted. Fortunately, most original records are not laden with mistakes, and you can generally use them without fear. Just be aware that some mistakes have been made in copied documents and in indexes, just as in original records, and watch out for them.

Secondary Records

For a number of reasons it is not always possible to use primary records. These include lack of time, too great a distance to travel, and the absence of existing original records. When no primary records exist, you will have to use secondary records that have been copied from the original sources. Secondary records certainly have their place in genealogical research and are a valuable source, despite being labeled "secondary." Records classified as secondary in nature are found in manuscript, typescript, or book form, in pamphlets, in newsletters, and in other materials that are copies of the originals. Always check secondary records against the original documents, whenever possible, to make sure that no mistakes were made when the records were copied. Checking copied records with the existing original document is especially important when records are written in a foreign language or in an unfamiliar script. People are human and do make mistakes, and a careful personal search of the original records is always advisable.

Sometimes it is not possible to check a secondary record against the original one because the original record may no longer exist. Original records may have been lost, destroyed in a courthouse fire, or be privately held. When a cemetery no longer exists, you must rely on any available transcripts of the cemetery records. When a courthouse and its contents have burned, any existing copies of those records must be used in place of the missing originals. Even though you may feel very fortunate to have found copies of those lost records, you should try to verify data by using other records. When you can verify secondary information by checking it against that found in a primary record, you feel much more confident about the validity of your proofs.

Valid Proof

Many kinds of records or documents can constitute valid proof in genealogy. Records made by the various agencies of government—federal, state, county, and local—are considered acceptable, valid genealogical proof of births, marriages, deaths, actions at law, military service, naturalization, and so forth. Original records made by churches and other organizations also can serve as valid proof for genealogical purposes.

A family Bible is often used as proof for dates and events in the lives of family members, but not every family Bible can be considered valid proof for genealogical purposes. Information recorded in a family Bible is considered valid proof only if each entry was made at the time the particular event took place, not recorded some time afterward. If the publication date of the Bible is *after* the recorded events occurred, you know that the data were either copied from another source or entered from memory. In such a case, the information may be entirely correct but the copied data makes the Bible a less reliable source. Note such a discrepancy in your family file and try to verify dates and events by using another contemporary source.

A photograph or photocopy of an original record is considered valid proof. Always try to get a photocopy of an original record from the custodian to ensure that neither you nor the custodian has made copying errors. Many clues can be gathered by poring over the photo of an original document. Photocopies can be obtained from the offices of the county court, county health offices, the State Board of Health, and from the National Archives, all for reasonable fees. If you want to get a copy of a document as proof for membership in a patriotic or hereditary organization, be sure to ask for a *certified copy* of the desired record. Certification by the county official or other custodian attests that the document is authentic. Most other custodians of original records—the churches, clubs, historical and genealogical societies, libraries, and the like—can make photocopies of original documents that are in their possession.

A courteous approach is always helpful when requesting genealogical information or photocopies. You should always be courteous, whether in person, by phone, or in a letter. Courtesy and consideration open more doors and lead to more information than a cursory demand does. Another courtesy involves requests by mail. Always send a self-addressed, stamped, legal-sized envelope (S.A.S.E.) with your letter of inquiry when you want an individual's reply. Fold the envelope in thirds or in half and insert it into the envelope with your letter.

Offer to repay the person for copying and mailing costs. A questionnaire is also helpful for obtaining the information you want and also for jogging the person's memory. When you contact a governmental unit or a public library the S.A.S.E. is not necessary because the facility includes mailing charges in its usual search fee. Besides, the courthouse or library might send you more material than your envelope will hold. A request made to a genealogical or historical society should probably include the S.A.S.E., however. These organizations are seldom tax-supported and all of them will welcome prestamped return envelopes. Expect to pay a small search fee for research made by any society.

Eyewitness Proofs

In a pinch, the written report of an eyewitness to an event, such as a birth, marriage, or death, can be used as valid proof. You cannot be a witness to your own birth, however, nor can your mother, unless she was awake and alert at the time of your birth. The doctor who attended her is the best witness, but a relative who witnessed the birth can often give such proof. If you don't have a birth certificate and no physician or witness exists, the census bureau will furnish your approximate age by consulting past census records. Your parent can also attest to your age as proof for some things, such as eligibility for Social Security or a pension. It is also possible to use school records giving a person's age in a certain year as proof of age for such purposes. If the present school system does not have such records, you may find them in the local historical or genealogical society library, in the local public library, or at the Indiana State Library in Indianapolis.

You sometimes find valuable eyewitness reports of births, marriages, and deaths in veterans' pension applications for service in the Revolutionary War and later wars. These depositions were needed by the veteran or his widow to prove that he had been married to the woman, and when, where, and by whom married; that he had received wounds in the war, could not work, and needed a pension; that he was deceased, and how, when, and where he died, and his widow was in need of a pension; or that the couple's minor children needed assistance because of his physical or mental disability. Such eyewitness depositions often give much valuable genealogical information which may not be available elsewhere. If you must use an eyewitness report in your genealogical records, be sure that you have the signature of the witness, the person's age and address, and a written statement as to the truth of the report, that is, how the person happened to witness the event and to know the information.

DOCUMENTATION

Documentation is absolutely necessary in genealogical research. Documentation records the source of information found on your family group sheets, pedigree charts, and your genealogy. Documentation of genealogical evidence includes identifying the *source* of a piece of information, either by the name of a person, a book, a record, a church register, a Bible inscription, a tombstone inscription, and so forth. Documentation also describes where the information was found and where it can be seen, used, and verified. Documentation must always accompany any information found in your genealogical records. You must document the name of the person, the place, the manuscript, book, volume, page number, microfilm reel, facility, et cetera, where information, such as a name, a date, a place, or a statement, was obtained. Any statement which appears in your genealogy or family history must be documented.

Data recorded on a pedigree chart or a family group sheet are documented by writing the source of the data on a separate sheet of paper, usually in the same location as the corresponding data on the chart or group sheet. The documentation sheet is placed immediately behind the family group sheet it identifies in your family notebook. A typical statement of documentation for, say, birthdate for Eliza Smith might be: "From the family Bible of Jacob Smith of Clinton, Indiana, published in 1842; inscription written by his wife, Sarah Dodson Smith." Or "From the personal knowledge of Emily Smith, who witnessed the birth." Or "From the book *Baltimore County Families,* by Robert Barnes, pages 233–34, Genealogical Publishing Company, Inc., Baltimore, Maryland." A marriage date might be documented thus: "Marriage Book A, Vermillion County, Indiana, page 76." A death date could be documented as "Tombstone inscription, Grave's Cemetery, Clinton County, Indiana," followed by plot and row numbers, if you know them.

Genealogical material is documented to show where information was found and to allow others to find and use the source to verify the information or to learn more about the subject. If, in the future, your descendants find new information which could change a name or date in your genealogy, they can check your identified source for study and comparison. Unless the source you used is well documented, your descendants will not be able to recheck the information. Without proper documentation your entirely proper work may seem questionable to others. Thus, you should document each and every bit of information that goes into your genealogy or family history.

Uniform Documentation

Before you begin gathering genealogical information about your family, inspect the various types of group sheets and charts available for recording data. Any genealogical supply house offers genealogical recording forms, and *The Genealogical Helper* carries ads for several kinds in their pages. Do not invent your own forms! Too many genealogies have been discarded by descendants because they could not understand the recording system used by the genealogist. Find a commercially designed form you like and use it, and try not to change forms in mid-genealogy. It is easy to become confused in such a changeover, especially when the old and new forms are very different. Recopying all of your material uses time that could often be spent on further research. Copying errors are also less likely if you stay with your original choice of forms. And you certainly don't want to have two or more types of group sheets in your notebooks. Not only would other people become confused by different forms, but you might, also. If you do find that your original choice of forms is inadequate, by all means select other forms, but do so carefully, and fill them out just as carefully. Remember the bugaboos caused by careless copying.

Genealogical information should also be recorded in a standard, uniform manner. Rather than devising your own record-keeping system, use one already devised for you. Wise and experienced genealogists have determined the most efficient way of recording genealogical material, which will save you the time and effort of devising your own system. Unless you are using a computerized genealogy program, the accepted method is as follows: Type or print material using a noncarbon typing ribbon or permanent black ink. Capitalize all surnames, and record a person's in the order it is spoken, "John SMITH," not the reversed "SMITH, John." Places are recorded from the smallest unit to the largest: village, neighborhood or town, township, county, state, and nation, as in "Lancaster neighborhood, Huntington County, Indiana." Record the nation only when it is not in the United States. Dates are also recorded from the smallest unit to the largest, beginning with the day, then the month, and then the year. Write the date October 12, 1813, as "12 Oct. 1813," never as "10/12/1813" or "12/10/1813," because either date could be misread as "10 Dec. 1813." Always use at least three letters of the month to avoid mistakes in reading the name of a month. "JU" could be either June or July, and "MA" might be March or May. Always write out the year in full, too, because you will soon be dealing with more than one century.

Accepted abbreviations used in genealogy are "ca." for "circa" and "abt." for "about." For an approximate date, use either "ca." or "abt.," as in "ca. 1798" or "abt. 1798." Choose which abbreviation you will use and use it consistently. You might make a key sheet giving the meanings of the abbreviations you use to place at the front of your notebook. Such a key could be helpful to anyone who might peruse your genealogy materials. Whenever you are not sure of a date, use "ca." or "abt." followed by a question mark placed in parentheses. Also, use a similar question mark after any unproved or supposed names, dates, places, and any other unproved data. For example, record an unverified death date as "d. ca. 1936(?)" or a questioned location as "Logansport(?), Cass County, Indiana." The addition of the question mark shows that you are not sure of the information and that until it is verified it should not be taken as fact.

The abbreviation "b." is used for "born," "d." for "died," "m." for "married," "bap." for "baptized," "chr." for ""christened," "bur." for "buried," "mo." for mother, "fa." for father, "sib." for "sibling(s)," "div." for "divorced," "ae" for "age," "w/o" for "wife of," "s/o" for "son of," "d/o" for "daughter of," "nee" (meaning "born") for "maiden name," "gr-fa." for "grandfather," and "gr-mo." for "grandmother." Currently, most genealogists use either the older, three-letter abbreviations for states (Ind. for Indiana) or the newer, two-letter ones (IN for Indiana) now used by the U.S. Postal Department.

Pedigree Charts

The word "pedigree" comes from the French words "pie de grue" (MF), meaning "foot of the crane." This name came to be used because the arrangement of lines on a pedigree chart resembles a crane's foot. It also resembles a square, bare-branched tree, with the trunk to the left and the limbs branching out toward the right. A pedigree chart contains only the names and the most important data about an individual's direct ancestors. None of your siblings, aunts, uncles, or cousins will appear on your pedigree chart. Information about these "collateral" relatives appears only on the family group sheets, where all family members are recorded, and on their own pedigree charts. If family group sheets with their worlds of data are considered the "meat" of a genealogy, then pedigree charts with their skeletal arrangement and direct-line content might be considered the "bones."

If a pedigree chart begins with you, then only you, your parents, your grandparents, your great-grandparents, and your great-great-grandparents will appear on that pedigree chart. The only information given for each individual is birthdate, birthplace, marriage date, death date, death place, and, sometimes, place of burial. Also given for the first person on the chart (person number 1) is the name of that person's spouse. The names, only, of the 16 second great-grandparents will appear on the first pedigree chart, with no other data about them. Further information about each of these 16 people will be found continued on 16 separate pedigree charts, one for each of the 16 individuals. Thus, a pedigree chart is really the "skeleton" of your genealogy, giving the bare essentials about your direct ancestry back to your 16 second great-grandparents.

On a five-generation pedigree chart person number 1 can be either male or female, but all succeeding males are given even numbers, and all females, odd numbers. If you are person number 1, then your father is person number 2, and your mother, number 3. The even-numbered individuals, 2, 4, 8, and 16, will all normally carry the paternal surname, and the odd-numbered ones, 3, 6, 12, and 24, will carry the maternal surname. Should a surname-change have occurred at some time in the lineage, the former name can be placed in parentheses at the generation when the name was altered.

The top half of a pedigree chart will contain the names of your father's direct ancestors, and the bottom half, the ancestors of your mother. Your father's father is given number 4, and his mother, number 5; your mother's father would be number 6, and her mother, number 7. Your paternal grandfather's father and mother would be numbers 8 and 9, and his maternal grandmother's parents, numbers 10 and 11. The final 8 people on the top half of the chart (numbers 16 through 23) are the second great-grandparents of person number 1. Persons number 16 and 17 are the parents of number 8; numbers 18 and 19 are the parents of his wife, number 9. Numbers 20 and 21 are the parents of number 10, and numbers 22 and 23 are the parents of his wife, number 11.

On your mother's part of the chart, numbers 12 and 13 are her paternal grandparents, and numbers 14 and 15, her maternal grandparents, who are the great-grandparents of you, person number 1. Numbers 24 and 25 are the parents of number 12, and persons numbers 26 and 27 are the parents of number 13, the wife of number 12; they are number 1's great-grandparents. Numbers 28 and 29 are the parents of number 14, and numbers 30 and 31 are the parents of number 14's wife, who is number 15. Numbers 24 through 31, which appear on the bottom half of the right column are all the maternal second great-grandparents of person number 1.

A five-generation pedigree chart begins with number 1 at the left side of the page in the center (where the horizontal "tree trunk" begins); the next column contains numbers 2 and 3 placed vertically, 2 above 3, and to the right of the column containing number 1 (where the first two "limbs" take off); numbers 4, 5, 6, and 7 are placed, in descending order from top to bottom, in the column to the right of 2 and 3, making four limbs branch off from number 2 and number 3. The next vertical column contains numbers 8, 9, 10, 11, 12, 13, 14, and 15, the four limbs branching out to form 8. The last column, located along the far right side of the chart contains numbers 16 through 31, adding another 16 "tree" branches. The five-generation chart is the standard format, but there are also charts which contain fewer or even many more generations. The larger charts are designed to be folded or to be used as wall decorations.

Each successive five-generation pedigree chart takes your ancestry back another five generations, adding another 30 individuals (number 1 on the second chart is a repeat of one of the names, numbers 16 through 31, on the first chart) when completed. Thus, each pedigree chart might be considered an "index" to your direct lineage for five generations, giving the vital information (dates and events of birth, marriage, and death) for the first fifteen individuals and only the names for the next sixteen people. Each added five-generation pedigree chart "indexes" another thirty people, giving birth, marriage, and death dates and places for the first fifteen, and only the names of the next sixteen people. Pedigree charts come in both vertical (8½ by 11 inches) and horizontal (8½ by 14 inches) arrangements, and are available from a number of genealogical supply companies.

GOOD HABITS PAY OFF

A better genealogy will be produced by the person who conducts research correctly and completely than by the person who does it haphazardly. After faulty or incomplete documentation of data, the next worst fault in genealogy is not analyzing and filing material immediately. Check the notebooks of most genealogists and you will find loose pieces of paper, scribbled-on envelopes, tiny scraps of data-laden paper, and unclassified, unsorted census sheets, family group sheets, and other miscellaneous sheets. The genealogical "hunt" is so much more engaging than the organization that most researchers keep hunting and neglect to organize and file their materials.

Sort your photocopied papers and research notes and file them in appropriate sections of your notebook as soon as you get home from a research trip. When you first begin family research, your family lines will probably fit into one notebook, and you will merely need dividers to separate the different families. You can file family material either chronologically, from the present to the past, or from the past to the present. It may be more convenient to keep the file for the family you are currently researching at the front of the notebook. Devise a system that you can work with, but change to another system if you discover one that is more useful. As you accumulate the data for more families, you may need a separate notebook for each line and can use dividers to separate the various types of forms and papers.

Place any written material about the family in a section of the notebook called Family History. Other sections might be headed Birth Certificates, Marriage Records, Death Records, Census Records, Military Records, Family Group Sheets, Pedigree Charts, and so on. If yours is a truly disorganized notebook, sort materials into piles according to subject matter and then type the data onto permanent sheets for your notebook. There will be some materials which you probably should not carry in your research notebook—photocopies of vital records, such as birth, marriage, and death certificates, military records, deeds and wills, and original documents.

File valuable family papers in a file cabinet or file box. You needn't rush out to buy a file box, however, A large detergent box works fine in the beginning, and later on you can use a big typing- or photocopy-paper box to hold your files. Place your valuable papers in the section reserved for each particular surname. As you amass more and more materials for a surname you may need further to divide the material into smaller categories, again using dividers between sections. The more minutely separated your material is, the easier it should be to find everything. Of course, if you invariably forget where you filed a particular paper, make a "what is filed where" list. It seems to work and saves a lot of time and grief when hunting an elusive document.

Some materials, such as framed photographs and other keepsakes, don't fit into a notebook or a file cabinet. An acid-free box will hold those items and keep them safe from deterioration. Wrap each item in acid-free tissue paper or separate them with acid-free cardstock. Keep the box of photos in a dry, cool place which is free of dust and out of direct sunlight or artificial light. You might also like to hang your framed family photos on an inside wall in a darkish room where they can be enjoyed. Other photos, the unframed ones, can be placed in acid-free sleeves in a permanent family album where they can be seen occasionally. Keep the photos clean, dry, and out of direct light so that they will be in good shape to be included in the family history when you write one.

COMPLETENESS COUNTS

Whenever and wherever you do research, be sure you research an item, an area, or an individual completely. Copy every bit of information which seems of value to your research. Xerox material whenever possible, regardless of the cost. Even a high fee can't be compared to the time saved by photocopying instead of handcopying. Document where and when you found any information, whether it was from a person, a book, or a government record. Make it clear how and where one can locate the data. When recording data, always use uniform charts and forms, a standard system of recording information, and accepted genealogical abbreviations. Remember that printed material isn't necessarily true just because it is printed in a newspaper, in a book, or even in government records. Be skeptical, also, when information doesn't "seem right." Try to verify any questionable information by checking it against some other kind of contemporary record.

Completeness and correctness in everything you do in your genealogical pursuit will assure you of a good and reliable end product. When you finish, you will know, with certainty, that the people you call your ancestors are truly your ancestors.

NOTES

1. INDIANA, A VARIED LAND

1. *The Northwest Ordinance,* Ordinance of July 13, 1787. An ordinance for the government of the territory of the United States northwest of the river Ohio.
2. George R. Wilson, *Early Indiana Trails and Surveys,* Indiana Historical Society, Indianapolis, (1919), 1986, 80–81.
3. Irvin S. Cobb, *Cobb's American Guyed Books,* Doran & Company, New York, 1924, 24.
4. John R. Hill, Director of Public Relations and Educational Services, Indiana University, Bloomington, in a talk before the Monroe County Historical and Genealogical societies, January 16, 1989, Bloomington.
5. Robert C. Kingsbury, *An Atlas of Indiana,* Department of Geography, Occasional Publication Number 5, Indiana University, Bloomington, March 1970, 4–15.
6. Hill.
7. Ibid.
8. Ibid.
9. Kingsbury, 18.
10. *Encyclopaedia Britannica,* volume 12, William Benton, Chicago, London, Toronto, etc., 1968, 79.
11. Ibid.
12. Ibid.
13. Ibid.
14. Ibid.
15. Ibid., 80.
16. R. Carlyle Buley, *The Old Northwest: Pioneer Period, 1815–1840,* volume 2, Indiana University Press with Indiana Historical Society, Bloomington, (1950), 1983, 491.
17. Ibid., 247.
18. Ibid., 248.
19. *Encyclopaedia Britannica*, 79.
20. Hill.

2. THE INDIANS OF INDIANA

1. *Encyclopaedia Britannica,* volume 12, William Benton, Chicago, London, Toronto, etc., 1968, 63.
2. Ibid.
3. James H. Kellar, *An Introduction to the Prehistory of Indiana,* Indiana Historical Society, Indianapolis, 1983, 24.
4. Ibid.
5. *Encyclopaedia Britannica*, 63.
6. Evelyn M. Sayers, *Indiana: A Handbook for U.S. History Teachers,* Indiana Department of Education, Indianapolis, 1987, 11.
7. Ibid., 12.
8. Ibid.
9. *Encyclopaedia Britannica*, 64.
10. Sayers, 13.

11. Kellar, 24.

12. James H. Madison, *The Indiana Way: A State History,* Indiana University Press, Bloomington, Indiana Historical Society, Indianapolis, 1986, 13.

13. Ibid.

14. John Francis McDermott, "French Settlers and Settlements in the Illinois Country in the 18th Century," in *The French, the Indians, and George Rogers Clark in the Illinois Country,* Indiana Historical Society, Indianapolis, 1977, 9.

15. George A. Rawlyk, "The Rising French Empire in the Ohio Valley and Old Northwest: The Dreaded Juncture of the French Settlements in Canada with Those of Louisiana," in *Contest For Empire, 1500–1775,* Indiana Historical Society, Indianapolis, 1975, 48.

16. Madison, 16.

17. Ibid., 17.

18. Ibid., 18–19.

19. Ibid., 21.

20. Charles Moore, *The Northwest under Three Flags, 1635–1796,* Harper and Brothers, New York and London, 1900, 320.

21. McDermott, 39.

22. Clarence Edwin Carter, editor and compiler, *Territorial Papers of the United States,* volume 3, U.S. Government Printing Office, Washington, D.C., 1934, 325.

23. McDermott, 28.

24. Ibid., 15.

25. Madison, 31.

26. Works Progress Administration, *Guide to Public Vital Statistics Records in Indiana,* Historical Records Survey, Washington, D.C., July 1934, 9–10.

27. Sayers, 51, 58.

28. Madison, 45.

29. Ibid., 125.

30. Jerry Wright Jordan, compiler, *Cherokee by Blood,* volume 2, Heritage Books, Bowie, Md., 1987, vii.

3. INDIANA BOUNDARIES

1. George R. Wilson, *Early Indiana Trails and Surveys,* Indiana Historical Society, Indianapolis, (1919), 1986, 58–59.

2. Carolynne L. (Wendel) Miller, *Indiana Sources for Genealogical Research in the Indiana State Library,* Indiana Historical Society, Family History Section, Indianapolis, 1984, 14–15.

3. Wilson, 56.

4. Ibid.

5. George Pence and Nellie C. Armstrong, *Indiana Boundaries,* Indiana Historical Collections, volume 19, Indiana Historical Bureau, State Department of Education, William B. Burford Printing, Indianapolis, 1933, 86.

6. Wilson, 62–63.

7. Ibid., 58.

8. Ibid., 65.

9. Ibid., 56.

10. Val D. Greenwood, *The Researcher's Guide to American Genealogy,* second edition, Genealogical Publishing, Baltimore, 1990, 326–330.

11. Miller, 14.

12. Marion County Surveyor's Office, *Surveying in Indiana,* leaflet, no date, no page numbers.

13. Evelyn M. Sayers, *Indiana: A Handbook for U.S. History Teachers,* Indiana Department of Education, Indianapolis, 1987, 44–46.
14. Wilson, 60.
15. Ibid., 64.
16. Miller, 14.
17. Ibid., 14–15.
18. Ibid., 14.
19. Wilson, 65.
20. Pence and Armstrong, 20.
21. Ellen T. Berry and David A. Berry, *Early Ohio Settlers: Purchasers of Land in Southwestern Ohio, 1800–1840,* Genealogical Publishing, Baltimore, 1986, x.
22. Pence and Armstrong, 20.
23. Ibid.
24. Sayers, 69.
25. Pence and Armstrong, 220.
26. Ibid., 152–154.
27. Ibid., 162–166.
28. Ibid., 166–176.
29. Ibid., 182–186.
30. Ibid., 196.

4. EMIGRANT TRAILS

1. George R. Wilson, *Early Indiana Trails and Surveys,* Indiana Historical Society, Indianapolis, (1919), 1986, 20–24.
2. Ibid., 16.
3. Marcus Lewis, "The Development of Early Emigrant Trails," *National Genealogical Society Quarterly,* June 13, 1946, 2.
4. Mark F. Seeman, *The Hopewell Interaction Sphere: The Evidence for Interregional Trade and Structure Complexity,* Pre-Historic Research Series, volume 5, number 2, 291–296.
5. Lewis, 7.
6. Works Progress Administration, *Guide to Public Vital Statistics Records in Indiana,* Historical Records Survey, Washington, D.C., July 1934, 9–10.
7. Lewis, 7–11.
8. Ibid., 4.
9. Ibid., 5.
10. Ibid.
11. Ibid., 8–9.
12. Ibid., 11.
13. Herrmann Schuricht, *History of the German Element in Virginia,* volume 1, Genealogical Publishing, Baltimore, (1898) 1977, 58.
14. Lewis, 7.
15. Ibid., 6.
16. Ibid.
17. Logan Esarey, *A History of Indiana from 1850–1920,* volume 2, third edition, Hoosier Press, Fort Wayne, 1924, 160–168.
18. Wilson, 8.
19. Ibid., 65.
20. Lewis, 11.
21. Wilson, 1.

22. Ibid., 65.
23. Ibid., 36–41.
24. Ibid., 12, 44–47.
25. Ibid., 33.
26. Ibid., 47.
27. Ibid., 48–49.
28. Ibid., 4–5.
29. Thomas J. Schlerith, *U.S. 40: A Roadscape of the American Experience,* Indiana Historical Society, Indianapolis, 1985, 64.
30. Lewis, 11.
31. Ibid.
32. Ibid., 12.
33. James H. Madison, *The Indiana Way: A State History,* Indiana University Press, Bloomington, Indiana Historical Society, Indianapolis, 1986, 80–82.
34. Wilson, 92.
35. Madison, 82.
36. Ronald E. Shaw, "The Canal Era in the Old Northwest," in *Transportation and the Early Nation,* Indiana Historical Society, Indianapolis, 1982, 89.
37. Ibid., 93–95.
38. Ibid., 93.
39. Ralph D. Gray, "The Canal Era in Indiana," in *Transportation and the Early Nation,* Indiana Historical Society, Indianapolis, 1982, 120.
40. Ibid.
41. Ibid.
42. Madison, 85.
43. Ibid., 154.
44. Evelyn M. Sayers, *Indiana: A Handbook for U.S. History Teachers,* Indiana Department of Education, Indianapolis, 1987, 96.
45. Robert C. Kingsbury, *An Atlas of Indiana,* Department of Geography, Occasional Publication Number 5, Indiana University, Bloomington, March 1970, 74–75.
46. Sayers, 99.
47. Ibid., 114.
48. Madison, 157–158.
49. Kingsbury, 78–79.
50. Ibid., 78.
51. Sayers, 100.

5. WHO CAME TO INDIANA?

1. James H. Madison, *The Indiana Way: A State History,* Indiana University Press, Bloomington, Indiana Historical Society, Indianapolis, 1986, 13.
2. Charles Moore, *The Northwest under Three Flags, 1635–1796,* Harper and Brothers, New York and London, 1900, 166.
3. *U.S. Federal Census for Indiana, 1850.*
4. Perret Dufour, *The Swiss Settlement of Switzerland County, Indiana,* Indiana Historical Commission, Indianapolis, 1925, Heritage Classic, 1987, Heritage Books, Bowie, Md., 1988, vii.
5. Moore, 69–72.
6. Arlene Eakle and Johni Cerny, editors, *The Source: A Guidebook of American Genealogy,* Ancestry Publishing, Salt Lake City, 1984, 356.
7. Madison, 116–117.

8. Robert M. Taylor, Jr., Errol Wayne Stevens, Mary Ann Ponder, and Paul Brockman, *Indiana: A New Historical Guide,* Indiana Historical Society, Indianapolis, 1989, 397.
9. Ibid., 289–290.
10. "Foreign Immigration into Indiana before 1860," *Indiana Source Book III,* Willard Heiss, editor, Indiana Historical Society, Family History Section, Indianapolis, 1982, 187.
11. *Encyclopaedia Britannica,* volume 9, William Benton, Chicago, London, Toronto, etc., 1968, 938–943.
12. John I. Coddington, "Patterns of Post Revolutionary Migration," talk given at the Indiana History Conference, November 1967, *Indiana Source Book II,* Indiana Historical Society, Family History Section, Indianapolis, 1981, 74.
13. Joel L. Swerdlow, "Erie Canal: Living Link to Our Past," *National Geographic,* volume 178, number 5, November 1990, 50.
14. Madison, 174.
15. Coddington, 74.
16. Henry A. Verslype, "The Belgians of Indiana," *Indiana Magazine of History,* volume 75, number 4, December 1989, 352–355.
17. Coddington, 74.
18. Ibid., 74–75.
19. Ronald D. Cohen, "Children of the Mill: Schooling and Society in Gary, Indiana, 1906–1960," *Indiana Magazine of History,* volume 86, number 4, December 1990, 421–422.
20. Madison, 237.
21. Francisco Arturo Rosales and Daniel T. Simon, "Mexican Immigrant Experience in the Urban Midwest: East Chicago, Indiana, 1919–1945," *Indiana Magazine of History,* volume 77, number 4, December 1981, 33–357.
22. Frances V. Halsell Gilliam, *A Time to Speak, 1865–1965,* Pinus Strobus Press, Bloomington, Ind., 1985, 3–4.
23. Ibid., 4.
24. Ibid., 4–5.
25. *Indiana Laws,* 46th Special Session, 1869, Section 3, 4.
26. Madison, 241.

6. MILITARY RECORDS

1. James H. Madison, *The Indiana Way: A State History,* Indiana University Press, Bloomington, Indiana Historical Society, Indianapolis, 1986, 23.
2. Ibid.
3. Robert M. Sutton, "George Rogers Clark and the Campaign in the West: The Five Major Documents." *Indiana Magazine of History,* volume 76, number 4, December 1980, 335.
4. James B. Walker, talk given at National Genealogical Society and Indiana Historical Society, Conference in the States, Indianapolis, May 14, 1982.
5. Val D. Greenwood, *The Researcher's Guide to American Genealogy,* second edition, Genealogical Publishing, Baltimore, 1990, 494.
6. Walker.
7. Madison, 29–30.
8. Ibid., 30–31.
9. Ibid., 44.
10. Evelyn M. Sayers, *Indiana: A Handbook for U.S. History Teachers,* Indiana Department of Education, Indianapolis, 1987, 72.

11. "Indiana Militia: Black Hawk War," *Indiana Source Book III,* Willard Heiss, editor, Indiana Historical Society, Family History Section, Indianapolis, 1982, 344.
12. Ibid., 351.
13. Carolynne L. (Wendel) Miller, *Indiana Sources for Genealogical Research in the Indiana State Library,* Indiana Historical Society, Family History Section, Indianapolis, 1984, 12.
14. Greenwood, 525.
15. Ibid.
16. Sayers, 78–79.
17. Miller, 11.
18. Gerald Weland, *The Last Post,* Heritage Books, Bowie, Md., 1990, 65–66.
19. Miller, 11.
20. Sayers, 86.
21. Greenwood, 529.
22. Arlene Eakle and Johni Cerny, editors, *The Source: A Guidebook of American Genealogy,* Ancestry Publishing, Salt Lake City, 1984, 275.
23. Greenwood, 528–529.
24. Eakle and Cerny, 275.
25. Greenwood, 225–226.
26. Reference Service Branch, *The National Archives,* Washington, D.C., 1984. Announcement of new procedure.
27. Eakle and Cerny, 281, 285.
28. Miller, 11.
29. Ibid., 12.
30. Ibid., 11.
31. Ibid., 12.
32. National Archives Trust Fund Board, *Guide to Genealogical Research in the National Archives,* U.S. General Services Administration, Washington, D.C., 1984, 105.
33. Eakle and Cerny, 265.
34. Ibid.
35. Miller, 12.
36. Eakle and Cerny, 265.
37. Ibid.
38. Ibid., 266.
39. Ibid., 267.

7. INDIANA CHURCH AND CEMETERY RECORDS

1. Val D. Greenwood, *The Researcher's Guide to American Genealogy,* second edition, Genealogical Publishing, Baltimore, 1990, 425.
2. Ibid., 423–424.
3. Ibid., 424.
4. James H. Madison, *The Indiana Way: A State History,* Indiana University Press, Bloomington, Indiana Historical Society, Indianapolis, 1986, 105.
5. Ibid., 99.
6. John Francis McDermott, "French Settlers and Settlements in the Illinois Country in the 18th Century," in *The French, the Indians, and George Rogers Clark in the Illinois Country,* Indiana Historical Society, Indianapolis, 1977, 28.
7. Madison, 99.
8. James J. Divita, "Using Catholic Records for Genealogical Research," *The Hoosier*

Genealogist, volume 30, number 3, September 1990, Indiana Historical Society, Indianapolis, 129.

9. Ibid., 131.
10. Ibid.
11. Ibid., 130.
12. John D. Barnhart and Dorothy Riker, *Indiana to 1816: The Colonial Period,* Indiana Historical Bureau and Indiana Historical Society, Indianapolis, 1971, 366–367.
13. Ibid.
14. Ibid., 367.
15. John Cady, *The Baptist Church in Indiana: The Origin and Development of the Missionary Baptist Church in Indiana,* Franklin College, Franklin, Ind., 1942, 25.
16. Ibid., 21.
17. Ibid., 46.
18. Ibid.
19. Ibid.
20. Arlene Eakle and Johni Cerny, editors, *The Source: A Guidebook of American Genealogy,* Ancestry Publishing, Salt Lake City, 1984, 141.
21. *Encyclopaedia Britannica,* volume 15, Chicago, London, Toronto, etc., 1968, 304–305.
22. Madison, 100–101.
23. Ibid., 102.
24. R. Carlyle Buley, *The Old Northwest: Pioneer Period, 1815–1840,* volume 2, Indiana University Press with Indiana Historical Society, Bloomington, (1950), 1983, 447–449.
25. Eakle and Cerny, 144–145.
26. Margaret R. Waters, Dorothy Riker, and Doris Leistner, *Abstracts of Obituaries in the Western Christian Advocate, 1834–1850,* Indiana Historical Society, Family History Section, Indianapolis, 1988, vii–viii.
27. Robert M. Taylor, Jr., Errol Wayne Stevens, Mary Ann Ponder, and Paul Brockman, *Indiana: A New Historical Guide,* Indiana Historical Society, Indianapolis, 1989, 174.
28. Ibid., 253.
29. Ibid., 275.
30. Ibid., 270–271.
31. Ibid., 339.
32. Buley, 447–475.
33. Barnhart and Riker, 327.
34. Greenwood, 342–348.
35. *Encyclopaedia Britannica,* volume 15, 159.
36. Ibid., 159–160.
37. Ibid., 160.
38. Ibid., volume 18, 460–465.
39. Buley, 420–422.
40. Barnhart and Riker, 367.
41. Eakle and Cerny, 145.
42. David B. Eller, "Hoosier Brethren and the Origins of the Restoration Movement," *Indiana Magazine of History,* volume 76, number 1, March 1980, 2.
43. Ibid., 3.
44. Ibid., 3, 5.
45. Ibid., 6.
46. Ibid., 20.
47. Ibid., 11.
48. Ibid., 1.

49. Ibid., 20.
50. Greenwood, 437.
51. Eakle and Cerny, 144.
52. Taylor et al., 493–494.
53. Ibid., 555.
54. Ibid., 588.
55. Eakle and Cerny, 144.
56. Miller, 22–27.
57. Buley, 468.
58. Tombstone inscription, Vernal Baptist Cemetery, Monroe County, Indiana, Richland Township, Section 34.
59. Greenwood, 546.
60. Eakle and Cerny, 64.
61. Gilbert Doane, *Searching for Your Ancestors,* Bantam Books, New York, London, Toronto, 1974, 82.
62. Ibid., 83.
63. Ibid., 64.
64. Ibid., 83–84.

8. INDIANA COUNTY RECORDS

1. John J. Newman, "Research in Indiana Courthouses: Judicial and Other Records," paper presented before the Indiana Historical Society, Family History Section, Spring Symposium, Indianapolis, April 11, 1981, 10.
2. George R. Wilson, *Early Indiana Trails and Surveys,* Indiana Historical Society, Indianapolis, (1919), 1986, 95–97, 99–109.
3. Arlene Eakle, and Johni Cerny, editors, *The Source: A Guidebook of American Genealogy,* Ancestry Publishing, Salt Lake City, 1984, 217.
4. Ibid., 219.
5. Val D. Greenwood, *The Researcher's Guide to American Genealogy,* second edition, Genealogical Publishing, Baltimore, 1990, 347.
6. Ibid., 348.
7. Ibid., 350.
8. Ibid., 351.
9. Ibid., 360.
10. Newman, 11.
11. Elizabeth Petty Bentley, *County Courthouse Book,* Genealogical Publishing, Baltimore, 1990, 79.
12. Ibid., 79.
13. Newman, 1–2.
14. Bentley, 79.
15. Newman, 11.
16. Eakle and Cerny, 177.
17. Ibid.
18. Ibid., 185.
19. Ibid., 178.
20. Ibid., 179.
21. Ibid., 178, 314.
22. Ibid., 183.
23. Huntington County (Ind.), Huntington, Indiana, Courthouse, Office of the County Clerk, *Will Record Book B*, 406–408.

24. Greenwood, 289.
25. Ibid., 292.
26. Ibid., 289.
27. Eakle and Cerny, 76.
28. Ibid., 80.
29. Works Progress Administration, *Index to Supplemental Marriage Transcript Records of Monroe County, Indiana, 1882–1920, Letters A–Z Inclusive,* n.d. [1930s], 262.
30. Eakle and Cerny, 75–76.
31. Ibid., 83.
32. Malinda E. E. Newhard, compiler, *Divorces Granted by the Indiana General Assembly Prior to 1852,* published by compiler, Harland, Ind., 1981, 4.
33. Malinda, E. E. Newhard, compiler, *Name Changes Granted by the Indiana General Assembly Prior to 1852,* published by compiler, Harland, Ind., 1981, 6.
34. Greenwood, 405.
35. Eakle and Cerny, 177.
36. John J. Newman, *American Naturalization Processes and Procedures, 1790–1985,* Indiana Historical Society, Family History Section, Indianapolis, 1985, 6.
37. Ibid., 6–7.
38. Ibid., 5.
39. Ibid., 15.
40. National Archives Trust Fund Board, *Guide to Genealogical Research in the National Archives,* U.S. General Services Administration, Washington, D.C., 1982, 63.
41. Newman, *Naturalization,* 18.
42. Greenwood, 412.
43. Newman, *Naturalization,* 18.
44. Ibid.
45. State Registrar of Vital Records, Indianapolis, 1991.
46. Newman, "Courthouses," 10.
47. County Records of Indiana Microfilming Project (CRIMP), Information Leaflet.
48. Ibid.
49. Willard Heiss, editor, *Indiana Source Book,* volume 1, frontispiece.
50. Ibid., *passim.*
51. Ibid.
52. Ibid.
53. Ibid.
54. Ibid.

9. CENSUS RECORDS

1. U.S. Constitution, Article 1, Section 2.
2. *U.S. Federal Census for 1790.*
3. Val D. Greenwood, *The Researcher's Guide to American Genealogy,* second edition, Genealogical Publishing, Baltimore, 1990, 186–196.
4. Ibid.
5. *U.S. Federal Census for 1800.*
6. George Pence and Nellie C. Armstrong, *Indiana Boundaries,* Indiana Historical Collections, volume 19, Indiana Historical Bureau, State Department of Education, William B. Burford Printing, Indianapolis, 1933, 20.
7. *Census of Indiana Territory for 1807,* Indiana Historical Society, Family History Section, Indianapolis, 1980, 29–42.
8. Ibid., 1.

9. Greenwood, 188.
10. Ibid., 182.
11. Marshals of the Several Judicial Districts, *A Census of Pensioners for Revolutionary or Military Services; with Their Names, Ages, and Places of Residence, as Returned by the Marshals of the Several Judicial Districts,* Washington, D.C., 1841, Genealogical Publishing, Baltimore, 1989, 185.
12. Schedule [form], U.S. Federal Census for 1850.
13. Schedule [form], U.S. Federal Census for 1870.
14. Greenwood, 225–226.
15. Schedule [form], U.S. Federal Census for 1900.
16. Greenwood, 221.
17. Ibid., 221.
18. Ibid., 221–223.
19. Marshals of the Several Judicial Districts, *A Census. . . .*
20. Arlene Eakle and Johni Cerny, editors, *The Source: A Guidebook of American Genealogy,* Ancestry Publishing, Salt Lake City, 1984, 103.
21. Carolynne L. (Wendel) Miller, *Indiana Sources for Genealogical Research in the Indiana State Library,* Indiana Historical Society, Family History Section, Indianapolis, 1984, 20.
22. (1840) *Census of Pensioners,* 1.
23. Eakle and Cerny, 105.
24. Miller, 19.
25. Ibid.

10. INDIANA COUNTY HISTORIES AND OTHER SOURCES

1. Arlene Eakle and Johni Cerny, editors, *The Source: A Guidebook of American Genealogy,* Ancestry Publishing, Salt Lake City, 1984, 398–400.
2. Ibid., 413.
3. Ibid., 407, 418.
4. Anita Cheek Milner, *Newspaper Genealogical Column Directory,* third edition, Heritage Books, Bowie, Md., 1987, viii.
5. Ibid.
6. Jane E. Darlington, "Indiana Genealogical Research Sources in Indianapolis," *The Hoosier Genealogist,* volume 29, number 3, September 1989, 129–131.
7. Ibid., 132–133.
8. Beth Rosenberg Zweg, "Fort Wayne Library a Leader in Genealogy," *Indianapolis Star,* "Focus," Sunday, June 24, 1990, F1, F6.
9. Alice Eicholz, *The Red Book: American State, County and Town Sources,* Ancestry Publishing, Salt Lake City, 1990, 175.

11. BASIC GENEALOGICAL PRINCIPLES

1. Allan J. Lichtman, *Your Family History,* Vintage Books, New York, 1978, 86–87.
2. Ibid.

BIBLIOGRAPHY

Barnhart, John D., and Dorothy Riker, *Indiana to 1816: The Colonial Period,* Indiana Historical Bureau and Indiana Historical Society, Indianapolis, 1971.

Bentley, Elizabeth Petty, *County Courthouse Book,* Genealogical Publishing, Baltimore, 1990.

Berry, Ellen T., and David A. Berry, *Early Ohio Settlers: Purchasers of Land in Southwestern Ohio 1800–1840,* Genealogical Publishing, Baltimore, 1986.

Buley, R. Carlyle, *The Old Northwest: Pioneer Period, 1815–1840,* volumes 1 and 2, Indiana University Press, Indiana Historical Society, Bloomington, 1950, 1983.

Cady, John, *The Baptist Church in Indiana: The Origin and Development of the Missionary Baptist Church in Indiana,* Franklin College, Franklin, Ind., 1942.

Carter, Clarence Edwin, editor and compiler, *Territorial Papers of the United States,* volume 3, U.S. Government Printing Office, Washington, D.C., 1934.

Cobb, Irvin S., *Cobb's American Guyed Books,* Doran & Company, New York, 1924.

Coddington, John I., "Patterns of Post Revolutionary Migration," talk given at the Indiana History Conference, November 1967, *Indiana Source Book II,* Willard Heiss, editor, Indiana Historical Society, Family History Section, Indianapolis, 1981.

Cohen, Ronald D., "Children of the Mill: Schooling and Society in Gary, Indiana, 1906–1960," *Indiana Magazine of History,* volume 86, number 4, December 1990.

Darlington, Jane E., "Indiana Genealogical Research Sources in Indianapolis," *The Hoosier Genealogist,* volume 29, number 3, September 1989.

Divita, James J., "Using Catholic Records for Genealogical Research," *The Hoosier Genealogist,* volume 30, number 3, September 1990.

Doane, Gilbert, *Searching for Your Ancestors,* Bantam Books, New York, London, Toronto, 1974.

Dufour, Perret, *The Swiss Settlement of Switzerland County, Indiana,* Indiana Historical Commission, Indianapolis, 1925, Heritage Classic, 1987, Heritage Books, Bowie, Md., 1988.

Eakle, Arlene, and Johni Cerny, editors, *The Source: A Guidebook of American Genealogy,* Ancestry Publishing, Salt Lake City, 1984.

Eicholz, Alice, *The Red Book: American State, County and Town Sources,* Ancestry Publishing, Salt Lake City, 1990.

Eller, David B., "Hoosier Brethren and the Origins of the Restoration Movement," *Indiana Magazine of History,* volume 76, number 1, March 1980.

Encyclopaedia Britannica, volumes 9, 12, 15, William Benton, Chicago, London, Toronto, etc., 1968.

Esarey, Logan, *A History of Indiana from 1850–1920,* volume 2, third edition, Hoosier Press, Fort Wayne, 1924.

Gilliam, Frances V. Halsell, *A Time to Speak, 1865–1965,* Pinus Strobus Press, Bloomington, Ind., 1985.

Gray, Ralph D., "The Canal Era in Indiana," in *Transportation and the Early Nation,* Indiana Historical Society, Indianapolis, 1982.

Greenwood, Val D., *The Researcher's Guide to American Genealogy,* second edition, Genealogical Publishing, Baltimore, 1990.

Heiss, Willard, editor, *Indiana Source Book,* volume 1, Indiana Historical Society, Genealogy Section, Indianapolis, 1977.

———, *Indiana Source Book II,* Indiana Historical Society, Family History Section, Indianapolis, 1982.

———, *Indiana Source Book III,* Indiana Historical Society, Family History Section, Indianapolis, 1982.

Jordan, Jerry Wright, compiler, *Cherokee by Blood,* volume 2, Heritage Books, Bowie, Md., 1987.

Kellar, James H., *An Introduction to the Prehistory of Indiana,* Indiana Historical Society, Indianapolis, 1983.

Kingsbury, Robert C., *An Atlas of Indiana,* Department of Geography, Occasional Publication Number 5, Indiana University, Bloomington, March 1970.

Lewis, Marcus, "The Development of Early Emigrant Trails," *National Genealogical Society Quarterly,* June 13, 1946.

Lichtman, Allan J., *Your Family History,* Vintage Books, New York, 1978.

Madison, James H., *The Indiana Way: A State History,* Indiana University Press, Bloomington, Indiana Historical Society, Indianapolis, 1986.

Marshals of the Several Judicial Districts, *A Census of Pensioners for Revolutionary or Military Services; with Their Names, Ages, and Places of Residence, as Returned by the Marshals of the Several Judicial Districts,* Washington, D.C., 1841, Genealogical Publishing, Baltimore, 1989.

McDermott, John Francis, "French Settlers and Settlements in the Illinois Country in the 18th Century," in *The French, the Indians, and George Rogers Clark in the Illinois Country,* Indiana Historical Society, Indianapolis, 1977.

Miller, Carolynne L. (Wendel), *Indiana Sources for Genealogical Research in the Indiana State Library,* Indiana Historical Society, Family History Section, Indianapolis, 1984.

Milner, Anita Cheek, Newspaper Genealogical Column Directory, third edition, Heritage Books, Bowie, Md., 1987.

Moore, Charles, *The Northwest under Three Flags, 1635–1796,* Harper and Brothers, New York and London, 1900.

National Archives Trust Fund Board, *Guide to Genealogical Research in the National Archives,* U.S. General Services Administration, Washington, D.C., 1982.

Newhard, Malinda E. E., compiler, *Divorces Granted by the Indiana General Assembly Prior to 1852,* published by compiler, Harland, Ind., 1981.

———, compiler, *Name Changes Granted by the Indiana General Assembly Prior to 1852,* published by compiler, Harland, Ind., 1981.

Newman, John J., "Research in Indiana Courthouses: Judicial and Other Records," paper presented before the Indiana Historical Society, Family History Section, Spring Symposium, Indianapolis, April 11, 1981.

———, *American Naturalization Processes and Procedures, 1790–1985,* Indiana Historical Society, Family History Section, Indianapolis, 1985.

Pence, George, and Nellie C. Armstrong, *Indiana Boundaries,* Indiana Historical Collections, volume 19, Indiana Historical Bureau, State Department of Education, William B. Burford Printing, Indianapolis, 1933.

Rawlyk, George A., "The Rising French Empire in the Ohio Valley and Old Northwest: The Dreaded Juncture of the French Settlements in Canada with Those of Louisiana," in *Contest For Empire, 1500–1775,* Indiana Historical Society, Indianapolis, 1975.

Rosales, Francisco Arturo, and Daniel T. Simon, "Mexican Immigrant Experience in the Urban Midwest: East Chicago, Indiana, 1919–1945," *Indiana Magazine of History,* volume 77, number 4, December 1981.

Sayers, Evelyn M., *Indiana: A Handbook for U.S. History Teachers,* Indiana Department of Education, Indianapolis, 1987.

Schlerith, Thomas J., *U.S. 40: A Roadscape of the American Experience,* Indiana Historical Society, Indianapolis, 1985.

Schuricht, Herrmann, *History of the German Element in Virginia,* volume 1, 1898, Genealogical Publishing, Baltimore, 1977.

Seeman, Mark F., *The Hopewell Interaction Sphere: The Evidence for Interregional Trade and Structure Complexity,* Pre-Historic Research Series, volume 5, number 2, Indiana Historical Society, Indianapolis, 1979.

Shaw, Ronald E., "The Canal Era in the Old Northwest," in *Transportation and the Early Nation,* Indiana Historical Society, Indianapolis, 1982.

Sutton, Robert M., "George Rogers Clark and the Campaign in the West: The Five Major Documents," *Indiana Magazine of History,* volume 76, number 4, December 1980.

Swerdlow, Joel L., "Erie Canal: Living Link to Our Past," *National Geographic,* volume 178, number 5, November 1990.

Taylor, Robert M., Jr., Errol Wayne Stevens, Mary Ann Ponder, and Paul Brockman, *Indiana: A New Historical Guide,* Indiana Historical Society, Indianapolis, 1989.

Verslype, Henry A., "The Belgians of Indiana," *Indiana Magazine of History,* volume 75, number 4, December 1989.

Walker, James B., "Military Records in the Old Northwest," talk given at the National Genealogical Society and Indiana Historical Society, Conference in the States, Indianapolis, May 14, 1982.

Waters, Margaret R., Dorothy Riker, and Doris Leistner, *Abstracts of Obituaries in the Western Christian Advocate, 1834–1850,* Indiana Historical Society, Family History Section, Indianapolis, 1988.

Weland, Gerald, *The Last Post,* Heritage Books, Bowie, Md., 1990.

Wilson, George R., *Early Indiana Trails and Surveys,* Indiana Historical Society, Indianapolis, 1919, 1986.

Works Progress Administration, *Guide to Public Statistics Records in Indiana,* Historical Records Survey, Washington, D.C., July 1934.

______, *Index to Supplemental Marriage Transcript Records of Monroe County, Indiana, 1882–1920, Letters A–Z inclusive,* n.d. [1930s].

Zweg, Beth Rosenberg, "Fort Wayne a Leader in Genealogy," *Indianapolis Star,* "Focus," Sunday, June 24, 1990, F1, F6.

SUGGESTED READING

GENERAL

Eakle, Arlene, and Johni Cerny, *The Source: A Guidebook of American Genealogy,* Ancestry Publishing, Salt Lake City, 1984.

Everton, George B., Sr., *Handy Book for Genealogists,* seventh edition, Everton Publishers, Logan, Utah, 1981.

Greenwood, Val D., *The Researcher's Guide to American Genealogy,* Genealogical Publishing, Baltimore, first edition, 1973, second edition, 1990.

Madison, James H., *The Indiana Way: A State History,* Indiana University Press, Indiana Historical Society, Indianapolis, 1986.

INDIANA AND ITS BOUNDARIES

Commissioner of the General Land Office, *Land Claims: Vincennes District,* House Document Number 198, Indiana Historical Society, Family History Section, Indianapolis, 1983.

Gioe, Joan Colbert, *Indiana: Her Counties, Her Townships, and Her Towns,* The Researchers, Indianapolis, 1979.

Pence, George, and Nellie C. Armstrong, *Indiana Boundaries,* Indiana Historical Collections, volume 19, Indiana Historical Bureau, State Department of Education, William B. Burford Printing, Indianapolis, 1933.

Taylor, Robert M., Jr., *The Northwest Ordinance, 1787: A Bicentennial Handbook,* Indiana Historical Society, Indianapolis, 1987.

Thornbrough, Gayle, editor, *The Correspondence of John Badollet and Albert Gallatin, 1804–1836,* Indiana Historical Society Publications, volume 22, Indiana Historical Society, Indianapolis, 1963.

INDIANA'S INDIANS

Darbee, Leigh, Tim Peterson, Eric Pumroy, and Linda Carlson Sharp, *Indiana and the Old Northwest,* An Exhibition in Honor of the One Hundred and Fiftieth Anniversary of the Indiana Historical Society, Bulletin Number 3, Indiana Historical Society, Indianapolis, 1980.

Law, Judge John, *The Colonial History of Vincennes under the French, British and American Governments,* Harvey, Mason and Company, Vincennes, 1858, Heritage Press, Bowie, Md., 1989.

McDermott, John Francis, George C. Chalou, George M. Waller, John H. Long, and Dwight L. Smith, *The French, the Indians, and George Rogers Clark in the Illinois Country,* Proceedings of the Indiana American Revolution Bicentennial Symposium, May 14–15, 1976, Indiana Historical Society, Indianapolis, 1977.

Moore, Charles, *The Northwest under Three Flags, 1635–1796,* Harper and Brothers, New York and London, 1900.

EMIGRANT TRAILS

Transportation and the Early Nation, papers presented at the Indiana American Revolution Bicentennial Symposium, Indiana Historical Society, Indianapolis, 1982.

Wilson, George R., *Early Indiana Trails and Surveys,* Indiana Historical Society, Indianapolis, (1919), 1986.

INDIANA SETTLERS

Barnhart, John D., and Dorothy L. Riker, *Indiana to 1816: The Colonial Period,* The History of Indiana, volume 1, Indiana Historical Bureau and Indiana Historical Society, Indianapolis, 1971.

Carter, Clarence Edwin, editor and compiler, *Territorial Papers of the United States,* volume 3, U.S. Government Printing Office, Washington, D.C., 1934.

Thornbrough, Gayle, *The Correspondence of John Badollet and Albert Gallatin, 1804–1836,* Indiana Historical Society Publications, volume 22, Indiana Historical Society, Indianapolis, 1963.

INDIANA MILITARY ENGAGEMENTS

Cooke, Jean, Ann Kramer, and Theodore Rowland-Entwistle, *History's Timeline,* Grisewood and Dempsey, London, 1981, Crescent Books, New York, 1982.

Law, Judge John, *The Colonial History of Vincennes under the French, British and American Governments,* Harvey, Mason and Company, 1858, Heritage Press, Bowie, Md., 1989.

Moore, Charles, *The Northwest under Three Flags, 1635–1796,* Harper and Brothers, New York and London, 1900.

Thornbrough, Emma Lou, *Indiana in the Civil War Era, 1850–1880,* The History of Indiana, volume 3, Indiana Historical Bureau and Indiana Historical Society, Indianapolis, 1965.

INDIANA CHURCHES

Barnhart, John D., and Dorothy L. Riker, *Indiana to 1816: The Colonial Period,* The History of Indiana, volume 1, Indiana Historical Bureau and Indiana Historical Society, Indianapolis, 1971.

Nolan, Ann, and Keith A. Buckley, *Indiana Stonecarver: The Story of Thomas R. Reding,* Indiana Historical Publications, volume 27, number 1, Indiana Historical Society, Indianapolis, 1984.

INDIANA'S COURT RECORDS

Baker, Ronald L., and Marvin Carmony, *Indiana Place Names,* Indiana University Press, Bloomington and London, 1975.

Bentley, Elizabeth Petty, *The Genealogist's Address Book,* Genealogical Publishing, Baltimore, 1991.

Eichholz, Alice, editor, *Ancestry's Red Book: American State, County, and Town Sources,* Ancestry Publishing, Salt Lake City, 1989.

Genealogist's Pocket Book, The Researchers, Indianapolis, 1979.

Kemp, Thomas J., *Vital Records Handbook,* Genealogical Publishing, Baltimore, 1988.

Where to Write for Records in Indiana, The Researchers, Indianapolis, 1979.

CENSUSES

Government Printing Office, *A Century of Population Growth, 1790–1900,* Government Printing Office, Washington, D.C., 1909, Genealogical Publishing, 1989.

Hamilton, Ann B., *Researcher's Guide to United States Census Availability, 1790–1910,* Heritage Books, Bowie, Md., 1987.

Thorndale, William, and William Dollarhide, *Map Guide to the U.S. Censuses, 1790–1920,* Genealogical Publishing, Baltimore, 1987.

COUNTY HISTORIES AND NEWSPAPERS

Filby, P. William, *A Bibliography of American County Histories,* Genealogical Publishing, Baltimore, 1985.

Miller, John W., *Indiana Newspaper Bibliography*, Indiana Historical Society, Indianapolis, 1982.

Peterson, Clarence S., *Consolidated Bibliography of County Histories in Fifty States,* Genealogical Publishing, Baltimore, 1980.

BASIC GENEALOGICAL PRINCIPLES

Doane, Gilbert H., *Searching for Your Ancestors,* Bantam Books, New York, 1974.

Dollarhide, William, *Managing a Genealogical Project,* Genealogical Publishing, Baltimore, 1988.

Stryker-Rodda, Harriet, *How to Climb Your Family Tree: Genealogy for Beginners,* Genealogical Publishing, Baltimore, 1983.

INDEX

MONA ROBINSON has written "Family Tree Leaves," a genealogical column in the Bloomington (Indiana) *Sunday Herald-Times* since 1974. She has been actively engaged in genealogical research on her own family for more than twenty-five years.